Forest Farmers and Stockherders

NEW STUDIES IN ARCHAEOLOGY

Series editors
Colin Renfrew, *University of Cambridge*
Jeremy Sabloff, *University of Pittsburgh*

PETER BOGUCKI   *Forbes College, Princeton University*

Forest Farmers and Stockherders

Early Agriculture and its Consequences in North-Central Europe

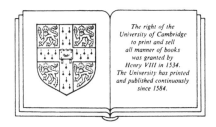

The right of the
University of Cambridge
to print and sell
all manner of books
was granted by
Henry VIII in 1534.
The University has printed
and published continuously
since 1584.

Cambridge University Press

Cambridge

New York   New Rochelle   Melbourne   Sydney

CAMBRIDGE UNIVERSITY PRESS
Cambridge, New York, Melbourne, Madrid, Cape Town, Singapore, São Paulo, Delhi

Cambridge University Press
The Edinburgh Building, Cambridge CB2 8RU, UK

Published in the United States of America by Cambridge University Press, New York

www.cambridge.org
Information on this title: www.cambridge.org/9780521103602

First published 1988
This digitally printed version 2009

A catalogue record for this publication is available from the British Library

Library of Congress Cataloguing in Publication data
Bogucki, Peter I.
Forest farmers and stockherders.
(New studies in archaeology)
Bibliography.
Includes index.
1. Neolithic period—Central Europe.
2. Central Europe—Antiquities.
I. Title. II. Series.
GN776.22.C36B64   1987   936   87-17858

ISBN 978-0-521-32959-0 hardback
ISBN 978-0-521-10360-2 paperback

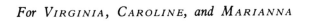

For VIRGINIA, CAROLINE, and MARIANNA

CONTENTS

FIGURES AND TABLES

Figures

Tables

PREFACE

This book has had a fairly prolonged gestation period, which began soon after the completion of my doctoral dissertation in 1981. To some degree, it was the inevitable result of thinking that had taken place on issues which surrounded my dissertation topic but which were too broad to warrant their inclusion in that work. At the time, I thought that I was sufficiently well informed on the Neolithic of central Europe to set these ideas to paper in fairly short order. Five years later, I have been disabused of such ambitious thoughts and instead have realized that ideas do not automatically translate themselves into prose.

When I attempted to characterize the approach taken in this book to a colleague, his reaction was, "so you're trying to hang a little theory on the data." European prehistorians for decades have had a practice of publishing copious volumes of data and hoping that from these data an image of prehistoric life will emerge. In recent years, the impact of anthropological archaeology has led to attempts to construct theoretical models of prehistoric society, often with little direct consideration of the relevant data or with a selective culling of those data which support the argument. My attempt in this volume is to try to synthesize these approaches, first by considering the empirical data on Neolithic adaptations in central Europe in some detail, then by linking those data directly to models drawn from anthropological theory.

The result is what appears at first glance to be a curious mix of both inductive and deductive argument. To some degree, this has been necessitated by the volume and complexity of the fundamental data and the need to organize them in a coherent manner. Essentially, this book seeks to examine the behavior of Neolithic communities in its environmental context and to propose some ideas to explain patterns of similarities and differences. There is considerable overlap between these two goals, and description and interpretation have sometimes become intertwined. This book is not a synthesis, nor is it a polemic. Rather, it represents a particular viewpoint on a body of archaeological data. The positions taken here are not incontrovertible, and their purpose is to lead others to endorse, to refine, or to reject them.

I am considerably indebted to my European and American colleagues who, through conversation and correspondence, have provided insights and information on recent fieldwork and interpretations. These include J. Lüning (Frankfurt), M. Dohrn-Ihmig (Frankfurt), M. Ilett (Paris), H. Schlichtherle (Hemmenhofen), A. Zimmerman (Frankfurt), D. Kaufmann (Halle), F. Hamond (Belfast), N. Starling (London), J.P. Farruggia (Paris), C. Bakels (Leiden), J. Bakker (Amsterdam), H.

Groenendijk (Groningen), M. de Grooth (Maastricht), L. Louwe Kooijmans (Leiden), P. Modderman (Arnhem), T. Wiślański (Poznań), S. Gregg (Ann Arbor), S. Milisauskas (Buffalo), T. Kaiser (Toronto), R. Grygiel (Łódź), J. Shibler (Basel), U. Willerding (Göttingen), G. Schwarz-Mackensen (Wolfenbüttel), U. Kampffmeyer (Karlsruhe), D. Heinrich (Kiel), P. Rowley-Conwy (Cambridge), and J. Shackleton (Cambridge). Many of these individuals provided reprints of recent articles from journals that are scarce on this side of the Atlantic. They should not, however, be implicated in any of the shortcomings of this book. Bernard Wailes (Pennsylvania) and Alasdair Whittle (Cardiff) took the time to make detailed comments on an earlier draft of this manuscript which helped considerably in improving the text. Some of the ideas presented here have been discussed with participants in the informal meetings of a group of American archaeologists who work in Eastern Europe.

I am grateful to my superiors at Princeton – Joan Girgus, Gene Lowe, and especially John Wilson – for allowing me to have the time necessary to complete this book when they could easily have found additional duties to add to my administrative portfolio. Peggy Hoffman permitted me to store files on her computer account, thus making it considerably easier to manage the manuscript. Robert Matthews of the Department of Physics Photo Lab helped with the reproduction of Figure 2.5.

Finally, my wife Virginia and daughters Caroline and Marianna have tolerated the writing of this book for the last few years. They have had to put up with lawns unmowed and outings missed, and to dedicate this book to them seems to be meager compensation for their patience.

1

Introduction: investigating the European Neolithic

The expansion of food production as an economic strategy across Europe over 7,000 years ago marked the most radical transformation of prehistoric society in this region since the retreat of the last glaciation. An economy based on non-indigenous cultigens and domestic forms of both local and foreign animal species was established rapidly and successfully across a broad belt stretching from the Ukraine to France and subsequently expanded north to the Baltic and North Seas and south to the Alps (Fig. 1.1). In the course of this process, new environmental zones were exploited for the first time and new ecological adaptations were made by both indigenous and colonizing populations. The landscape of central Europe was markedly different from that found where agriculture had been previously established. Instead of the park-forest and steppe of the Near East and Balkans, the early farming cultures of Europe encountered a countryside which several thousand years later Tacitus would describe as "covered with bristling forests and foul swamps." Beneath these superficial features lay a mosaic of soil types and landforms unlike any previously encountered by agricultural groups, including the loess blanket of the central European uplands and the glacially deposited soils of the North European Plain. The nature of the adaptations made by these early farming communities and their immediate successors, as well as the implications which these adaptations had for other aspects of human behavior, forms the subject of this book.

In the past 20 years, there has been a renewal of interest in the early agricultural communities of central Europe. Many large and important sites have been excavated and, more importantly, researchers have begun to adopt a regional perspective, focusing on many sites within well-defined study areas. There has been an increased interest in the recovery and analysis of subsistence data, although in many areas poor preservation conditions have hindered this pursuit. There has been an awakening of interest in topics such as trade and social structure, previously considered to be profitable areas of research only in connection with more complex societies. Finally, regional syntheses have appeared which combine many types of data to produce models of early farming societies.

All of this work has resulted in great strides in our understanding of the early agricultural communities of central Europe. Yet, despite this research, a coherent picture of early food-producing adaptations in central Europe has yet to emerge. This book presumes at least to make a start in that direction in that it considers the ecological adaptations of the early farming communities of this area and the implications of these adaptations for economic and social organization. As such, it

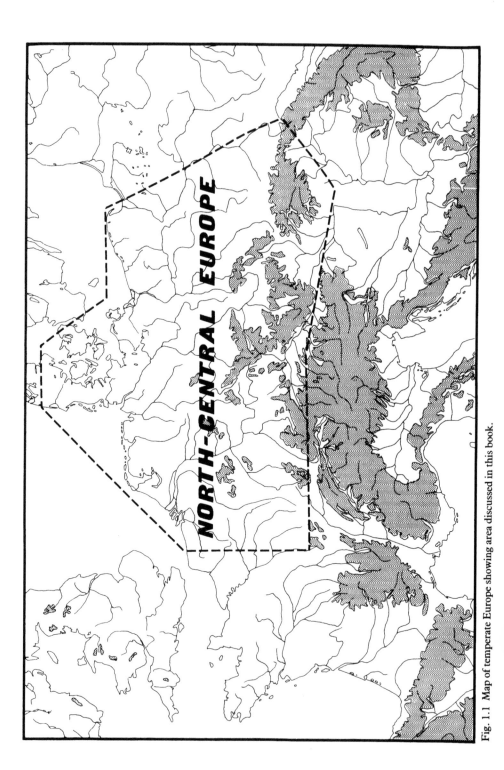

Fig. 1.1 Map of temperate Europe showing area discussed in this book.

NORTH-CENTRAL EUROPE

takes a particular theoretical approach, although many other interpretations of the same data are also possible. In writing this book, I have examined a number of current ideas about early agricultural adaptations in central Europe. Some have been found to make sense, while others have been found wanting. In the latter cases, I have tried to present alternative hypotheses which I believe fit the available data somewhat better. The term "hypothesis" is important and should be kept in mind by the reader throughout this book. Many of the current ideas of early food-producing adaptations in central Europe are untested hypotheses. Few, if any, have been subjected to rigorous verification. But at the same time, many of these hypotheses have replaced earlier ones, which have been subjected not to deductive testing but to the sometimes more demanding inductive procedure of considering how well they account for the available data. In the last 15 years, for instance, our ideas of the farming systems of Neolithic Europe have changed largely as a result of the generation of new data and the inability of the earlier hypotheses to account for these data.

A major aspect of this book will be its emphasis on the archaeologically observable dimensions of human behavior which bear on the social relationships of prehistoric communities. The modelling of subsistence and settlement systems is not viewed as an end in itself, but rather as an intermediate step in the understanding of Neolithic societies in central Europe. In bridging the gap between the archaeological record and the social dimensions of these cultures, it will be necessary to invoke models derived from other branches of anthropology and human ecology. The underlying rationale is not to seek direct analogies but to indicate that certain insights into the archaeological record can be derived from examining human responses to similar conditions of resource distribution, abundance, and scarcity.

Some words of explanation are in order concerning the selection of the geographical arena of this study, referred to here as "central Europe", although "north-central Europe" would probably be more precise (Fig. 1.1). The underlying rationale was that it is the area in which the archaeological record between 4500 and 2500 bc is most directly related to the materials with which I had direct field experience. Moreover, it had a coherent set of well-defined environmental zones, namely the loess belt and the North European Plain. The Alpine Foreland of southern Germany and Switzerland should properly be included in such a study, but upon reflection I decided that lacking direct experience with the sites and materials (save for museum collections) I would be unable to write more than derivative synopses of the relevant data. My feeling, however, is that there are a number of parallels in the process of the establishment of agrarian communities between the North European Plain and the Alpine Foreland, an idea that a reader may wish to consider further.

Beyond palaeoeconomy

For a number of years, the study of early agricultural societies in central Europe has been focused on an "economic approach to prehistory." As originally proposed by Grahame Clark in the 1950s, this approach represented a major departure from previous attempts at classification and systematics and provided a number of fresh insights into prehistoric lifeways in temperate Europe. As carried further by Eric Higgs and his students, the study of economic prehistory yielded a considerable corpus of new data and new analytical techniques for many parts of Mediterranean and temperate Europe. These include the systematic collection and analysis of faunal and botanical samples from many sites in specific regions and the development of interpretive approaches such as site catchment analysis.

The trajectory of palaeoeconomic studies, however, has led to two major shortcomings, especially from the perspective of anthropological archaeology. The first of these was the exclusive emphasis on subsistence questions and the reliance on subsistence alone as an explanatory framework. This resulted in a tendency to interpret most patterns of human behavior which left their traces in the archaeological record in a framework of "alimentary determinism." This is not to argue that questions of subsistence did not play a major, if not key, role in much prehistoric decision-making. The issue is that they should not be seen as the sole factor that determined the configuration of the archaeological record. It is fair to note that many of Higgs' students have taken up fresh approaches to prehistoric life which represent departures from the earlier subsistence-centered treatments, exploring topics such as resource exchange and social organization (e.g. Barker 1981).

The other fundamental shortcoming of many current approaches to economic prehistory is that it does not explore the social implications of its observations nor does it even consider them to be germane to the study of prehistoric change. This issue is addressed by Jarman, Bailey, and Jarman (1982: 4–5), who argue that since social behavior depends so much on economic behavior, and given the limitations of archaeological data, it makes more sense to limit the scope of the enquiry and the degree of direct causation sought by archaeologists. They maintain that "social factors ... seem to be of secondary rather than primary importance among the long-term determinants of human behavior" (1982: 5). Prehistory, in their view, must "perforce deal ... in terms of evolutionary forces and guiding principles which operate in the long term, while sociology and kindred subjects are constrained to concentrate upon the short term and proximate causative factors" (ibid.). It is interesting to note that whereas the original goals of economic prehistory, as articulated in the programmatic statements of Clark (e.g. 1953), were to bring prehistory *closer* to the study of culture, the recent emphasis on palaeoeconomy has taken much the opposite course.

There is, however, a different perspective that can be taken, which sees short-term, local variation as very interesting and as a necessary part of anthropological archaeology. In fact, it is largely through the study of such phenomena that cross-cultural generalizations can be made about human behavior in specific situations. Historically, anthropology, and with it anthropological archaeology, has been more interested in proximal causal factors rather than the broader factors which may have *conditioned* the nature of human adaptations. Although archaeology is in a unique position among the social sciences to examine long-term social change, it is just as valid to study changes that occurred over several decades or centuries as it is to examine major transformations that took millennia to complete.

Ecological approaches in anthropological archaeology

The theoretical position taken in this book is that cultural behavior can be understood in terms of its relationship to its natural and social environment. From the start, the social aspects of this relationship will be treated as being equally important as the relationship of the early European farmers to their natural environment. In this sense, this book represents somewhat of a departure from the traditional approach to ecological issues in European prehistory. Many studies of European archaeological problems which profess to have an "ecological perspective" have been primarily concerned with man-natural environment relationships, particularly in terms of the local flora and fauna. There has been a general tendency to equate an "ecological perspective" with a reconstruction of the *habitat* of the archaeological cultures in question. There are, of course, ecological aspects to habitat reconstruction, in that the flora and fauna of the prehistoric environment all interacted in some way, and thus formed a segment of the web of relationships that linked prehistoric man to his environment. Since many of these relationships were implicated in the subsistence behavior of human beings, there has been a tendency to equate the reconstruction of subsistence systems with the primary goals of an ecological approach to archaeological analysis.

The position taken here is drawn primarily from the agenda of recent ecological approaches in anthropology (e.g. Jochim 1979b, 1981; Hardesty 1977; Thomas, Winterhalder, and McRae 1979; Ellen 1982; Butzer 1983; Bronitsky (ed.) 1983; Minnis 1985). To some degree, their anthropological perspectives on ecology differ from those of strictly biological ecology in that they take cultural behavior into account. Human beings have any number of extrasomatic means of assuring their survival and for dealing with situations that threaten their survival. The natural environment presents a set of conditions to which human beings must respond and adjust. The study of these mechanisms for adjusting the relationships between humans and their environments forms the substance of much of ecological anthropology.

Jochim (1979b: 82) has pointed out that there are two fundamental approaches to ecological research in anthropology. The first entails a focus on the behavior of sociocultural systems as whole entities that are either stable or changing. The other involves the study of the behavior of various groups and individuals who make up these larger systems. Jochim argues that the first approach lends itself to the description of changes within the system, but that the second approach enables change to be understood and explained. He points out that change in human sociocultural systems is largely the result of "various groups and individuals pursuing different advantages and options with a variety of constraints and goals in a variety of natural and social environments." The behavior of the system as a whole is largely the cumulative result of what can be viewed as a myriad number of individual and group microeconomic decisions in the face of environmental limitations and challenges.

Green and Sassaman (1983) have argued that the social and political dimensions of these decisions must be taken into account. The model that they propose has three interactive dimensions: political economy, resource management, and environment. These three components have a dynamic relationship, changing themselves and causing change in each other. Political economy, in their view, is defined by the social and technological organization of the society in question, while the resource management patterns of that society manifest themselves in the subsistence and settlement systems. Both of these relate to each other directly as well as through the environment within which the particular cultural system operates (Fig. 1.2).

To a large degree, such a model provides the programmatic underpinnings of this book. Ecological models of early European agrarian communities must go beyond the study of the subsistence and settlement systems and encompass social and political aspects of these societies. The focal point of this book will be on the intersection of these three dimensions in order to try to better understand the adaptations of the earliest food-producing communities of central Europe. If palaeoeconomy can be considered to be the study of the acquisition, distribution, and consumption of resources, there will be a conscious effort made here to expand that perspective to include the decision-making processes and institutions which governed such resource procurement and allocation.

This book could also be called an attempt to define the "ecological niche" of the early European farming communities and to document the changes in that niche over the first 2,000 years of settled agricultural life in this area. "Niche" here is used in its ecological sense, in that it does not refer only to the *habitat* of the prehistoric communities but rather has a much broader meaning that includes not only the physical environment but also the functional relationships of these communities with other households and groups. Love (1977: 32) has defined the ecological niche of a human group as an "aggregate representation of the relations of its members to income-generating resources at a point in space and time." He has identified the critical dimensions of the niche of a human group as land, water, labor, capital, space, and time. To these, I would add "information", in that access to and control of this resource is often a critical aspect of the microeconomic decisions made to allocate other resources. It is the decisions made which allocate these resources which make up various behavioral subsystems, and it is the scarcity of these resources that leads to the problems whose solutions may often force evolutionary change in human culture.

Although the ecological approach described here portrays humans as interacting in a web of interrelationships with their natural and social environments, there are generally a number of behavioral subsystems which lend themselves to direct examination from this point of view. These include subsistence, settlement forms and patterns, demography, social organization, and political economy. Of course, these are themselves all linked together in this web, yet they can be considered to represent a sort of cumulative hierarchy of relationships. Subsistence can be viewed as the fundamental survival mechanism of the human organism, while political economy represents an adaptive strategy in which communities and regional populations engage within an environment containing neighboring groups of various sizes and organizational structures.

The links in this hierarchy are the decisions made by individuals and groups as

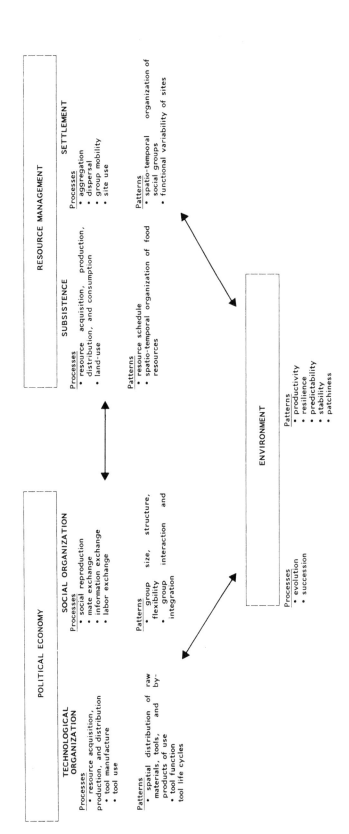

Fig. 1.2 The relationships among aspects of political economy, resource management, and the environment (after Green and Sassaman 1983: fig. 1).

they respond to challenges to their survival. These decisions are made on the basis of information and the goals and motivations of the individuals and groups involved. They may not necessarily be the best from a long-range strategic point of view, but rather they may be simply local, short-lived responses to ephemeral conditions. Thomas et al. (1979) have identified a number of categories of human behavioral responses to environmental conditions. These include avoidance, modification of environment, buffering, distribution, resistance, conformity, and systemic change. The selection of the appropriate response by an individual or group poses a set of problems whose solution raises further challenges to be addressed. Jochim (1979b: 105) has raised the possibility that cultural evolution may in fact represent a chain of solutions and secondary problems. If human cultural behavior is viewed as largely being problem-solving, the solutions to problems generally grow out of decisions made in the context of these types of responses. More than one response is often possible for a given problem, but the long-range implications of these responses may be markedly different. The solutions to problems may be interrelated themselves and may pose secondary problems to be faced.

This focus on human adaptation as the concatenation of solutions to environmental problems will be the underlying theme of this book. This issue is particularly germane to the early farming cultures of Europe, where small communities, employing a subsistence system which was largely alien to the environment of central Europe, were forced to make fundamental decisions which affected their survival as groups. These groups were not simply acting passively as a part of a larger system of agicultural dispersal but rather were faced with choices about crops, animals, settlement locations, settlement forms, resources, information, and a myriad of other variables. Individuals and groups were driven by different motivations and values, yet all were coping with very similar environmental characteristics.

Decision-making
The position taken in this book is that human cultural advances represent the cumulative results of decisions made in the face of stresses of various types. These stresses can be physiological, such as the results of famine or communicable diseases. They can also be social, resulting from conflicting expectations and motivations. Finally, they can be environmental, stemming from continental- scale climatic variation or from changes in local habitats. These stresses are essentially beyond the ability of human populations to suppress. Rather, when faced with specific stresses, as well as uncertainty about environmental conditions, human communities are presumed to have developed behavioral patterns which reduced the amplitude of these stresses and also made them more predictable in space and time. In one sense, this book is about the sorts of cultural buffers adopted by the Neolithic populations of central Europe in their efforts to cope with various types of stresses.

These decisions often involve microeconomic choices in the allocation of scarce resources. In this context, however, it is necessary to take an expansive view of what constitutes "economic" behavior. In our culture, it is generally thought that the maximization of expected utility lies behind such decisions. Other cultures, however, often place a greater value on things like prestige and rank. Some simply wish to minimize risk and uncertainty. Decisions made to cope with stress may involve trade-offs and compromises which do not reflect strictly "economic" considerations.

The nature of such responses to stress is conditioned by the decision-making system of a community or culture. Decisions can be made in climates of certainty, uncertainty, and risk (Levin and Kirkpatrick 1975). Certainty prevails when one can predict what will happen in the period affected by the decision, whereas in conditions of uncertainty, one can not determine the probabilities of a set of outcomes. Risk occurs in cases where the probability distribution of several possible outcomes, some more favorable than others, can be established. From a cultural standpoint, dealing with uncertainty would appear to be more crucial than dealing with risk, for the possibility of uninformed maladaptive choices is greater with the former. As certainty decreases, humans employ increasingly complex decision-making processes, but each time a decision is made, it limits the number of options available in the future. As a result, decisions are more often compromises among an array of competing prerogatives and choices.

The models of human behavior discussed in this book owe relatively little to optimization principles, such as the "Law of Least Effort" (Zipf 1949), which suggest that humans will organize their behavior so as to obtain the maximum return for a minimum of effort. Rather, the decision-making model of human social ecology used here presumes that households and communities will have to make compromises between a number of different factors. These decisions are complicated further by the unpredictability of resource locations and abundance, and still more by the fact that the operational environment of a human group is formed in terms of the group's perceptions rather than actual conditions. The position taken here is that prehistoric decisions are basically rational, but that this rationality is not necessarily predicated upon the optimizing principles of modern "Economic Man" (see also Leibenstein 1976 for a discussion of what he calls "selective rationality").

Such models of human adaptation are not completely novel in archaeological research. Isbell (1978) proposed a similar explanation to account for the development of state-level societies in the Andes, while Jorde (1977) and Minnis (1985) have examined buffering behavior in the Southwestern United States. Their models assume that there is an adaptive advantage to behavior which provides for interaction between geographically separated human populations, as well as the development of facilities to "even out" environmental fluctuations over time by the "banking" of key resources. It is not unreasonable to assume that similar issues faced the Neolithic inhabitants of central Europe. The question is how they responded in the context of the environmental and social conditions which confronted them.

Adaptive units

Throughout this book, it will be important to keep in mind the size of the human groups making the decisions which determined the nature of early agricultural adaptations in Europe. Clearly, individuals were ultimately responsible for the decisions themselves, but the issue here is the effective size of the groups that put these decisions into operation. Although individual initiatives were of fundamental importance, it was their effects on the behavior of larger groups that resulted in their impact on prehistoric society and the extent to which they are visible archaeologically.

Three levels of social groupings have been used by archaeologists to characterize the social units adjusting to particular circumstances. These can be termed the "culture", the "community", and the "household." Such units cannot be used interchangeably, so it is important in any discussion to know the dimensions of the social units in question.

European archaeologists have been traditionally concerned with the adaptive strategies of archaeological cultures. Earlier definitions of the "culture" in European prehistory (e.g. Childe 1957: vi) have been expanded to include the subsistence system and settlement patterns which are associated with consistently recurring archaeological assemblages found in continuous geographical areas. There are two fundamental problems with this approach. The first is that it creates a sort of "package deal" mentality, as Barker (1976) has pointed out, in which "culture = economy." In other words, finds of the material remains of an archaeological culture have been automatically assumed to constitute *prima facie* evidence for the practice of a particular subsistence strategy, where there is really no compelling reason to assume that this was actually the case.

The second, and more serious, problem with discussing prehistoric adaptations in Europe strictly in terms of archaeological cultures is that the culture is *an archaeological unit of study.* It is not necessarily a real social grouping, although many archaeologists have made the leap-of-faith to assume that a culture is a reflection of human group territoriality (as noted by Shennan 1978: 114). If the focus here is on adaptation as decision-making and problem-solving, then the archaeological culture is not the most useful unit of analysis, for it is not itself capable of behavior except of an exceedingly abstract sort. One cannot completely discard the concept, however, for the variation in material culture reflected in the Neolithic cultures of central Europe is nonetheless significant. It is simply that cultures cannot be taken by themselves as decision-making organizations.

Rather, the adaptive units which will have greater relevance for this study are the "household" and the "community." It is in the contexts of groups such as these that the crucial decisions were made. Of course, it is not possible to speak of communities and households in the same degree of concreteness as seems possible with cultures, for as "real" social groupings, they represent an inference from archaeological data, not the archaeological data themselves. These smaller groups do not have names, nor can their exact bounds be precisely established. A household can be presumed to have been the equivalent of a residential group occupying a single Neolithic house with its associated features, while a community can be presumed to have been the equivalent of an agglomeration of households in a defined area at a specific moment in time. Sometimes, the community can be considered to equal the occupants of a single site, but there is also the possibility of dispersed households that may have acted in concert from time to time. Beyond their archaeological correlates, however, it is impossible to give these households and communities concrete dimensions. In many cases, the discussion of them will be in the abstract, couched in terms of "virtual communities" and "virtual households", as opposed to definite entities which are completely observable archaeologically.

Tringham (1983) has made the following observation:

> The importance of the household is that it is the minimal (and can be maximal) unit of economic production and/or social reproduction and thus enables the archaeologist to analyse in a quantifiable way the co-operative organization and social relations of production, consumption, and distribution of resources, and even their transmission (Wilk and Rathje 1982). The investigation of these functions at a micro-level enables the investigation of social change with a credibility that enquiry at more macro levels into kinship relations and manifestation of political power cannot achieve.

The position is taken here that the quantifiable aspects of the archaeological household are perhaps less important than the fact that it is a social unit which appears to have had significance for the Neolithic inhabitants of central Europe, based on the spatial patterning of their settlements, and hence can be inferred to have been the social unit in which the key decisions about resource allocation and consumption were made. In light of the fact that in many modern-day agrarian societies the primary productive unit is the household (e.g. Barlett (ed.) 1980; Meillassoux 1972), this inference does not seem unreasonable. This is particularly true under conditions of subsistence agriculture, where no form of cash-cropping has yet entered the economy. Although the household has at its core a family unit, there may be other individuals who participate in its activities. Households in agrarian societies often include distant relatives who provide labor in return for their keep but who do not have full managerial or decision-making rights.

Households, of course, do not usually stand in total social isolation, and they are usually grouped into larger communities. Of course, the line between these units of analysis is often arbitrary, and they should not be considered to represent completely different entities. In nucleated settlements, such as one finds in the Primary Neolithic cultures of central Europe (see below), the community can be presumed to be generally congruent with individual settlement sites, although outlying sites may also have been attached. In dispersed settlement patterns the definition of the community is difficult, and it should probably be considered in terms of the populations of particular microregions.

Primary and Consequent Neolithic
Chronology and culture history are difficult aspects of European Neolithic cultures to discuss, for the simple reason that so many different chronological schemes have

been developed over the years. Although there is a broad consensus concerning the overall sequence of cultures, each researcher has usually found it possible to divide them into phases, groups, and periods slightly differently from the next one. Before discussing the chronology of any one area, it is necessary to know *whose* chronology will be the common language of the proceedings. Site-based chronologies abound, especially during the later part of the period under discussion in this book, and in the absence of large numbers of radiocarbon dates from these same sites it is often difficult to link these chronologies together. The matter is further complicated by the lack of one single "yardstick" chronology to which regional sequences can be tied, in the way that Reinecke's periodization of the European Bronze Age permitted to some degree. The decades-old "Danubian" sequence of Childe is so broad that it does not really fill this role for the Neolithic.

Another major difficulty is that geography and political boundaries color researchers' concepts of what is "Early", "Middle", or "Late." For instance, "Early Neolithic" in Czechoslovakia is considered to be only *Bandkeramik*, while in Poland it includes Lengyel as well (Bogucki, in press; Kulczycka-Leciejewiczowa 1979). In Denmark, however, "Early Neolithic" refers to neither of these cultures, for they do not extend this far north, but rather is equivalent to the Funnel Beaker Culture – which in Czechoslovakia is placed in the "Early Eneolithic", a term rarely used elsewhere in central Europe.

There has been a tendency for many archaeologists to see chronology and culture history as ends in themselves, and as the archaeological record of central Europe becomes progressively better understood, the cultural picture becomes even more complex. The fundamental reason for this is that many "cultures" and "groups" were identified prior to World War II on the basis of materials from one or a few sites, widely separated from coeval sites by areas where few or no data relating to the same period had been recovered. The fragmentary nature of the data base made materials from particular regions appear more distinct than they really were. Given the perceived discreteness of these cultures, it was easy to make the leap to considering them as "ethnic" entities which had a concept of themselves as a distinct people whose identity was manifested in their material culture. The diachronic study of these archaeological cultures led to the development of a loose historical narrative in which these entities divided, merged, and procreated as though they were organisms. At the same time, these cultures were assumed to have particular sorts of economies which were the same everywhere that the culture appeared, with an implicit "culture = economy" equation. The overall result was that a "chest-of-drawers" approach was taken to the prehistory of central Europe, much like the situation described by Barker (1981) for Italian prehistory. The different cultures were like the drawers in slots, opening and closing sequentially through time.

The cumulative results of archaeological research in central Europe, especially in the last 20 years, have shown that the cultural patterns were considerably more complex than the chest-of-drawers model permits. Cultures and groups overlap, often reflect patterns of archaeological research rather than the prehistoric reality, and sometimes abruptly appear and disappear from the literature. At the same time, we must ask ourselves whether culture history is the real goal of archaeological research at all. I would suggest that a different paradigm be adopted, one which cuts through the forest of cultures and groups and looks at broader adaptive patterns. There would be two ways to treat chronology in such a context. The first would be to consider the range of variation in the adaptations of each of these cultures individually. Such an approach would probably promote the sort of Balkanization of European prehistory that this book seeks to avoid. Another would be to impose simpler categories on the complicated picture and use these to unite the various cultural entities into overall adaptive patterns. The second approach is the one which is proposed here.

Although it is usually risky to propose neologisms where a standard nomenclature is already in place, the type of discussion presented in this volume makes it necessary to do so. Therefore, when considering the early food-producing populations of central Europe, I propose to employ two generic terms. "Primary Neolithic" refers to the pioneer food-producing groups of central Europe and their immediate descendants, while "Consequent Neolithic" designates the food-producing communities which continued the process of adjustment to the central European environment and entered habitats not previously colonized by Primary Neolithic groups, as well as those groups of foragers which had adopted food production. This usage differs fundamentally from the old, and now outmoded, term "Secondary Neolithic" used in western and northwestern Europe. The use of these terms is simply to facilitate the discussion presented in this book, and I would hope that they do not enter general archaeological usage, at least not for now.

For these terms to be of any use at all, it will be necessary to relate them to the archaeological cultures which they represent. Included in the central European Primary Neolithic is, above all, the Linear Pottery Culture (*Linearbandkeramik*) and its congeners, including the *Rubané Récent* of the Paris Basin and the Omalian of Belgium, along with the plethora of "styles" which characterize the late stages of this culture. In addition, the Stroke-Ornamented Pottery Culture (*Stichbandkeramik*) of Germany, western Poland, and Bohemia, the Lengyel, and Rössen cultures can also be considered under the heading of Primary Neolithic, for these appear to represent direct continuations of Linear Pottery adaptive patterns. Finally, the "Limburg Pottery" of the Benelux and France is a phenomenon so closely connected with Linear Pottery as to be inseparable from it, although it does represent the penetration of new ecological zones. 4500–3500 bc (5400–4400 BC) is a reasonable span for the Primary Neolithic.

The Consequent Neolithic, on the other hand, is represented primarily by the Funnel Beaker Culture and its congeners, including Michelsberg. In addition, it also includes the various Dutch coastal agrarian communities such as Swifterbant and Hazendonk, and a variety of groups in Baden-Württemburg and Bavaria such as Aichbühl and Schussenreid, which are coeval with the Pfyn and Cortaillod cultures of the Alpine Foreland. In short, the Consequent Neolithic of central Europe exhibits a much greater degree of cultural and economic variation than does the Primary Neolithic, but this is to be expected as these cultures occupied habitats hitherto unexploited by Primary Neolithic groups. A rough dating of the

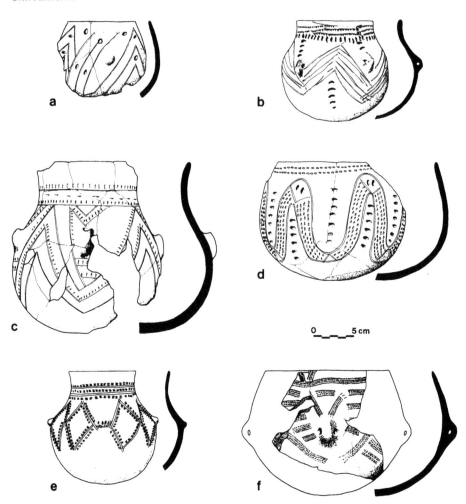

Fig. 1.3 Examples of Primary Neolithic ceramics. Key: a – Ludwigsburg-Poppenweiler (after *Fundberichte aus Baden-Württemburg* 10 (1985): plate 11); b – Elsloo, grave 106 (after Modderman 1985: fig. 37); c, d – Langweiler 9 (after Kuper, et al. 1977: plates 36 and 39); e – Anning II Eschlbach (after Bayerlein 1985: plate 23); f – Irchonwelz (after Farruggia, Constantin, and Demarez 1982: fig. 3).

central European Consequent Neolithic would be approximately 3500–2500 bc (4400–3300 BC). The end of the Consequent Neolithic is not very well defined here, to avoid creating an artificial stopping point. There appear to be a number of changes in subsistence and settlement in the late third millennium bc (ca. 3000 BC), but these are beyond the scope of this book.

Such a division into "Primary" and "Consequent" Neolithic, of course, obscures a considerable amount of chronological and regional diversity which is reflected in the fine-grained subdivisions of these units commonly found in European prehistory. Given that the focus of this book is on adaptation and social organization, a detailed discussion of the culture history of this area would detract from the main arguments. Yet the two broad categories identified here appear to reflect a very real separation in the adaptive patterns seen in the archaeological record. The separation was not sharp. There exist situations which appear to fall

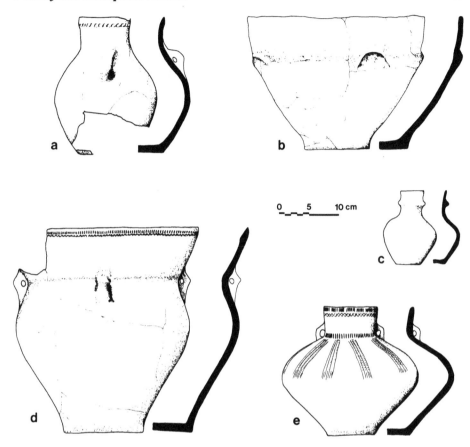

Fig. 1.4 Examples of Consequent Neolithic ceramics. Key: a – Ludwigsburg "Im Schlösslesfeld" (after Lüning and Zürn 1977: plate 39); b – Mrowino (after Tetzlaff 1981: fig. 1); c – Heliodorowo (after Wiślański 1979: fig. 92); d – Niedzwiedz (after Burchard 1981: fig. 5); e – Milicz (after Wiślański 1979: fig. 96).

between. One such case is the Brześć Kujawski Group of the Lengyel culture in the Polish lowlands (Bogucki 1982), essentially Primary Neolithic in its settlement plan but exhibiting a subsistence pattern which presaged the Consequent Neolithic pattern of the North European Plain.

The expression "continuity and change" has become somewhat hackneyed by its constant use in recent positions on the European Neolithic, yet it actually does reflect the fact that there were both long traditions of cultural development coupled with marked shifts in human adaptation in central Europe. The chronological scheme in use here should not be viewed as suppressing the regional variation in adaptation which in fact is a very important dimension of the cultural mosaic of these times. Nor should it be taken as an attempt to discard the efforts of countless prehistorians over the last century in the development of a coherent chronological structure. Rather, it provides a frame of reference within which the significant developments in social and economic organization in Neolithic Europe can be discussed without the distraction of sharp and often arbitrary separations between cultures, groups, and periods.

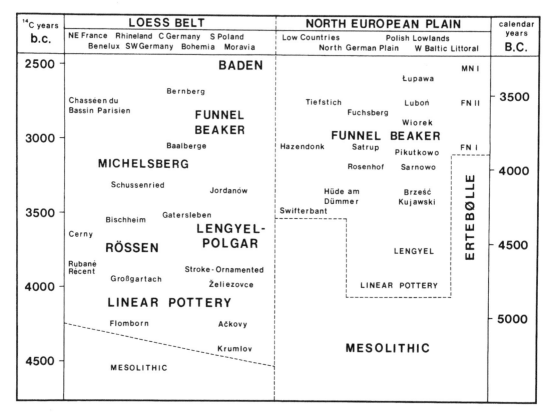

¹⁴C years b.c.	LOESS BELT			NORTH EUROPEAN PLAIN				calendar years B.C.
	NE France Rhineland C Germany S Poland Benelux SW Germany Bohemia Moravia			Low Countries Polish Lowlands North German Plain W Baltic Littoral				

Fig. 1.5 Chronological chart showing Primary and Consequent Neolithic sequences for major regional units in study area. Names in capitals are major archaeological cultures, while those in lower case are smaller cultures, groups, ceramic styles, and distinctive local assemblages.

Conclusion

It appears that two poles are emerging in the study of early European society. Many of the current approaches in European prehistory seem to consider social organization to begin to be interesting only when it approaches ranking and social differentiation. Their focus has been on the later part of the Neolithic, when mortuary practices and exchange networks indicate some nascent social complexity. Earlier agrarian communities are often presumed to be acting under social conditions dictated by their subsistence economies, devoid of motivations and decision-making power. The prime movers of early European agriculture have been reduced to demographic pressures or soil depletion, without any sort of social context. There is thus a polarization of archaeological interests into the "palaeoeconomy" camp on one hand and the "ranking, resource, and exchange" group on the other. Cultures with egalitarian organizing principles have been largely ignored from a social perspective. Hierarchy is where the action has been of late.

But the earliest farmers of central Europe did have some form of social relationships, and the fact that they may not have been hierarchical does not mean that they are any less interesting. These agrarian communities had to relate to neighboring social groups, organize their activities and procure resources, and deal with an imperfectly known environment. Communities and households had to respond to the challenges posed by the European habitat and make adjustments.

The ecological approach taken in this book appears to make the most sense for this type of study. The data that are available for these early European farming communities can be analyzed from this perspective with a relative minimum of speculation and conjecture. More importantly, it is a form of analysis that permits the introduction of comparative, cross-cultural data into the discussion, not in a naive form of direct analogy but rather in an effort to examine similar ecological responses.

2

Primeval central European habitats

The ecological emphasis of this book necessitates a fairly detailed consideration of central European landforms, soils, drainage, potential vegetation, and native fauna. Although the perspective taken is an anthropocentric one that looks at the characteristics which are most relevant for human existence, the following discussion will be fairly wide-ranging. As I noted in Chapter 1, many so-called "ecological" approaches to prehistoric adaptations have confused "niche" with "habitat". The following section will explore the potential habitats encountered by the earliest food-producing communities on several scales, ranging from large parts of the European continent to individual habitats within specific microregions.

Continental environmental conditions 5000–2500 bc

The Blytt-Sernander climatic division of the European Postglacial, which still forms the basis for the periodization used today, is based on the vegetational associations which occur at various points in the palynological record of northern and central Europe (Fig. 2.1).

There seems to be little question that these variations in vegetation are due to climatic factors, for they can be recognized in many parts of Europe. Of Blytt and Sernander's five climatic divisions, two are of particular interest to this study: the Atlantic and the Sub-Boreal.

The beginning of the Atlantic period is conventionally dated to about 6000 bc, continuing to about 3000 bc (Lamb 1984: 372). The succeeding Sub-Boreal period lasted until ca. 800 bc. On the basis of their palynological investigations of Scandinavian peat bogs, Blytt and Sernander concluded that the Atlantic period was warm and damp, while the Sub-Boreal was characterized by a drier and somewhat cooler climate. The characterization of the climate throughout these periods has been broadly assumed to have been similar throughout central Europe, since similar changes in the palynological record have been noted over much of the continent. Although the same climatic divisions of the Holocene can be recognized over all of Europe, a question which is not frequently asked by researchers is whether these periods had similer climatic characteristics over the entire continent or whether there was greater regional differentiation.

Magny (1982) has called attention to discrepancies between the standard assessments of the Atlantic and Sub-Boreal climates in Scandinavia and in the sub-alpine zone of central Europe. His palynological evidence indicates that the Atlantic in central Europe was possibly drier than has been hitherto thought, and moreover, that rather than a decrease in precipitation during the Sub-Boreal in

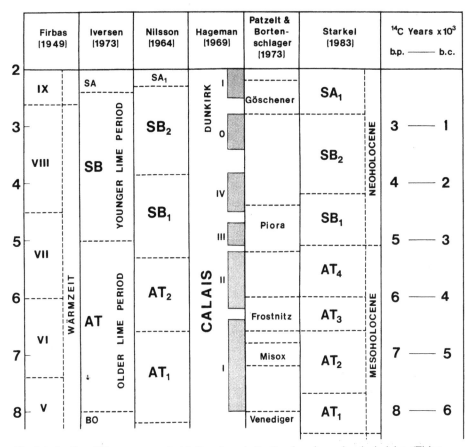

Fig. 2.1 Outline of European postglacial climatic periodization, based on palynological data (Firbas 1949; Iversen 1974; Nilsson 1964), marine transgressions in NW Europe (Hageman 1969), and Alpine climatic oscillations (Patzelt and Bortenschlager 1973). Starkel 1983 is a composite periodization. Key: BO – Boreal; AT – Atlantic; SB – Sub-Boreal; SA – Sub-Atlantic. Chart adapted from Starkel (1983: fig. 10).

central Europe, there was actually a marked increase in dampness. Magny argues convincingly that the differences between the Scandinavian evidence and that from central Europe can be explained in terms of the patterns of atmospheric circulation over northern and central Europe. During the Atlantic, he maintains, the maritime polar air masses were located far to the north, with much of continental Europe under the influence of tropical air. The apparent dampness of this period is the result of the perturbation zone of depressions caused by the polar front meeting the warm air being located over southern Scandinavia. Meanwhile, during the Sub-Boreal, the polar air masses were displaced southwards, leading to what Magny calls "climatic deterioration" in central and southern Europe. The perturbation zone moved south over central Europe, while the area of northern Europe in its wake came under the influence of cooler continental air masses and the cold, dry polar air. There is thus no contradiction between the Scandinavian record and that of central Europe, but rather a difference in which temperature and precipitation are affected by atmospheric circulation at different latitudes (Fig. 2.2).

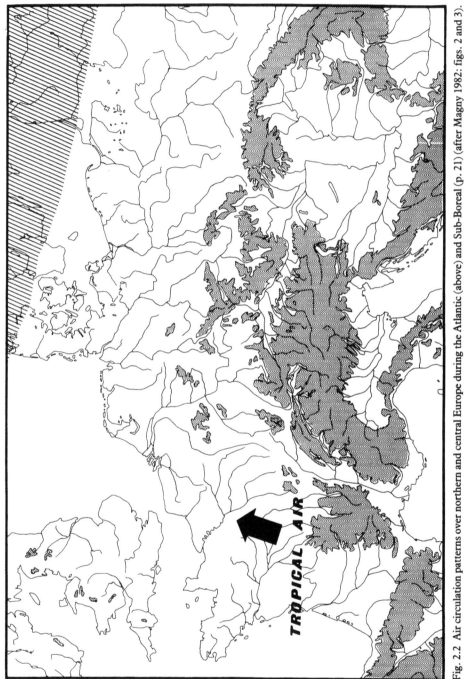

TROPICAL AIR

Fig. 2.2 Air circulation patterns over northern and central Europe during the Atlantic (above) and Sub-Boreal (p. 21) (after Magny 1982: figs. 2 and 3). Hatched area indicates zone of climatic perturbation along southern fringe of the polar front.

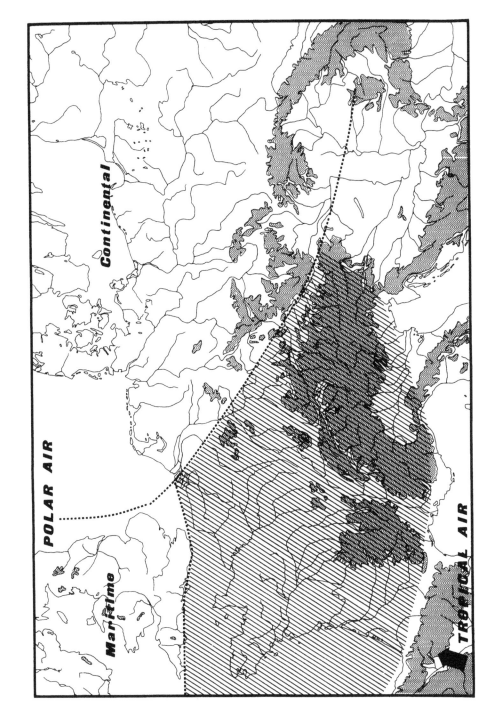

POLAR AIR

Continental

Maritime

TROPICAL AIR

Frenzel (1966), relying on high-altitude data that may be more sensitive to incremental changes than the indicators at lowland sites, has summarized the botanical evidence for climatic changes in central Europe during the transition from the Atlantic to the Sub-Boreal. He noted that the early part of the Sub-Boreal was characterized by essentially the same climatic conditions that prevailed during the Atlantic, and the "deterioration" normally associated with the Sub-Boreal did not occur until later in this period, ca. 2000–1500 bc. During the first part of the Sub-Boreal, winter temperatures were lowered a little and those of summer increased, with the net result being no change in mean annual temperatures. Frenzel pointed out that the overall effect of this transition on vegetation was rather weak and that it was often camouflaged by local conditions, including human activity. It seems fair to conclude that the net change between the Atlantic and the Sub-Boreal was not so radical as to cause major transformations of human culture by itself.

Of greater importance, however, is the period of the transition, approximately between 3400 and 3000 bc. On the basis of pollen analysis and radiocarbon, Zöller (1977) identified a number of post-glacial climatic oscillations in the southern Alps, the most recent of which, the "Piora Oscillation", is dated between 3400 and 3000 bc. The occurrence of a cold spell during this period is confirmed by other indicators, including increased variation in the thickness of tree rings from central and northern Germany (Schütrumpf and Schmidt 1977: 41) suggesting variable and unsettled climatic conditions (Fig. 2.3). The actual duration of the Piora Oscillation cannot be adequately determined, but it seems to have focused on the period around 3200 bc. While the net impact of this cold spell, when considered in terms of the "average" climate of the Atlantic and Sub-Boreal, was relatively weak, the increased annual variation in temperatures and rainfall would have had major implications for human adaptation. If climatic conditions were not within a predictable range from one year to the next, then crop yields would be similarly unpredictable. In evaluating similar data from the American Southwest, Minnis

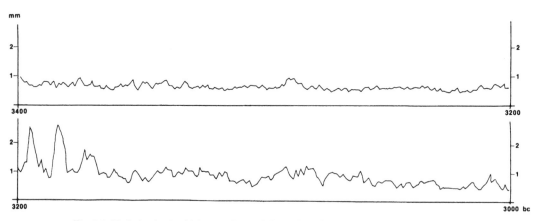

Fig. 2.3 Variation in the thickness of annual rings of oak found at Heidenoldendorf, Germany (after Schütrumpf and Schmidt 1977: fig. 9). Note the greater annual variation in the sequence between 3200 and 3000 bc than in that from the preceding 200 years.

(1985) has attached considerable significance to annual climatic variation and its effect on agrarian societies.

Terrain and landforms

The area of central Europe that concerns us here can be rather grossly divided into two main zones, with transitional areas between them and considerable internal variation. These are the North European Plain, and the loess belt through the Hercynian uplands of central Europe (Fig. 2.4). Within these zones, there is much regional variation. The discussion below will focus on the habitats within these zones which have the most relevance for the establishment of agrarian communities during the Neolithic.

The North European Plain

The northern part of the region considered here is the area known generally as the "North European Plain", which stretches from northern France, through the Low Countries and northern Germany, up into Denmark, and east into Poland and beyond. The North European Plain includes those areas which were either covered by the ice sheet of the Weichsel glaciation or by outwash sands and gravels in front of it. The actual southernmost extent of the Weichsel glaciation around 20,000 BP reached a line that begins over the North Sea in the west, runs southeast along the Elbe river before turning east across East Germany south of Berlin, and reaches its southernmost point in Silesia near Leszno (ca. 52° N) before running northeast across central Poland north of Warsaw into European Russia. The area immediately to the south of the ice experienced permafrost and tundra conditions especially during the winter, then was covered by glacial outwash during the warmer months as meltwaters streamed off the ice. The areas where this condition prevailed correspond to the plains of northern France, the Low Countries, and West Germany, and a thin band through East Germany, spreading out into the broad Mazovian outwash plains of central Poland. In addition to the glacial outwash, the major rivers of central Europe such as the Elbe, Oder, and Vistula alluviated wide floodplains as their waters were diverted by the ice front. The resulting band of flat terrain with sandy and gravelly soils of marginal fertility ranges in width from less than 50 kilometers to over 200.

As the Weichsel ice sheets retreated further north, the downcutting of the river valleys through the outwash plains resulted in a lowering of the water table. The result was that in areas primarily covered by sandy soils, dune formation began. This process was especially pronounced during the Older and Younger Dryas periods (Maruszczak 1983) in the terminal Pleistocene. Much of central Poland is covered by dunes originating during this period, as is the outwash belt through Germany into the Low Countries.

By about 11,000 BP, the ice sheet had retreated well to the north of continental Europe, leaving a glacially-modified landscape in its wake. The retreat of the Scandinavian ice sheets between 20,000 and 10,000 BP was so relatively rapid that large areas of northern Poland, Germany, and Denmark escaped being turned into outwash plains as had happened further south. Rather, a flat ground moraine was

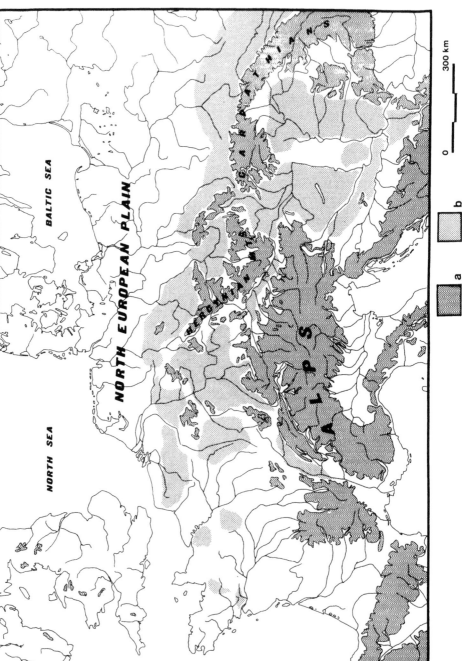

Fig. 2.4 Ecological zonation in temperate Europe, including terrain forms and drainage. Key: a – areas over 500 meters above sea level;

left in many areas, generally composed of boulder clay. The retreating ice also scoured finger-lakes in north-central Poland and left terminal moraines which so disrupted drainage that more lakes resulted. The lake belts of northern Poland and East Germany are the result of such terminal moraines. The retreating ice also left behind blocks of dead ice which subsequently melted to form shallow kettle lakes. Similar processes sometimes occurred in the periglacial outwash areas as well, where water which accumulated in low areas during warm spells froze, was covered by later sediments, and then melted to form shallow lakes such as the Dümmersee in north Germany (Seehafer 1980).

The rivers of the glaciated parts of the North European Plain, particularly the Elbe, Oder, and Vistula, found their way out to the nascent Baltic and North Seas late in the Pleistocene by progressively cutting channels through the ground moraine. The Vistula near Chełmno in northern Poland, for instance, cut a trough 50–60 meters below the level of the surrounding ground moraine. The result is that as they get closer to their mouths, the Oder and Vistula are relatively constricted streams with narrow floodplains, whereas further south they are broader and more meandering as they cross the outwash plains.

The coastal regions of the North European Plain, while appearing very uniform, are quite varied in their structure. The primary distinction can be made between those areas which lay beyond the reach of the maximum extent of the Weichsel ice sheets ca. 20,000 BP and those which lay under the ice. The areas in the former category include the coasts of Belgium, the Netherlands, northwest Germany, and southwest Denmark, while the latter includes northern and eastern Denmark, and the East German and Polish coasts.

The coastal areas not covered by the ice sheets were generally part of the glacial outwash belt lying before the ice front. As such, they were subject to the same glaciofluvial processes as the inland outwash plains and were subsequently affected by similar dune formation processes. As a result, much of the northern parts of Belgium, Holland, West Germany, and western Denmark are covered by sandy soils. Sometimes, these take the form of active dunes along the coast, but in higher areas, there are more stable soils known as cover-sands. The Holocene depositional history of this area is exceedingly complex, for even minute changes in sea level can trigger a complex of ecological effects reaching back into the hinterlands. The major post-Pleistocene marine event in this area was the progressive drowning of much of the once-dry land where the North Sea is today, as a result of the world-wide rise in sea levels after the retreat of the glaciers. A general approximation of today's coastline was reached by about 6000 bc. Since then, there have been a number of marine transgressions and regressions, all of which had profound effects on human settlement in the coastal zone (Louwe Kooijmans 1976, 1980a). Louwe Kooijmans (1980a: 107) defines six environmental belts in the Dutch coastal zone, including sandy coastal barriers with sand dunes, tidal flats, salt marshes, estuarine creeks, peat zones, and alluvial plains. The nature of the outwash belt has resulted in a rather broad coastal zone in this part of northwestern Europe, ranging up to 50 kilometers in places such as the Rhine-Maas delta. The above six zones interdigitate with each other to create a tremendously diverse environment. The configuration of these zones and the changing sea levels has resulted in a very dynamic coastal environment in northwestern Europe during the last 8,000 years.

The east Danish, East German, and Polish coasts are configured somewhat differently, since these areas lay beneath the ice sheets and have undergone considerable eustatic and isostatic movement following the removal of the burden of the ice. The initial response to deglaciation was a rebounding of the land surface, followed by a compensating lowering as parts of Scandinavia rebounded. The eventual lowering of the land was accompanied by the general Holocene rise in sea levels. The result was that about 80 to 100 kilometers of the early Holocene coastal plain in northern Poland have been drowned, and a similar amount of land was lost in East Germany and Denmark. The rising sea levels in relation to the land surface also caused a silting up of the deltas of the lower Oder and Vistula rivers. The alluvium along the lower Oder is 25 meters deep at its thickest and that along the lower Vistula is up to 50 meters deep. The major difference between the coastline of this area and that of western Europe is the morainic character of the Danish, East German, and Polish littoral. Rather than the extensive sandy areas of the Dutch and West German coastal dunes, the areas further east have somewhat more marked relief and less dune formation, even though the soils are generally sandy. The dunes, peatbogs, and estuaries are all of very recent origin and confined to a narrow strip less than 10 kilometers wide along the coast. Considerable environmental variation within the ground moraine exists, however, largely as the result of numerous sub-glacial channels, many of which are dry but some of which carry small rivers draining into the Baltic. There are also numerous kettle lakes in the ground moraine of the Polish littoral.

The loess belt
South of the band of glacial outwash is a zone which was largely unaffected by the glacial ice and the fluvial processes associated with it, but where periglacial conditions nonetheless prevailed during the Weichsel glaciation. This zone coincides, in large part, with the Tertiary hills of central Europe. Much of this area is covered by loess soils deposited during the Weichsel. Loess is fine soil whisked up by winds from the periglacial expanses of western Europe and deposited where the wind was broken by the uplands. The loess lands of central Europe take several different configurations, largely determined by the underlying topography. Along the southern margin of the North European Plain in northern Germany, there are flat expanses of loess in the areas around Soest, Hannover, and Magdeburg. In these areas, the border between the loess and the glacial outwash immediately to the north of it is difficult to perceive topographically, yet probably would have been reflected by a sharp vegetation difference in the Atlantic primeval forest.

Further south, in the basins and river valleys of the rolling upland areas of Brabant, Limburg, central Germany, southern Poland, Bohemia, and Moravia, there are patches of loess which often cover substantial areas. These loess landscapes are usually dissected by streams which have a dendritic pattern, and their rolling terrain is quite distinguishable from the outwash plains which border them to the north. Although these areas are often pictured on maps as being continuous belts, a closer examination of soil maps will show that they are really discontinuous, separated by varied landforms such as rocky ridges, *karst,* and the Tertiary mountain ranges of central Europe. The areas covered by the loess tend to have a fairly homogeneous soil cover, but it is important to note that the edaphic variation caused by the terrain results in different levels of productivity, ranging from very high in the valley bottoms to moderate on the drier loess-covered watersheds.

In some areas which lie outside of the loess belt proper, it is still possible to find loess soils in the form of redeposited loess-derived alluvium in the valley bottoms. This so-called *Schwemmlöss* often forms a veneer a meter or so in thickness on the gravel terraces of valleys such as the Aisne in northeastern France.

The ecological differences between the lowlands of the North European Plain and the loess belt are most apparent when one examines LANDSAT imagery of the two regions (Fig. 2.5). The lowlands on the Plain are an extraordinarily patchy environment, with numerous lakes and bogs, and meandering streams. The loess uplands, on the other hand, have a more uniform tone in the LANDSAT image that reflects the homogeneity of the loess substrate, and the dendritic drainage pattern is conspicuous. The valley bottoms in these areas are clearly the most productive habitats. Some might argue that the ecological differences which appear in LANDSAT imagery are strictly anthropogenic, the result of recent land-use practices. There is probably an element of truth in this, but the modern land-use patterns are probably conditioned by the underlying terrain and soils. Moreover, the infrared images in Figure 2.5 do not reflect the sizes of individual fields and their crop cover but show the vigor of the vegetation cover on a somewhat coarser scale.

Potential natural vegetation of central Europe

The soils of continental central Europe supported a complex mosaic of mature vegetation associations, with the dominant tree species varying according to soils (especially their acidity), edaphic conditions, and local climatological factors. The present vegetation of the areas discussed here offers very little evidence of what the primeval Atlantic forest was like. Even where stands of virgin forest have survived, their proximity to anthropogenic vegetation has inevitably cost them some of their original character. Perhaps the closest approximation of the Atlantic forest can be found in the deeper reaches of the Białowieża Forest in eastern Poland. Even here, however, it must be remembered that the Białowieża woods are growing under a climatic regime different from that of the Atlantic and Sub-Boreal periods.

The primeval deciduous forest of central Europe is often characterized as oak woods mixed with lime and beech (e.g. Fitter 1978). Recently, however, the argument has been presented that the "mixed oak forest", or *"Eichenmischwald"* was not a universal vegetation type, and that many tracts, especially on the North European Plain, were covered by forests in which lime (linden) was the primary constituent (e.g. Iversen 1973, Andersen 1978, Greig 1982). Greig (1982: 25–6) attributes the under-representation of lime *(Tilia)* in pollen samples to several

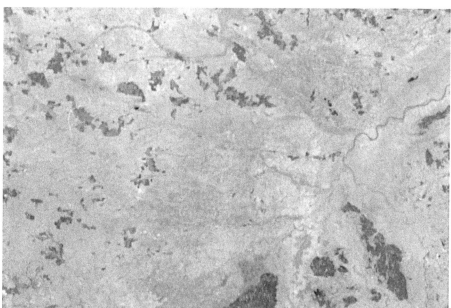

Fig. 2.5 LANDSAT images of sections of the North European Plain (A) and the loess uplands (B). These are black-and-white prints of original false-color composite infrared images. (A) is a part of north-central Poland known as Kuyavia with Vistula river at upper right and glacial finger lakes in center of image (NASA LANDSAT E.2104-09080.5), while (B) is the loess plateau northeast of the city of Kraków in southern Poland with Vistula river at center-right and loess plateau occupying center of image (NASA LANDSAT E.30448-08520). Black areas in both images are forests. Note the greater degree of "patchiness" in the image from the North European Plain and the dendritic drainage pattern of the loess landscape.

factors, including the general unsuitability of the soils immediately around pollen sampling sites for the growth of lime and the low pollen production of *Tilia* itself. Upland peats and lake beds are generally found in areas which would not support substantial lime growth, while in wet lowland basins, there would have been more oak growing closer to the actual sampling sites. In addition, dense riparian vegetation in the lowland pollen basins can physically screen out the pollen from the dryland forests nearby (Tauber 1965). *Tilia* pollen productivity is generally low, and its transport mechanisms do not promote its wide dispersal. When compared in pollen diagrams with the prodigious output of oak pollen, it appears to be insignificant. Greig has argued that when these factors are taken into account, it is possible to demonstrate that lime-rich forests, rather than "mixed oak forest" was the dominant vegetation type in many areas of temperate Europe during the Atlantic period.

In many parts of the Atlantic primeval forest, the closed canopy did not permit the infiltration of much light to the forest floor. In Białowieża forest today, only about 10% of the sunlight available above the canopy can actually can penetrate to the understory vegetation (Pirożnikow 1983: 147). During the spring, however, there is a brief period between the warming of the weather and the closing of the canopy by leaves, during which the understory plants can flower and grow. This vernal efflorescence of the forest floor, although short-lived each year, would have been visually striking in addition to providing much-needed food for prehistoric man at a critical time of the year. The actual seed bank in the soils of deciduous forests is small, however, in comparision with that of arable fields and grasslands (Pirożnikow 1983: 162). There would have been some time lag between the clearance of the tree cover and the development of markedly different vegetational associations if a field were not immediately planted with crops. It is therefore difficult to imagine the deliberate clearance of forest exclusively for pasture as opposed to arable land.

Clarke (1976) has called attention to the great natural productivity of the lowland forest ecosystems in Europe during the Atlantic period. The annual leaf-fall resulted in a dense ground layer of humus and decaying wood, which supported populations of edible fungi, mosses, and liverworts. Above this forest floor community was a layer of herbaceous grasses and other plants, including seed-bearing perennials and root and tuber plants. Bracken (*Pteridum aquilineum*) would have been a major constituent of this layer, since its large leaf area makes it the most efficient interceptor of the small amounts of sunlight filtering through the forest canopy (Riley and Young 1968: 13). The average annual productivity of this species is between 20 and 50 tons/km^2, most of it in the form of edible rhizomes. Higher up, there would have been a layer of hazel bushes, berry shrubs, and brambles. This layer would have been the most productive along the edges of the forest beside glades, lakes, and streams, since it requires more sunlight than the small plants of the lower layers. Finally, there were the trees of the forest canopy, which provided acorns and beech mast, as well as fertilizer for the whole system in the form of leaf litter. This vertical diversity would have been coupled with horizontal diversity as a result of the patchy distribution of the glacial soils of the

North European Plain. This ecosystem would have been effectively shut down for between three and five months each year, however, so the productivity was not constant throughout the course of the year.

The major limitation on the productivity of the understory vegetation described above was the degree to which sunlight was intercepted in the forest canopy by trees such as linden, elm, and oak. During the Atlantic, the thinly wooded areas and ecotones probably became more densely forested, and much productive understory vegetation would have been shaded out. The spread of climax forests would have impinged both on the wild animal populations of these woods and on the human foraging populations who relied on the forest resources.

The natural vegetation of the central European loess belt during the Atlantic period has long been the topic of considerable discussion. Gradmann (1933) argued that the distribution of Neolithic and Bronze Age settlements in central Europe was largely congruent with the modern distribution of steppe vegetation communities, and that this was due to the deliberate selection of these areas by prehistoric communities. In these *Altsiedlungsgebiete*, Gradmann argued, the primeval forests had been opened up by the drier and warmer Atlantic climate. Firbas (1949) pointed out a number of theoretical problems with Gradmann's argument and, on the basis of limited palynological evidence, concluded that the moister loess areas (where annual precipitation exceeds 500 mm today) had closed forests, while the drier loess upland areas (primarily the watersheds) had open woods and even parkland covering them. Loess is a fine-grained, permeable soil, and it evaporates more soil moisture than any other type of sediment (Butzer 1971: 577). As a result, loess soils are very dry, especially if well-drained, and they do not generally favor dense forest growth. According to Butzer, the Bohemian basin, the Elbe-Saale basin, and the upper Rhine all qualify as dry loess areas which were probably only lightly wooded during the Atlantic period. To these can probably be added the higher interfluves of the southern Polish loess areas along the north slopes of the Carpathians.

The malacological studies of Mania and his colleagues in the Elbe-Saale *Trockengebiet* would appear to support this model of loess vegetation during the Atlantic period (Mania 1973; Mania and Preuss 1975). Mania found that, in horizons datable to the Atlantic period, the chernozems formed on loess yielded a mollusc community typical of open, unwooded vegetation. In fact, he was able to conclude that chernozems, which are often thought to be the result of soil formation under Neolithic land clearance (e.g. Kruk 1973), already existed at the beginning of the Atlantic period, ca. 6200 bc. The mollusc analysis "showed the widespread nature of the richest and lushest forest communities of the Holocene, but in the center of the (Elbe-Saale) dry area – congruent with the extent of the chernozem – next to gallery and meadow-woods, [there existed] only different varieties of open, tree-poor, or tree-free landscape, even true steppe elements" (Mania 1973: 39, PB translation). Gradmann was perhaps not entirely wrong.

Palynological data from other parts of the loess belt, however, indicate that many areas supported quite dense vegetation. Bakels (1978) has studied pollen profiles from the lower Rhine and Danube basins which come from deposits near early

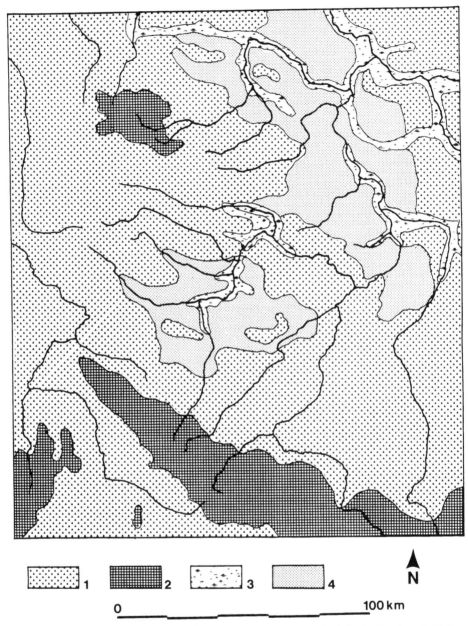

Fig. 2.6 Reconstructed vegetation zones in the Elbe-Saale area during the Atlantic climatic period (after Mania and Preuss 1975). Key: 1 – thermophilous mixed-oak forest; 2 – montane mixed forest; 3 – meadow and swamp woods; 4 – open, tree-poor landscape.

Neolithic sites. Such deposits generally are found in low-lying areas, and as a result, they probably do not reflect the vegetation of the interfluves. The areas around the bogs and lakes which yielded the data studied by Bakels would have been well-watered and well supplied with nutrients, precisely the areas where dense riparian forests would have grown. *But*, these are also the areas where many early Neolithic settlements of the loess belt are found.

From Bakels' analyses, it would appear that different parts of the loess belt had different sorts of forest types, with the areas along the lower Rhine and Maas differing somewhat from those closer to the center of the continent. Many of the wetter low-lying areas in the river valleys of the Rhine-Maas area, where the water table was very high, were covered by alder carrs. This sort of vegetation has a dense understory layer and is difficult to penetrate. The drier areas of the watershed margins in the Rhine-Maas area were probably covered by mixed deciduous forests belonging to the Alno-Padion association, a collection of lime, ash, sycamore, elm, and oak. Finally, there are the forests of the loess interfluves in the Rhine-Maas area, where Bakels has argued for the existence of a lime, or oak-lime, forest. The Atlantic forests of the loess uplands at their northwestern corner, then, would probably not have been markedly different from those in parts of the North European Plain where rich, dry soils occurred.

The more continental loess areas probably had a slightly different sort of forest cover. Bakels has reconstructed the loess forest near Hienheim in Bavaria as having been a deciduous forest in which oak was predominant, but with some amount of lime as well – essentially a more continental variant of the forest covering the loess in the Rhine-Maas area. On the alluvium of the river valleys themselves, Bakels has proposed that mixed deciduous forests of the Alno-Padion type were found, although the specific composition of this forest in any one area was quite variable.

When the malacological and palynological data are considered together, it appears that the natural vegetation of the loess belt during the Atlantic period was a varied mosaic of different arboreal densities and that some areas were lightly wooded or not wooded at all. The sparseness of the tree cover in some areas would have meant a smaller accumulation of leaf litter, and hence a poorer forest floor environment. In comparison with many other ecosystems, such as tundra and deserts, the productivity of the loess belt would still rate high, but not so high as that of the lowland forests. The diversity of the ecosystem in the loess areas would have been conditioned more by variations in texture, pH, mineral components, and water content than by the actual source material of the underlying soils.

The elm decline

A remarkable feature of the palaeoecological record at the end of the Atlantic and the beginning of the Sub-Boreal is the sharp decline in elm pollen found in many pollen diagrams across northern Europe. Although radiocarbon dates for the "elm decline" are not entirely uniform, they indicate that at approximately 3200 bc (unrecalibrated) there was a sudden decrease in the amount of elm pollen deposited in the bogs and lakes of temperate Europe. Prior to this date, the hardwood forests of northern Europe included a great many elms, and within a few decades some stands lost half the members of this species while the proportions of other arboreal taxa remained constant. The selective nature of the elm decline is its most intriguing aspect, one which has produced considerable discussion since it was first recognized prior to World War II.

The initial perception of the elm decline in the pre-radiocarbon era was as a climatic event which separated the Atlantic from the Sub-Boreal. Working against this hypothesis, however, is the fact that not all pollen diagrams contain elm declines, and in those that do other taxa which are even more temperature-sensitive do not show a simultaneous fluctuation. For instance, ash, a very cold-sensitive species, remains constant or even increases at a horizon coeval with the elm decline. Moreover, the decline is not absolutely synchronous over large areas, as would be expected if it has been caused by climatic change. An alternative explanation for the elm decline which involves natural causes was that it was the result of an epidemic disease of elms. The disease hypothesis is appealing, for it is consistent with the eventual recovery of the elm populations within a few centuries following the decline, much as other hardwood species with have been struck by epidemics in historic times have recovered. Nonetheless, Heybroek, a forest pathologist, has examined the disease hypothesis and found it untenable (Heybroek 1963). He argues that once a plant disease is established on a continent it is there to stay, and there is evidence to indicate that Dutch elm disease was introduced to Europe from southwest Asia within the last few centuries.

The most popular explanations for the elm decline involve anthropogenic causes. In some cases, the elm decline is considered to be coeval with the initial appearance of Neolithic agriculture, since it is often accompanied by the pollen of open-habitat species associated with cultivation. It is important to differentiate the elm decline from Iversen's classic *landnam* model of vegetation change and regeneration which accompanied the establishment of agriculture in the forests of northern Europe. The *landnam* model represents an episode of land clearance usually several centuries *later* than the elm decline and is characterized by displacements in whole groups of plant species. In much subsequent discussion, however, elm declines have been identified as *landnam* episodes, causing much confusion in the literature on this topic.

Actually, the only anthropogenic explanation for the elm decline which has gained any currency is that of Troels-Smith (1960) who proposed that the elms were not cleared but rather lopped or pollarded to provide fodder for domestic cattle belonging to semi-agrarian populations in the forests of Denmark and the North European Plain. Excessive lopping would have removed the pollen-generating flowers, thus causing a decline in pollen production and suppressing the regeneration of elms. Garbett (1981) has also recently argued in favor of the lopping hypothesis and against the climatic and disease explanations for the elm decline. Rowley-Conwy (1982: 205–6), on the other hand, has taken a position against the lopping hypothesis on the basis of the scale of the operation which would be necessary to depress pollen production to the point where it would so markedly affect the pollen diagrams. A decline of elm pollen by one half, according to his calculations, would imply the pollarding of 47-80 million elm trees in Denmark alone, supporting a population of close to a million cattle. Such figures seem impossibly high for early agrarian societies in Denmark and elsewhere on the North European Plain. In addition to Rowley-Conwy's reservations, it should also be noted that the elm decline normally predates the appearance of the earliest domesticated animals and plants in areas where it occurs by several centuries.

Although it seems that Rowley-Conwy's position against the lopping hypothesis

is a cogent one, the climatic and disease explanations also appear to be unacceptable. There is yet one more anthropogenic explanation which may be proposed,
however. At a number of pollen sites in temperate Europe, there is evidence for
pre-agricultural disturbances in the natural vegetation (see Chapter 3 below). The
purpose behind such manipulation would have been the improvement of hunting
conditions and the maintenance of productive sub-climax vegetation associations
(Mellars 1976). It seems possible that the elm decline is a part of the same
phenomenon. Elms would have been most common on lower areas with shallower
ground water, along lakes, bogs, and streams. These would be precisely the areas
which would have made the largest contributions to pollen deposits in these same
basins, as well as likely sites for the manipulation of the vegetation using fire.
Human activity that would have affected the vegetation in these edge areas may
have selectively affected elms among the arboreal component of the vegetation.
Since elms take such a long time to regenerate, the destruction of flowering elms by
fire may have had a magnified impact on pollen profiles in comparison with that of
the other members of these communities, many of which are fast-growing pioneer
species. Differences in burning regimes may account for the variations in the
timing and magnitude of elm declines. A sharp and sustained decline may have
been caused by extensive and repeated firing, while a gradual drop could indicate
less frequent episodes of burning. If such a model can be ultimately accepted as the
cause of the elm decline, it may have important implications for the process of the
introduction of food-production to north-central Europe, for it would reflect an
intensification of food collection immediately preceding the introduction of plants
and animals to this area.

Native fauna of central Europe
The wild animal populations of both the lowlands and uplands of central Europe
were characterized by essentially the same types of species. Among the larger
mammals, red deer, aurochs, and wild boar were the most common, with elk (the
North American moose) being confined to the areas with many lakes, such as parts
of the North European Plain and the Alpine Foreland. The European brown bear
(*Ursus arctos*) occurred in the lowland forests as well as in the mountainous areas.
Among the smaller herbivores, the roe deer (*Capreolus capreolus*) was very
common, capable of reaching very high population densities in the lowland
environment (Chaplin 1975: 41). In lowland areas with many lakes and streams,
there were large populations of beaver, marten, and otter. Human clearance of the
vegetation would have benefited the major wild herbivore species, but the bears
and smaller fur-bearing animals probably retreated from areas of human settlement.

An important reptilian species found in Neolithic Europe was the pond tortoise
(*Emys orbicularis*), which has become virtually absent from the area in recent
millennia following the deterioration of climate after the Sub-Boreal (Degerbøl and
Krog 1951: 92–6). The pond tortoise requires warm, dry summers and relatively
open vegetation so that the eggs can be buried without troublesome roots and so
that the soil in which the eggs are buried is exposed to the sun. Today, the

northernmost limit of non-breeding *Emys orbicularis* is approximately the 18° C
July isotherm in Germany and the 20° C July isotherm in France, while breeding
populations exist only in southern and eastern Europe (Fig. 2.7). Pond tortoise
remains frequently occur on Neolithic sites in temperate Europe, and their
presence can provide information on climate, seasonality, and even land clearance
(Degerbøl and Krog 1951; Bogucki 1982: 74–6).

Waterfowl would have been especially prevalent in the marshy meadows of the
North European Plain, particularly in areas such as the Rhine-Maas delta and the
estuaries and floodplains of the other major rivers. Birds of prey, including hawks
and eagles, would have been found in areas where the vegetation was open enough
to permit their hunting of small animals. These types of birds would have found
their environment enhanced by human clearance of land for cultivation.

The rivers, lakes, and ponds of central Europe supported considerable fish
populations. In addition to the members of the eel, carp, and perch families which
are found today, trout and salmon were also present in the major river systems.
Anadromous fish may have comprised an important food resource in Neolithic
Europe (e.g. Hartmann-Frick 1969), although the evidence for their exploitation is
slim. Fish bones are difficult to find archaeologically without the use of wet-
sieving, and this has rarely been done on most central European Neolithic sites.
Most evidence for Neolithic fishing comes from evidence such as fish-hooks,
net-weights, and fish-traps. In particular, fish-traps such as the one at Bergschenhoek (Louwe Kooijmans 1980b: 109) would have been especially suited for
the capture of anadromous fish.

There is some evidence for the exploitation of coastal fauna, particularly along
the west Baltic littoral. It has, in fact, been proposed that the richness of these
coastal resources – including oysters, seal pups, swans, and ducks – was a powerful
disincentive to the adoption of agriculture by the indigenous foragers of this region
(Rowley-Conwy 1984). The utilization of coastal fauna continued into the
Neolithic, although the marine component appears to have become significantly
less important (Skaarup 1973; Tauber 1981).

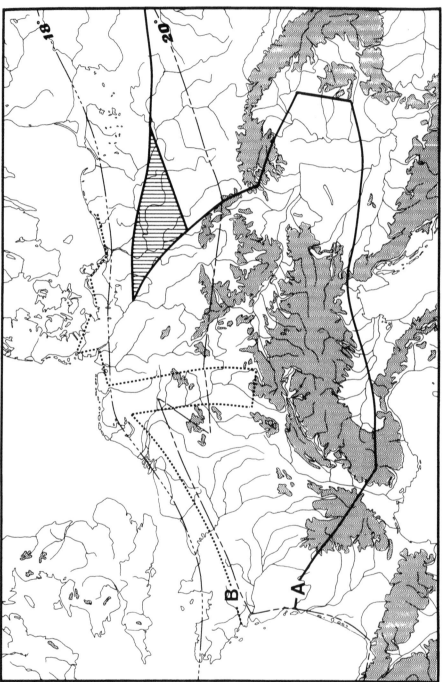

Fig. 2.7 Present distribution of the pond tortoise (*Emys orbicularis*) and the 18 and 20° C July isotherms (after Degerbøl and Krog 1951).
Key: a – northern limit of modern breeding populations (shaded area indicates region where this species was virtually extinct by the early twentieth century); b – northern limit of which non-breeding individuals have been found in modern times.

3

Indigenous foraging populations

Any discussion of the habitats encountered by the earliest European farmers would be incomplete without some mention of the indigenous foraging communities that inhabited many parts of central Europe. These groups formed a significant component of the ecosystem, and the early agricultural communities in Europe needed to accommodate them in some way. Two aspects of the postglacial foraging communities are especially important for the study of early agricultural adaptations. The first is the distribution of hunter-gatherer populations as reconstructed from the density of Mesolithic sites, and the other is the evidence for the modification of natural ecosystems by these groups.

Mesolithic settlement distribution
Within the major habitat zones of central Europe settled by the early food-producing communities, it has long been observed that the overall density of Mesolithic settlement was markedly lower in the dry loess areas than either in the sub-Alpine zone or on the North European Plain (Tringham 1968; Clarke 1976, among others.) The reasons for this lie in the generally lower natural productivity of the loess habitats, particularly the upland watersheds, when compared with that of the diverse glacial soils of the North European Plain. The loess landscape was certainly not barren, but it lacked the capacity to support foraging populations to the extent that other habitats could. I would urge caution, however, in downgrading the suitability of the loess belt for hunter-gatherer settlement. Above all, the assumption should not be made that the loess belt was totally devoid of habitation prior to the arrival of agriculturalists.

Many Mesolithic sites *have* been found in the loess belt (e.g. Milisauskas 1977; Geupel 1981). These are often located along rivers or in areas where subsequent land use did not obliterate traces of them (Fig. 3.1). It is important to remember that the Mesolithic exploitation patterns during many times of the year probably resulted in the creation of ephemeral, short-term exploitation sites (some might call them "stations" – cf. Binford 1980). Such sites would increase in archaeological visibility only as repeated use of particular loci resulted in "palimpsest" accumulations of occupation debris. If the overall Mesolithic population density in the loess belt was low to begin with, then the opportunities for such palimpsest site formation to occur would also have decreased proportionally. Compounding the situation is the fact that the suitability of the loess belt for grain cultivation has led to its being the most intensively farmed area of central Europe for the last six millennia. Many ephemeral Mesolithic sites would have stood very little chance of survival under the ensuing conditions of cultivation and erosion. A collection of Mesolithic artifacts still relatively *in situ* on a sand dune is much more visible archaeologically than an isolated scraper or microlith in a ploughed field of dark chernozem in the loess belt. A belief that the earliest farming cultures of central Europe did not encounter indigenous peoples from the outset is, in my view, mistaken. As the early food-producing communities of central Europe began to penetrate new ecological zones such as the Alpine Foreland and the North European Plain, the opportunities for contact with indigenous peoples multiplied significantly.

Pre-Neolithic vegetation disturbances

Over the past 20 years, evidence has been accumulating from many parts of northern Europe which indicates that natural vegetational communities were deliberately altered by indigenous foraging communities. Although this phenomenon has been best documented in the British Isles (Simmons 1969; Smith 1970; Mellars 1975; 1976), it is probable that Mesolithic populations across central Europe were engaged in it as well. It has been established that the documented disturbances of the vegetation were brought about largely, if not entirely, through the agency of fire, very much like similar exploitative strategies which have been documented for North America (summarized in Lewis 1973) and in Australia (Jones 1973; Hallam 1975).

The major limitation on the productivity of the oak/hazel/bracken plant association described in Chapter 2 above was the degree to which sunlight was intercepted in the forest canopy by climax tree species such as lime. The role of sunlight and the stages of plant succession are such basic aspects of forest ecology that any foraging group exploiting forest plant resources could not fail to have at least a basic cognizance of them. The differences between the productive plant associations of the more thinly wooded tracts and forest margins and the unproductive interiors of the climax forest would have been vivid, as would have been the termination of the vernal efflorescence of the forest floor by the closing of the forest canopy in late spring.

The deliberate burning of limited parts of the woodlands would increase both the plant and animal resources available to Mesolithic populations. Mellars (1976: 22–6) estimated that plant and animal food-yields could be increased by 500–900% in a woodland environment with a planned policy of deliberate burning. The effects of such strategies of deliberate burning in woodland habitats have been summarized by Mellars and Reinhardt (1978: 260):

1. It increases the mobility of human populations by destroying dense undergrowth;
2. It increases the growth of vegetable resources, particularly seed-grasses like *Chenopodium* (goosefoot), nut bushes like hazel, and tuber plants like bracken;
3. It improves hunting conditions by reducing the amount of cover available to animals;

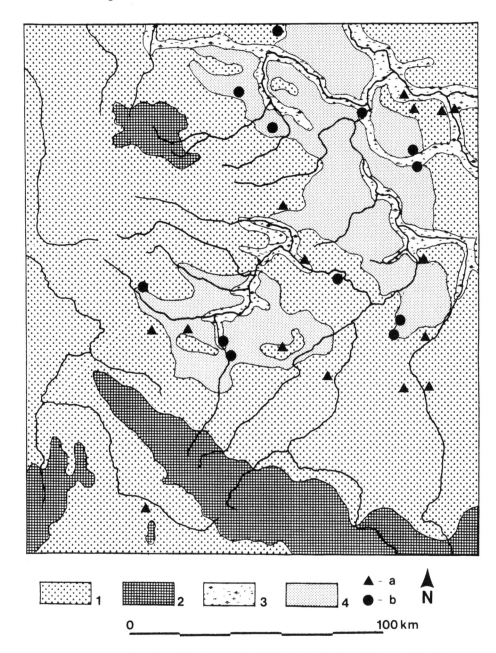

Fig. 3.1 Distribution of late Mesolithic and early Neolithic sites in the Elbe-Saale area of East Germany (after Geupel 1981: fig. 1). Key: 1 – 4 as in Fig. 2.6; a – late Mesolithic; b – early Neolithic ("earliest Linear Pottery").

4. It increases the total numbers and population densities of animal populations by increasing the quality and quantity of forage resources;

5. It increases the growth rate of young animals and the maximum size attained by mature animals;

6. It controls the distribution of animals, making hunting more predictable and thus more efficient.

An important consideration is the type of woodland which lends itself to being deliberately fired. On the North European Plain, those areas covered by damp clays and silts probably supported a dense lime forest during the Atlantic period. Simmons (1969: 111), writing about similar soils in England, notes that only rarely would such woods have provided good conditions for burning since they would have been rarely dry enough to support an extensive fire and the thick canopy would have suppressed the growth of fuel-producing ground vegetation. Burning in such woods would have to be performed in the sunnier ecotones along lakes, bogs, and streams, while the deeper parts of the woods would have been almost fire-proof.

On the sandy and gravelly glacial outwash soils, such as those of the meltwater valleys of the North European Plain and the outwash plains further south, the conditions for burning were better. On such soils, the woodlands would have been richly endowed with bushes, shrubs, and bracken on the forest floor. Such plants are the principal fuels for spreading fires in forested environments. There would have been numerous inflammable conifers mixed among the deciduous trees. Moreover, the permeable structure of the sandy soils would have allowed the forest, especially the undergrowth, to dry out during periods of little or no rain. In the loess belt, it is also probable that there were very good conditions for deliberate burning, given the drier nature of these areas and the thinness of the forest cover in many parts. The low overall density of Mesolithic population, however, might have made it unnecessary to resort to burning in order to increase subsistence resources.

Until now, most of the empirical evidence for pre-Neolithic vegetation manipulation has come from the British Isles. In particular, Smith (1970) considered the secondary *Corylus* (hazel) maximum which occurs in some British pollen diagrams close to the Boreal/Atlantic transition to be the effect of human activity, as is the appearance of *Plantago lanceolata* (plantain) before the Boreal/Atlantic transition. In continental Europe, few researchers have investigated this topic, but Smith (1970: 83) suggested that the pollen diagrams from Aamosen and Hohen Viecheln show evidence of artificial expansion of hazel growth. In Poland, the hazel advance is coeval with the elm decline, and isopollen maps indicate that these two events occurred in more or less the same areas, particularly in north-central Poland in the fourth millennium bc (Ralska-Jasiewiczowa 1983). It has been proposed that hazel nuts may have played a role in the Mesolithic economy across continental northern Europe (e.g. Price 1978: 107, 1981: 230; Clarke 1976: 376). Hazel is not a climax species, and in a natural vegetational succession, one would expect that it would be quickly closed out. In many pollen diagrams, however, it remains constant throughout the Atlantic, suggesting that the vegetation was being deliberately maintained at a sub-climax level. Hazel is particularly benefited by burning (Lewis 1973: 61–5), and many years ago, Rawitscher (1945: 303) suggested that if fire had been used extensively by the Mesolithic inhabitants of central Europe, "a prevalent hazel vegetation would not be unexpected."

In this connection, it may also be possible to view the elm decline which occurred about 3200 bc as the result of Mesolithic subsistence practices which involved burning. Both climatic change and disease appear to be unacceptable as explanations to account for the elm decline, leaving human activity as the most likely cause. The use of lopped elm branches for fodder is problematical due to a lack of traces of domestic livestock in the archaeological record coeval with the elm decline in most areas. Mesolithic burning, however, may still be a viable explanation, for the elms which would have made the primary contributions to the pollen-bearing deposits were those located on forest margins in the basins of lakes and bogs. Burning in these areas, rather than in the depths of the climax forest, may have selectively depressed elm pollen values leaving the proportions of other arboreal species relatively unchanged. The relative contemporaneity of elm decline episodes in the pollen diagrams of northern Europe may be a reflection of the demands made on Mesolithic subsistence in the last centuries of the fourth millennium bc.

The effects of the activity of Mesolithic populations on the vegetation are only beginning to be investigated by European palaeoecologists. There is a shift away from the view that the forest was an "ecological barrier" (Kozlowski 1975: 18–19) which Mesolithic man was unable to penetrate, control, and change. Rather than being dominated by the forest and remaining a passive beneficiary of its largesse, it can now be suggested that the Mesolithic foraging populations of central Europe played an active role in the modification of the ecosystem to suit their own needs. The earliest agricultural communities in this area, then, did not adapt to a completely pristine environment, but one which several millennia of human activity had altered to varying degrees. There was probably a degree of correlation between the extent to which the environment was modified and the density of Mesolithic populations. The implications of pre-Neolithic vegetation manipulation would have been most crucial when agricultural communities began to be established in areas such as the North European Plain, for it may have been in these artificial glade communities along the lakes and bogs of central Europe that the domestic crops were most easily introduced.

Mesolithic resource management and political economy
On the North European Plain, there was an increasing diversity in the material culture of foraging groups during the Boreal and Atlantic climatic periods (Kozlowski 1975). Several regional groups have been identified, usually on the basis of the variation in their flint assemblages, and the pattern of diversification is amplified over time. The areas occupied by these groups are generally on the order of 100 to 200 kilometers in diameter (Price 1981a: 219). To many archaeologists who deal with the Mesolithic, the presence of such groups indicates the existence of "social territories" (Clark 1975, Gendel 1984), and some have hypothesized that this may imply some notion of group differentiation and identity (e.g. Champion, Gamble, Shennan, and Whittle 1984: 111; Fig. 3.2). Vang Petersen (1984) has also addressed the question of regional differentiation in material culture during the late Mesolithic of eastern Denmark. It is difficult, however, to separate this hypothesis from the Childean view that the archaeological culture could also be equated with a clearly defined ethnic identity. Discussions of Mesolithic territoriality should

differentiate between actual social territories and territories conditioned by natural barriers to information exchange and decreasing population densities away from foci of human settlement. Binford (1983: 28–34) has noted that for many hunter-gatherers the concept of "territory" may not be a culturally specified idea but rather a notion which derives from the patterns of land use over the lifetime of individuals. It is possible, however, to maintain that regional distributions of tool types represent patterns of information exchange (e.g. Wobst 1977), and from this position, it may be possible to link settlement and land use patterns with the development of local decision-making structures. The section which follows represents an attempt to explore the Late Mesolithic groups of central Europe from this perspective.

There is a frustrating lack of empirical data on Mesolithic subsistence from many parts of central Europe, and hence it is difficult to develop models of resource procurement which are supported by seeds, shells, and bones. Price (1981a) has attempted to fill some of the gaps in the data base by employing "predictive" models similar to those employed by Jochim (1976) in his studies of Mesolithic subsistence in Baden-Württemberg. Price deals specifically with the Mesolithic groups of the Boreal period in the Netherlands, but his general model probably applies to Atlantic foraging communities as well. Price's model suggests five economic "seasons" in the patterns of resource use:

1. Winter (January-March) – primary utilization of red deer, small game, and wild pig;
2. Spring Transition (April-May) – use of fish and plants in addition to large herbivores like red deer and aurochs;
3. Summer (June-August) – plants, small game, fish, and aurochs;
4. Fall Transition (September-October) – plants, aurochs, red deer, and wild pig;
5. Late Fall (November-December) – small game, wild pig, aurochs, and red deer.

A problem exists in that there is still relatively little empirical evidence for plant use, but intuitively it would seem that gathered plants probably played a major role in the Mesolithic diet at most times of the year other than during the winter shutdown of the ecosystem.

It is quite possible that hazel nuts played a major role in the winter subsistence pattern, since they were eminently storable. Moreover, hazel groves would have been a localized resource, and their expansion (as would seem to be indicated by the palynological data) would be a powerful impetus toward the development of Mesolithic populations which were tied to specific territories over time. The problem is that although nuts produce high yields, they have a very low degree of long-term predictability (Ford 1979: 236) within any one particular locality. Communities exploiting such climax forest products need to have access to a number of collecting areas in order to minimize the risk from local shortfalls in resource production.

The late Mesolithic diversification of resource use, especially in the collecting of the products of the climax forest, had demographic implications as well. For instance, children may have ceased to be liabilities and have become assets to the

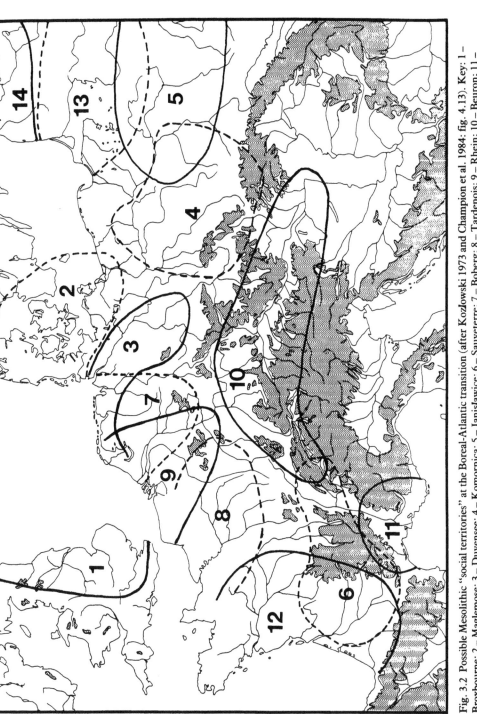

Fig. 3.2 Possible Mesolithic "social territories" at the Boreal-Atlantic transition (after Kozłowski 1973 and Champion et al. 1984: fig. 4.13). Key: 1 – Broxbourne; 2 – Maglemose; 3 – Duvensee; 4 – Komornica; 5 – Janisławice; 6 – Sauveterre; 7 – Boberg; 8 – Tardenois; 9 – Rhein; 10 – Beuron; 11 – Châteauneuf; 12 – Cuzoul; 13 – Neman; 14 – Kunda.

Mesolithic groups. Many climax forest resources are within easy reach of children, and they may actually make a substantial contribution towards their maintenance (Ford 1979: 236). If populations became more localized, children would no longer have been an impediment to group mobility, and it is quite possible that birth spacing decreased among Mesolithic populations during the Atlantic period.

Settlement data appear to support such a hypothesis (Meiklejohn, et al. 1984: 78; Constandse-Westermann and Newell 1984; Newell 1984). It is clear that there were larger aggregations of human population during the Atlantic period. Newell (1973) has documented a shift to larger settlements ca. 5000 bc in the western part of the North European Plain. In the inland continental areas of the North European Plain, there does not appear much regional variability in site sizes. Nonetheless, there seems to be a spatial concentration of Mesolithic settlements in specific microregions, such as the Plonia Valley in NW Poland (Czarnecki 1981; Fig. 3.3) and Satrup Moor (Schwabedissen 1957/8, 1981). In light of this agglomeration of population, the case for Mesolithic manipulation of the vegetation becomes stronger. Burning would have increased the spatial concentration and predictability of many plant species, thus permitting the maintenance of local high population densities in particular microregions.

The diversification of Mesolithic subsistence resources (Newell 1984: 71) would suggest that the later Mesolithic populations of the North European Plain exhibited what Binford (1980) would call "logistical organization." The concept of logistical organization refers to the degree to which accommodations are made to situations where consumers are near to one critical resource but far from other equally critical resources. Binford (1980) contrasts logistical organization with an alternative procurement strategy which he calls "mapping-on" to critical resources. In a logistically organized system, the community is organized into task groups which bring diverse resources to the settlement and store them for future use, while in a mapping-on system, the community moves frequently, searching out one critical resource after another. The former type of system generates a more diverse set of archaeological occurrences than does the latter. In addition to residential bases and "locations" (isolated artifact occurrences), Binford (1980: 10) has identified field camps, stations, and caches as components of the archaeological manifestation of a logistically organized system. Field camps are operational centers for task groups, while stations are observation points for information gathering (for instance, observing game movement). Caches are temporary storage facilities away from the main residential base. Although the number of Mesolithic sites which have provided information on their functions is relatively small, the model of Mesolithic adaptations on the North European Plain presented by Price (1981a) seems to fit the expectations of a logistically organized system more than those of a mapping-on system.

Binford (1983) has suggested that long-term land use among such hunter-gatherer populations may be more extensive than has been hitherto believed. In his view, many hunter-gatherer groups achieve subsistence security by having a number of "annual ranges" available for use. Although in any single year, the area exploited may be relatively small, the effective area utilized over the lifetimes of the

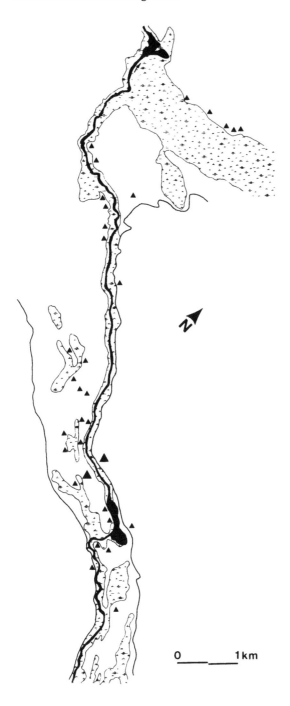

Fig. 3.3 Distribution of Mesolithic settlement in the Płonia valley of NW Poland (after Czarnecki 1981: fig. 2).

members of that group can be several times larger. The additional territory which is encompassed in a group's "lifetime range" may actually be quite necessary to that group's long-term survival, as resources within individual annual ranges are depleted. The implication of this, Binford suggests, is that hunter-gatherer groups which practice such long-term patterns of regional mobility may be very sensitive to incremental demographic changes (1983: 50). The addition of daughter communities to these systems would reduce the options for alternative annual ranges. Subsistence security would then have to be derived from the intensification of procurement strategies within a reduced range. The burning of vegetation in an effort to increase plant and animal productivity may have been one such intensification option.

In an interpretation of societies employing a procurement system broadly similar to that in parts of Late Mesolithic Europe, Green and Sassaman have proposed that the Late Archaic cultures of the Carolina Piedmont had evolved a rudimentary degree of status differentiation (1983: 277–80). Several features of Late Archaic society which Green and Sassaman use to support their argument have counterparts in Late Mesolithic Europe. These include larger and more permanent settlements, use of permanent installations such as houses and storage pits, and the elaboration of burial rituals. The agglomeration of settlement has already been discussed above. Newell (1981) has documented the large numbers of Late Mesolithic dwelling structures, although he notes that features at many sites identified as dwellings are probably tree-falls. A number of Late Mesolithic burials are known, some of which are quite elaborate. Particularly significant are the grave at Janisławice in Poland (Chmielewska 1954; Cyrek and Cyrek 1980; Fig. 3.4) and the cemetery at Vedbaek (Albrethsen and Brinch Petersen 1976; Price and Brinch Petersen 1987).

Green and Sassaman propose that local high population densities observed in Late Archaic settlement patterns in the Carolina Piedmont were nonetheless supported by a logistically organized "collecting" procurement strategy, which in turn necessitated higher levels of group organization. They argue that "as settlement density increases, informal exchange of information (i.e. nonhierarchical decision making) becomes less effective in integrating the settlement strategies of individual groups" (1983: 274). As Binford has also noted (1983: 50), the costs of pursuing subsistence options increase as settlement density increases, for the costs of settlement relocation also increase. It becomes increasingly difficult to mitigate local subsistence shortfalls through settlement moves and generalized reciprocity with kin in adjacent regions. The result is the need for structures to promote and control information flow and to organize procurement systems within local groups – specifically, decision-making hierarchies.

Similar developments can be postulated for the Late Mesolithic of central Europe, particularly on the North European Plain. The aggregation of Late Mesolithic settlements in areas such as the Płonia Valley and the Satrup Moor suggests that the exploitation of these areas required greater intragroup cooperation in the procurement of local resources. If the Green and Sassaman model can be adapted still further, this degree of local interaction would have led to the

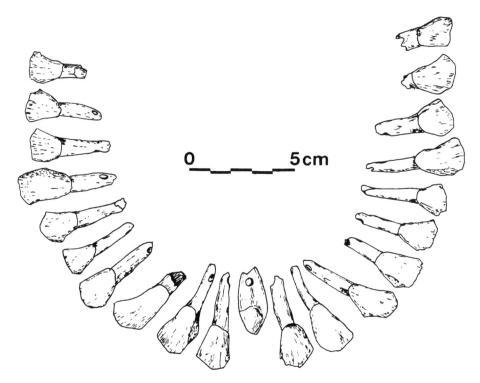

Fig. 3.4 Necklace of animal teeth from the Mesolithic burial at Janislawice (after Cyrek and Cyrek 1980).

emergence of localized settlement and mating networks, which, in turn, would have reduced the number of subsistence options available to individual groups. The flexibility of settlement relocation and moving in with distant kin would have been reduced. Such risks placed a premium on information and the transactions involved in obtaining it, which may have led to social inequalities on a rudimentary scale of the sort described by Green and Sassaman for Late Archaic cultures. Generalized reciprocity as a means for evening out subsistence shortfalls would have been replaced by alliances between local groups, relying on more specific and localized reciprocal arrangements.

A consequence of the development of local decision-making hierarchies, according to Green and Sassaman (1983: 282), is a greater social demand on production. Both subsistence and non-subsistence resources would have been important as "currency" in transactions involving resources and information and for the maintenance of alliances between local groups. Perhaps it is in this context that the systems of deliberate burning described above begin to make sense. If increased production was demanded by the hierarchy and alliance structures, rather than simply by local population increases (that could have been alleviated by other types of adjustments), then controlled burning would have been an effective means of meeting these demands in the absence of agriculture and stock-herding.

The application of this model to the Late Mesolithic societies of north-central Europe is, of course, still in the realm of hypothesis. Despite the vagueness of the data, it seems nonetheless to have a great degree of potential for explaining the social aspects of Mesolithic adaptations in north-central Europe. Instead of a strict focus on subsistence and settlement, there needs to be an explicit recognition that the social aspects of resource procurement and management must be considered if we are to understand fully the nature of prehistoric societies.

Conclusion

The Mesolithic hunter-gatherer populations of temperate Europe were clearly not starving foragers waiting to be enlightened by the appearance of food production. Rather, over the course of several millennia, they had made a set of complex adaptations to the European forests that we are only now beginning to comprehend. More importantly, they continued to deal with the twin variables of increasing forest density during the Atlantic period and increasing populations, apparently successfully. In some areas, the foraging adaptation was so successful that there was a considerable delay before the adoption of agriculture and stock-herding, and it has been proposed that only environmental changes caused the shift to a food-producing economy on the Danish littoral (Rowley-Conwy 1984; Zvelebil and Rowley-Conwy 1984). Mesolithic communities had a social existence beyond their subsistence pursuits, and it is possible that towards the end of the Mesolithic some form of decision-making hierarchy emerged. Newell (1984: 75) has noted that there are also indications that group identity and border maintenance was intensified toward the later part of the Mesolithic.

Such considerations have considerable relevance for the understanding of the process of the establishment of agrarian communities on the North European Plain in particular. The issue of contact between agriculturalists and hunter-gatherers becomes of considerable importance. As Dennell (1985: 136) has noted, there is a need for a better understanding by specialists in both the Mesolithic and the Neolithic of what is on the other side of the frontier. It may well be that this frontier was much more porous than hitherto imagined.

4

Primary Neolithic subsistence and settlement

4.1 Introduction

The first farmers of central Europe form one of the most striking archaeological manifestations of later prehistory. One cannot fail to be impressed by the richness of their ceramic decoration, the technical achievements of their longhouse construction, and the fundamental fact that they introduced an economy based on novel plants and animals into an ecosystem which required substantial modification. At the same time, there are fundamental aspects of Primary Neolithic subsistence, settlement, and social organization that are not completely understood.

In *The Dawn of European Civilization* V. Gordon Childe characterized the Primary Neolithic cultures of central Europe as "perhaps the most classically neolithic in the ancient world" (Childe 1957: 106). Whether one agrees that his assessment of "classically neolithic" has any utility given the diversity of prehistoric farming cultures, Childe's description of the "Danubian I" cultures still stands as the benchmark for subsequent discussions of early agricultural adaptations in central Europe. In Childe's cultural-evolutionary framework, the earliest cultivators in any one area could be expected to "practise the simplest conceivable sort of farming" (Childe 1957: 105). Not surprisingly, Childe then constructed a model of "a system of nomadic cultivation that does look really primitive – such as the earliest food-producers, undisciplined by environmental limitations, might be expected to invent" (1957: 105).

Childe was impressed by the considerable uniformity of the Linear Pottery culture "from the Drave to the Meuse and from the Dniester to the Baltic" (1957: 106). Moreover, he measured the amount of cultural deposits on Linear Pottery sites against the standard of the Vinča tell on the Danube near Belgrade with its long occupation sequence while simultaneously noting the relatively dense concentrations of sites of this culture across central Europe. In the 1920s, the "short" chronology for the European Neolithic to which Childe adhered permitted only a span of about 200–300 years for Linear Pottery and about the same period for the balance of the Primary Neolithic. The cumulative effect of these observations was that the Primary Neolithic sites of central Europe were seen as the product of a constantly migrating population. By 1957, the first radiocarbon dates had led Childe to extend the beginning of Linear Pottery to before 4000 bc, yet he kept the Lengyel sequence between 3000 and 2600 bc, thus leading to a 4- or 5-fold increase in the time available for Linear Pottery. The longer chronology, however, did not affect Childe's perception that many sites were occupied for only short periods of time, although he did note Sangmeister's (1951) estimate of a 450-year occupation span for Köln-Lindenthal (which did not necessarily imply *continuous* occupation.) Childe took the apparently short occupations of Primary Neolithic sites as evidence of the "crude agricultural technique" of the Danubians, in which following the exhaustion of the soil, they "shifted bag and baggage to a new site on fresh virgin soil" (Childe 1957: 106).

Childe was quite interested in the social aspects of the Primary Neolithic cultures as well as their economic dimensions. He suggested that the residential group which occupied a Primary Neolithic longhouse was "more like a clan than a pairing family" (1957: 106). He also argued that the Danubian communities were basically egalitarian, with no evidence of chieftainship. Childe noted the striking lack of Primary Neolithic figurines in central Europe, a contrast with the coeval cultures of the Balkans.

It is important to remember that as late as the mid-1950s only one fully investigated Primary Neolithic site had been published in a western language, the Linear Pottery settlement at Köln-Lindenthal (Buttler and Haberey 1936). (The Lengyel settlement at Brześć Kujawski had been published in Polish (Jażdżewski 1938) immediately before World War II.) Since 1957 there has been a growth both in the amount of empirical data on Primary Neolithic subsistence and settlement and in the elaboration of the archaeological, anthropological, and ecological approaches to agricultural adaptations. The data on subsistence available to Childe came from very few sites. By 1985, over 80 Linear Pottery sites had yielded carbonized seeds, and a large number of well-analyzed faunal assemblages have been reported. Settlement pattern surveys began in the late 1960s and have broadly expanded our knowledge of Primary Neolithic adaptations in central Europe.

A fundamental premise of this discussion is that the initial introduction of food production into central Europe was accomplished through the colonization of a specific set of habitats by peoples who were not indigenous to this area. Such has long been the "orthodox" view of the situation, based on the radical differences in material culture, economy, and settlement patterns between the indigenous hunter-gatherers of the area and the incoming Primary Neolithic populations. It is important, however, to understand the spatial and temporal limits of this model, especially in light of recently published positions on the topic. Dennell (1983), for instance, has advanced the idea that the earliest food production in Europe was not at the hands of immigrants from the Near East but rather by indigenous peoples of the Balkans, a position with which I am in considerable sympathy. Although a careful reading of what he writes shows that Dennell does not interpret the central European data in the same light, some less familiar with the subtleties of European prehistory may not make this distinction. At the other end of the continent, there has been a parallel tendency to treat the development of agriculture in places like Denmark and coastal Holland as local events prompted by the adoption of exotic cultigens by local peoples, again a position which I support and which I hope to document more in Chapters 6 and 7. At the same time, it must be realized that these developments are beyond both the spatial and chronological range of what has been defined here as "Primary Neolithic" in central Europe.

The discussion in this chapter, therefore, is confined to the period roughly between 4500 and 3250 bc (5400–4000 BC). Although some Primary Neolithic sites occur on the North European Plain, by far the majority of them are found in the central European loess belt (Figure 4.1). It cannot be emphasized too often that the Neolithic cultures of central Europe cannot be taken as a "package deal" and that there is considerable spatial and chronological diversity even at the early stages of the introduction of food production in this area.

The real research frontier in the study of Primary Neolithic communities in central Europe lies not so much in their subsistence economy, although more data will always help, but rather in their social aspects. This was an area that clearly fascinated Childe but which is frustratingly difficult to apprehend. Two important problem areas are the nature of the interaction between farming communities and indigenous hunter-gatherers and the social organization of the farming communities themselves. The goal of such research, of course, should be to respond to V. Gordon Childe's challenge to Grahame Clark (Clark 1974: 55):

"Yes, Grahame, but what have you done about Society?"

Empirical data on Primary Neolithic subsistence
Primary Neolithic subsistence is a difficult topic to discuss in a few pages. The empirical data on seeds and bones must be considered in some detail before it can be interpreted to construct models of subsistence systems. A fundamental problem lies in the unevenness of the data base. Interest in the systematic collection of subsistence data has arisen only recently, although the basic complex of Primary Neolithic cultigens and domesticates has been known since the early part of this century. Flotation and wet-sieving as a means of recovering seeds and small bones have been employed on comparatively few Primary Neolithic sites. Rather, there has been a reliance on trench-collected bones and seeds, with a resultant bias toward the larger mammalian species and domesticated cereals. Fish, amphibians, reptiles, and small mammals are poorly represented in most collections, as are the smaller seeds of grasses and fragmentary items such as hazelnut shells. It is possible that such taxa were not widely exploited by Primary Neolithic communities, but without more comprehensive recovery techniques, we shall never know. Another gap in our knowledge of Primary Neolithic subsistence stems from the fact that bones are not well preserved in loessic soil. This condition is especially pronounced in sites where the archaeological remains lie fairly high in the soil profile, in the zone where decalcification has occurred. For instance, at the well-known Linear Pottery settlement of Bylany in Bohemia, the quality of bone preservation was abysmal. Poplin (1975: 180) estimated that if there had been good bone preservation at Bylany, there should have been 500,000 to 1,000,000 recovered specimens! The total number of specimens identified by Clason (1967), however, was only 587, of which 354 were tooth fragments more resistant to the acidic loess. Deeper sites and those not situated on loess have better preservation of faunal materials, leading to further bias in the knowledge of Primary Neolithic faunal exploitation.

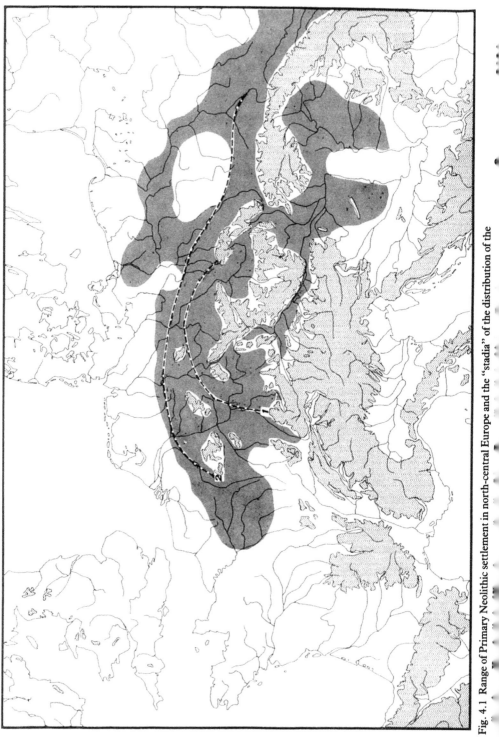

Fig. 4.1 Range of Primary Neolithic settlement in north-central Europe and the "stadia" of the distribution of the

Seed and bone assemblages from Primary Neolithic sites in temperate Europe tend to be small and do not approach the size of coeval collections from southeast Europe. As a result, one must generate a composite picture of the distribution of plant and animal taxa on these sites rather than generalize from the data from any single site. At the same time, one can identify marked regional differences, especially in the distribution of grain species, that should not be suppressed in the quest for synthesis. The identification of these regional differences militates against the notion that the Primary Neolithic subsistence system in central Europe was a "package deal" in which the same complex of cultigens and livestock was utilized wherever Primary Neolithic communities settled. Rather, it appears that different communities in different parts of central Europe chose different items from the same "menu" of plants and animals as they found appropriate for local conditions. This observation can be attributed primarily to the broader corpus of data on Primary Neolithic plant and animal exploitation which has become available in the last twenty years. Particularly important is the fact that numbers of assemblages are available from particular regions, such as the botanical data from the Rhineland (Knörzer 1973; Willerding 1980). Unfortunately, regions which have yielded large quantities of plant remains have not been so productive of animal bones and vice versa, a situation which shows little promise of being rectified in the near future.

Primary Neolithic botanical remains
In the last two decades or so, most archaeologists in central Europe have begun to appreciate the fact that carbonized plant remains are much more reliable indicators of prehistoric plant exploitation than impressions of seeds on pots. Unfortunately, the use of carbonized seeds as indicators of the prehistoric economy of a site is not without its problems either. Whereas consumption refuse such as animal bone is *expected* to appear archaeologically by virtue of its inedible nature, carbonized plant remains are preserved as the result of accidents in the prehistoric use of the seeds or the fortuitous charring of chaff, pits, or other plant refuse. In other words, plant materials are not inherently durable as bone is, but rather they require an additional transformation between their use by the prehistoric inhabitants of the site and their appearance in the archaeological record.

Plant remains on open sites in central Europe tend to occur in basically one kind of context: the trash-filled pit. This situation contrasts with that in southeast Europe and the Near East, where a variety of contexts such as rooms, caches, middens, floors, and pits are encountered. Bakels (1979: 9) has characterized the plant remains found on European open sites as relatively heterogeneous in composition and generally low in density, a kind of "noise" in the archaeological record of a prehistoric settlement. The low density of the plant remains (and the small size of the samples from any single context), when coupled with the complex transformation processes leading to their deposition, has the result that the numerical composition of any single sample is "largely meaningless and usually accidental" (Hubbard 1980: 51). In order to perceive patterns in the heterogeneous small samples from central European sites, it is necessary to go beyond the site as the basic unit of analysis and use a method of study which considers plant remains over a wider area. For this purpose, the method of "presence analysis" proposed by Hubbard (1975, 1980) has some merit, and it is adapted below to the corpus of Linear Pottery botanical data presented by Willerding (1980). Essentially, the proportion of sites with remains of a particular taxon is calculated as a percentage of the total number of samples of the relevant culture.

Interest in Primary Neolithic botanical remains has been focused on those from Linear Pottery sites, with somewhat less attention paid to data from those of Rössen and other later groups in the Primary Neolithic sequence. Over 80 Linear Pottery sites from central Europe have yielded samples of carbonized plant remains, although the circumstances of their collection vary markedly. In Table 4.1, the number of sites where a taxon has been identified is expressed as a percentage of the total number of sites in the sample. A marked regional separation in the distribution of Linear Pottery cultigens emerged during the syntheses of these data. The plant remains from the Rhineland and further west showed a markedly different composition from those found to the south and east. Accordingly, in addition to the presence-values for the lumped data from all sites, the samples from the Rhineland and Dutch Limburg were considered separately from the other Linear Pottery botanical samples from central Europe.

Emmer, *Triticum dicoccum*, appears to have been almost ubiquitous across the Linear Pottery area, occurring at 81% of the sites with carbonized plant remains. Einkorn, *T. monococcum*, was somewhat less widely used, being found in 60% of

Table 4.1. *Frequency with which carbonized remains of cultivated plants and hazelnuts occur on 85 Linear Pottery sites in central Europe.*

A – total sample (n=85); B – samples from east and south of Rhineland (n=57); C – samples from Rhineland and Dutch Limburg (n=20); D – samples from northeastern France and Belgium (n=8); * – occurrence of *H. vulgare nudum* attested at Wange in Belgium and Menneville in France on the basis of small number of grains; small number of samples may cause it to be overrepresented in this tabulation. Data from Willerding (1980), Bakels (1983/4, 1984), Bakels and Rousselle (1985).

	A	B	C	D
Triticum monococcum (einkorn)	60%	54%	75%	37.5%
Triticum dicoccum (emmer)	81	77	90	87.5
Triticum spelta (spelt)	1	2	–	–
T. aestivum (bread wheat)	5	7	–	–
T. aest.-compactum (club wheat)	7	10.5	–	–
Hordeum vulgare (barley)	19	28	–	–
H. vulgare nudum (naked barley)	6	5	–	(25)*
Secale cereale (rye)	2	3.5	–	–
Panicum miliaceum (millet)	6	9	–	–
Pisum sativum (peas)	26	19	35	50
Lens esculenta (lentil)	15	16	20	–
Linum usitatissimum (flax)	15	10.5	35	12.5
Papaver somniferum (poppy)	10.5	–	45	–
Corylus avellana (hazel)	25	7	60	62.5

the samples overall. These two wheat types seem to have been the primary cultigens throughout central Europe at this time. The regional separation mentioned above is found in the distribution of the various subsidiary species utilized by Primary Neolithic communities, namely barley *(Hordeum vulgare)*, millet *(Panicum miliaceum)*, and rye *(Secale cereale)*. (The last-named species may not have been deliberately cultivated during the Primary Neolithic, but rather could have occurred as a weed-of-cultivation (Hubbard 1980).) These species are hitherto unknown from sites in the Rhineland and Dutch Limburg, although barley occurs at 28% of the Linear Pottery sites further east, millet at 9%, and rye at 3.5%. Recent analyses of samples from northeastern France and Belgium have identified barley at two sites, Wange in Belgium and Menneville in the Aisne valley of France (Bakels 1984, Bakels and Rousselle 1985), although Wange in particular is quite late in the Linear Pottery sequence. Hexaploid wheats, such as *T. spelta, T. aestivum, and T. aestivo-compactum*, are also absent from the western sites, although the last species occurs at 10.5% of the Linear Pottery sites to the east and south of the Rhineland. It is doubtful that these differences are due to preservation or recovery factors, since enough sites in the Rhineland and Limburg have been studied by Knörzer and Bakels for these species to have been identified at least once (Knörzer 1971, 1973, 1974; Bakels 1978, 1979). There are also no apparent ecological reasons for the absence of these species, since all were subsequently grown successfully in this area. (There is the possibility, of course, of the varying perceptions of different analysts, especially since the differentiation of different wheat species from carbonized grains is difficult.) The place of these cultigens appears to have been filled by einkorn, which appears in 75% of the Linear Pottery samples in the Rhineland and Dutch Limburg. Recent analyses of botanical material from late Linear Pottery sites in Belgium and France have identified small quantities of barley, indicating that there was some time lag in the spread of this cultigen into the western range of Linear Pottery (Bakels 1984, Bakels and Rousselle 1985). In addition, peas *(Pisum sativum)* and poppy *(Papaver segiterum)* are found more frequently on sites in the Rhineland than on those to the east. The higher proportion of these smaller seeds in samples from the Rhineland is due largely to the fact that while most Primary Neolithic botanical samples are generally trench-collected during trowelling, the materials from the Rhineland have been water-separated. On the other hand, this same difference in recovery technique makes the absence of barley, millet, rye, and the hexaploid wheats from the Rhenish and Limburg sites all the more striking, since they would stand an even better chance of being found under such circumstances.

In the latter half of the Primary Neolithic sequence, the regional variation appears to fade. Barley is the principal component of a number of Rössen botanical assemblages in the Rhineland (Knörzer 1971), and bread wheat makes its first appearance in this region as well. At Wahlitz in East Germany, excavations in the 1950s resulted in the trench-collection of large botanical samples, which appear to be composed primarily of club wheat, *Triticum compactum* (Rothmaler and Natho 1957). Interestingly, barley is absent from these samples, although it was previously common on East German Linear Pottery sites. In the south German part of the loess belt, botanical samples from late Primary Neolithic sites at Endersbach (Piening 1979) and Schernau (Hopf 1981) yielded botanical samples with a broad composition in single features. For instance, the pit at Endersbach contained emmer, einkorn, barley, and peas, with einkorn as the most abundant taxon. Feature 22 at Schernau had several hundred carbonized grains from einkorn, emmer, barley, spelt, and bread wheat, along with a weed spectrum.

The recognition of the regional and temporal variability in the Primary Neolithic botanical record militates against the notion that the Primary Neolithic agricultural system was exactly the same across central Europe. It should be noted, however, that few of the sites with carbonized plant remains date from the very earliest phase of the Linear Pottery culture, which does not occur in the Rhineland or further west. Four sites of the earliest phase of Linear Pottery have yielded plant remains. These samples are quite small: Eitzum, with less than 10 specimens of emmer and less than five of barley; Dresden-Nickern, with 21 grains of emmer; Ammerbuch-Pfaffingen, with a single grain of wheat, probably emmer; and Eilsleben, where samples include emmer and peas (Bakels 1978: 66; Schultze-Motel 1980). There are thus very few empirical data on the agricultural base of the earliest Primary Neolithic communities in central Europe.

The more comprehensive Primary Neolithic plant remains from the Rhineland have enabled Knörzer (1971) to identify a consistently recurring weed association which, he argues, was found in the fields alongside the crops. Bakels (1978, 1979) has found a similar combination of weed species at Hienheim in Bavaria and at sites in Dutch Limburg. Knörzer has termed this weed association the Bromo-Lapsanetum praehistoricum, after its primary constituents – chess (*Bromus secalinus*) and nipplewort (*Lapsana communis*). Other members of this association include goosefoot (*Chenopodium album*), black bindweed (*Polygonum convolvulus*), barren brome (*Bromus sterilis*), cleavers (*Galium spurium*), sorrel (*Rumex* sp.), pink persicaria (*Polygonum persicaria*), timothy (*Phleum* sp.), meadow-grass (*Poa* sp.), and coarse vetch (*Vicia* cf. *hirsuta*). The characteristic plants of the Bromo-Lapsanetum are all either plants with tall stalks in the vicinity of 80-100 cm (such as goosefoot, nipplewort, sorrel, and chess), whose seed-bearing parts would be approximately the same height as the ears of wheat, or climbing plants (such as vetch, bindweed, and cleavers), which could climb up the grain stalks. Knörzer has concluded that the consistent recurrence of these species in association with wheat indicates that they form an anthropogenic community propagated during wheat cultivation. Their presence in the carbonized seed assemblages, to the virtual exclusion of plants with shorter stalks, indicates to Knörzer that the grain was harvested by cutting off the ears high up on the stalk rather than near to the ground, with the weeds of similar height having been reaped in the same process. Some of the seeds of these weed species would have found their way into the seed grain used the following year and sown along with the crop plants, while the shorter plants would have been crowded out and not propagated in this fashion. Although most of the species in this segetal association were probably already present in pre-agricultural central Europe, Knörzer believes that several, especially the climbers such as vetch, bindweed, and cleavers, were not and were probably introduced as agriculture spread. Knörzer's recognition of this association and his plausible explanation for its recurrence on archaeological sites imply that Primary Neolithic grain crops were not pure stands but rather had some competition in the fields. The effect of this competition on crop productivity is unknown, but it probably did not promote higher grain yields. Knörzer's research also suggests that Primary Neolithic fields were also small. Both nipplewort and barren-brome are shade-demanding species, and since their seeds occur frequently, Knörzer believes that large areas of the fields were overshadowed by higher vegetation, either by forest edges surrounding the fields or by trees left standing among the crops.

The next research frontier in the collection of data on Primary Neolithic subsistence lies in the identification of edible plants which do not produce parts which lend themselves to carbonization, such as tubers, rhizomes, and fungi. The potential productivity of such plants has been noted by Clarke (1976) and it is inconceivable that they were ignored by Neolithic farmers, especially in the season prior to the ripening of the crops. Unfortunately, these plants leave few traces which can be recovered archaeologically. One promising line of research is through phytolith analysis (Rovner 1983), but so far this technique has not been applied on central European Neolithic sites. For the time being, we are left with a record biased toward the cereals, when in reality these may have contributed somewhat less towards the Primary Neolithic diet than it appears at present.

Primary Neolithic faunal remains

Primary Neolithic faunal assemblages are as difficult to compare as the seed collections. Not only are there different standards of recovery and degree of identification from site to site, but the methods of reporting the primary data also vary from researcher to researcher. In the first half of this century, it was common for faunal analysts, usually zoologists by training, to present "laundry lists" of identified species which were appended to site reports. It then became common for counts of identified specimens to be given and compared from which conclusions about the relative economic importance of various taxa were drawn. The result was a bias toward the larger mammalian species and those in which the living animal contained more bones. Dissatisfaction with this method of counting led to the borrowing of the concept of "minimum numbers of individuals" from palaeontologists for the quantification of faunal assemblages. The effect of this measure was to "overrepresent" the species for which there were only a few bones and "underrepresent" the species for which there were large numbers (for a fuller discussion, see Grayson 1979.) A promising, but hitherto little-used, compromise would be the "diagnostic zones" method proposed by Watson (1979), but this technique has not gained wide acceptance. Some researchers have attempted to convert specimen counts and MNI into "kilograms of available meat" and compare the figures so derived to ascertain the relative economic importance of different species (e.g. Milisauskas 1978). This "weight method", first proposed by Kubasiewicz (1956), has a number of serious drawbacks (Casteel 1978). The ratio of bone weight to meat weight is not constant from animal to animal and from species to species. Moreover, it also assumes that meat was the the sole reason why domesticated stock was kept, ignoring the economic value of products like milk and wool.

The most common denominator among Primary Neolithic faunal reports from central Europe is that counts of identified specimens are usually presented alongside other methods of quantification. Therefore, in spite of their inherent biases, the most widely applicable basis of comparison of these assemblages would be based on such counts. In order to synthesize these data as economically as possible, the focus here will be on two main aspects of these data. The first is the relative proportions of bones from domestic and wild animals, while the second is the relative numbers of bones from the four main domestic subsistence species: cattle, sheep, goat, and pig.

Figure 4.2 depicts the relative percentages of wild and domestic bones in the faunal assemblages from 25 Primary Neolithic sites with faunal assemblages greater than 100 identified specimens. The pattern is strikingly consistent across central Europe: the bones of wild mammals are very rare in Primary Neolithic contexts especially when fragment counts are the basis of quantification. Of course, a major problem exists in the fact that one analyst's aurochs or wild boar is another's cow or domestic pig. The point of separation between the domesticates which are indigenous to central Europe and their wild relatives has long been a disputed point (see Grigson 1969: Clason 1972; Boessneck 1977, among others). The situation of the aurochs/domestic cattle bones from Müddersheim is a case in point. The original analysis by Stampfli (1965) indicated that 28.8% of the 201 identified mammal bones belonged to wild animals, based on his assessment that 33 of them were those of aurochs, *Bos primigenius*. This observation was incorporated into the argument by some that the Primary Neolithic communities along the lower Rhine and Maas engaged in a greater amount of hunting than elsewhere in Europe (e.g. Newell 1970). Clason's reinterpretation of the Müddersheim cattle bones indicated that only two were of aurochs and that the proportion of wild to domestic specimens was not much different from that found at other Primary Neolithic sites in central Europe.

Not only are the bones of wild mammals relatively rare in Primary Neolithic contexts, but those of reptiles, amphibians, and fish are also scarce. Much of this can be attributed to recovery practices, since the proportions of such species rises markedly in sieved samples (see Meadow 1976). Another factor to account for the scarcity of such bones may lie in the way in which the meat from such animals is handled. Often, the entire animal would have been cooked, bones and all. The cooked bones would have been discarded at the location of consumption, not of preparation, and thanks to their small size, they do not lend themselves to systematic collection and disposal. A fish vertebra is much easier to tread into a dirt floor than a cow femur. The cooked bones would also be more susceptible to weathering and decay than the bones of larger mammals which were either uncooked or shielded from the heat by a thicker layer of muscle and fat. One is led to suspect that the bones of non-mammalian wild species are underrepresented on Primary Neolithic sites in proportion to their actual frequency of use. A hint of the problems created by differential disposal of the bones of different taxa on open sites

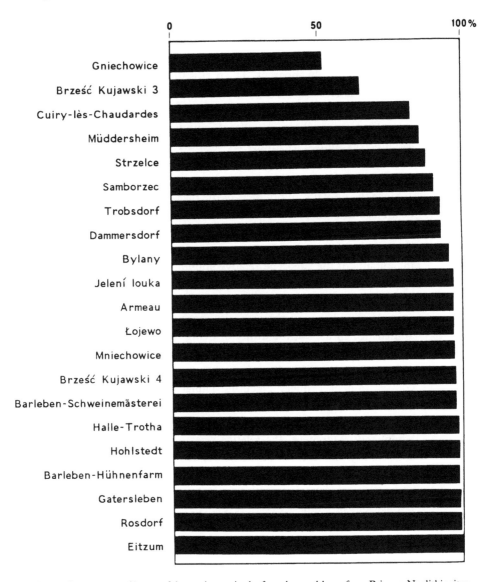

Fig. 4.2 Percentages of bones of domestic taxa in the faunal assemblages from Primary Neolithic sites in central Europe, based on numbers of identified specimens. Note that in almost all cases, the percentage is over 80%, often over 95%.

comes from the Lautereck rock shelter in southern Germany (Taute 1966). Here, Primary Neolithic occupation areas were spatially restricted by the confines of the rock shelter, and a comprehensive sample of faunal remains was obtained which included fish bones. Arguably, they were found because all bones were discarded within the same confined space. At the same time, however, it may also be argued that this was a special-purpose exploitation camp which would not reflect larger trends in faunal exploitation.

The second striking regularity among Primary Neolithic faunal asemblages is found in the relative frequency of the three main domesticates: cattle, sheep/goat (considered together due to the difficulty of separating them osteologically) and pig. The data from 25 Primary Neolithic sites with faunal assemblages larger than 100 identified specimens are summarized graphically in Figure 4.3. Two consistent patterns are readily apparent. The first is that virtually everywhere domestic cattle form the major component of the faunal assemblages. The only exception to this occurs in several of the larger assemblages reported by Müller (1964) from Saxo-Thuringia, where sheep/goat outnumber the cattle. If, however, all 71 assemblages studied by Müller are considered together, cattle outweigh sheep/goat by a ratio of 1.7:1, for the smaller assemblages which do not lend themselves singly to quantitative comparison are comprised largely of cattle bones.

Since the only useful products of the pig (meat, skin, lard, and bone) require the death and dismemberment of the animal before they are available, the number of pig bones on a site should, barring problems of preservation and disposal practices, be a relatively accurate reflection of the economic importance of this species to the inhabitants of the site. The relative abundance of cattle and sheep/goat bones, on the other hand, may *underrepresent* the economic importance of these taxa, due to the products such as milk, blood, and wool which can be taken from living animals. The bones of these species represent the final utilization of slaughtered animals for meat, but the utility of living cattle, sheep, and goats results in these creatures having longer "useful lives" than do pigs.

It is similarly difficult to interpret the data which bear on the sex and age composition of Primary Neolithic faunal assemblages, especially for the cattle bones. This problem is directly related to the small size of the assemblages, and when they are lumped together, any vestige of statistical reliability vanishes completely. Moreover, the relative sizes of males, castrates, and females can be consistent within local populations but can vary widely across geographical zones. The argument has frequently been made that the kill-off patterns observed in archaeological faunal assemblages can indicate the use to which the living populations of animals were put (e.g. Payne 1973). Unfortunately, this approach may work only when large assemblages which can be reliably separated into males and females are available. Such is not the case on Primary Neolithic sites, and only general kill-off patterns have been reported from a few sites (e.g. Bogucki 1982). Even when such data are available, their interpretation is often ambiguous. It is important to remember that an archaeological faunal assemblage represents a collection of dead animals, not a living herd. Data on kill-off patterns of Primary Neolithic cattle come from the Polish Lowlands (Bogucki 1982) and East Germany (Müller 1964). At Brześć Kujawski, over 90% of the Linear Pottery cattle were slaughtered beyond their 18th month and 70% survived their 36th month and lived to an advanced age. There are very few juvenile cattle bones represented in this assemblage. On the East German sites, however, Müller found 60.5% adult, 11.5% subadult, and 28% juvenile individuals (on the basis of an estimated minimum of 143 individuals from these sites). These data suggest a higher degree of calf slaughter than found at Brześć Kujawski. In both cases, however, there is little evidence of an emphasis on the slaughter of animals in the 48-month age group, the age at which cattle reach their optimal meat weight (Higham and Message 1969).

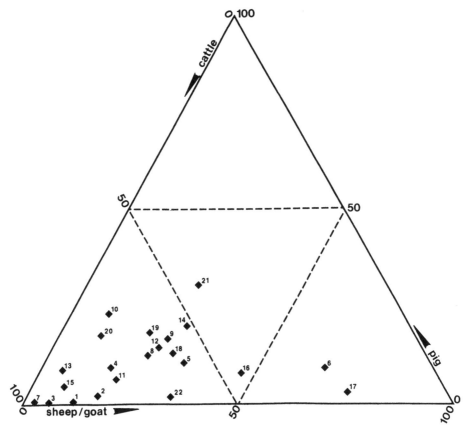

Fig. 4.3 Relative percentages of cattle, sheep/goat, and pig bones at 22 Linear Pottery sites, based on numbers of identified specimens attributed to *Bos taurus, Ovis aries/Capra hircus,* and *Sus scrofa* (after Bogucki 1984, fig. 3). Key: 1 – Brześć Kujawski 3 (n=82); 2 – Brześć Kujawski 4 (n=514); 3 – Strzelce (n=77); 4 – Iojewo (n=594); 5 – Barleben-Schweinemästerei (n=223); 6 – Barleben-Hühnenfarm (n==168); 7 – Eitzum (n=46); 8 – Armeau (n=928); 9 – Cuiry-lès-Chaudardes (n=501, data to 1976); 10 – Samborzec (n=384); 11 – Gniechowice (n=158); 12 – Jelení louka (n=532); 13 – Bylany (n=540, all Linear Pottery periods); 14 – Gatersleben (n=252); 15 – Halle-Trotha (n=357); 16 – Trobsdorf (n=345); 17 – Dammersdorf (n=199); 18 – Hohlstedt (n=351); 19 – Hienheim (n=72); 20 – Müddersheim (n=184, according to Clason 1972); 21 – Reichstett (n=125); 22 – Miechowice (n=1449).

The considerably smaller numbers of sheep/goat and pig bones on Primary Neolithic sites do not permit any similar observations of sex and age distribution. In the case of the pig bones, however, the majority are usually those of juvenile individuals, reflecting a standard kill-off pattern for domestic pigs found in both prehistoric and modern times. Finally, the wild animals represented on Primary Neolithic sites are too few in number to even begin to investigate sex and age distributions, and it is therefore not possible to reach any conclusions about systematic culling of wild animal populations.

The form and distribution of Primary Neolithic settlements
The configurations of Primary Neolithic settlement
Discussions of the forms of Primary Neolithic settlements in central Europe in the archaeological literature have tended to treat them, as with the subsistence

economy, as a "package deal." Primary Neolithic settlements are presumed to have been universally characterized by large numbers of longhouses which form villages. These descriptions are usually acompanied by spectacular ground plans of Linear Pottery, Lengyel, or Rössen settlements showing a number of longhouse plans which are oriented in roughly the same direction and which often overlap, indicating several phases of occupation. It has generally been taken for granted that this represents the typical, in fact the sole, configuration of Primary Neolithic settlements across central Europe.

There are two major identifiable "horizons" of the Linear Pottery culture during its initial expansion across central Europe. The first of these is the Earliest (*"älteste Linearbandkeramik"*), also known as the "Krumlov" style, which is found as far west as the Neckar and upper Danube rivers in Germany (Quitta 1960) and reaches north to the Hannover-Magdeburg area of central Germany (Kaufmann 1983; Schwarz-Mackensen 1983). The Earliest Linear Pottery was quickly succeeded by a second horizon, the Earlier Linear Pottery (*"ältere Linearbandkeramik"*), also known as the "Flomborn-Ačkovy" style, which extends even further into the Rhine Valley, Dutch Limburg, and southern Poland. Later Linear Pottery phases (*"jüngere Linearbandkeramik"*) saw the expansion of this culture into eastern France, Belgium, Normandy, and the North European Plain.

Until very recently, it was possible to say that no finds of the Earliest Linear Pottery had ever been unequivocally associated with longhouses, but the discovery of longhouses datable to this phase at Schwanfeld in Lower Franconia indicates that such structures were constructed from the very beginning of the Linear Pottery sequence (Lüning and Modderman 1982). Such early houses are quite rare, and most Earliest Linear Pottery sites have not yielded traces of "classic" Linear Pottery structures. Longhouses began to appear regularly in the "Earlier" phase of Linear Pottery. The first longhouses at Bylany (Soudský 1962: 192) are associated with "Ačkovy" ceramics. Along the lower Rhine, there are longhouses associated with Flomborn ceramics at Niedermerz (Dohrn-Ihmig 1979: 234) and in Dutch Limburg at Geleen, Elsloo, and Sittard (Modderman 1970). It should be noted that the *majority* of the longhouses at these sites do not date from the older Linear Pottery phases but rather from the younger ones (Modderman 1972). In the Polish Lowlands, the earliest Linear Pottery materials are datable to the *Notenkopf* phase and are unaccompanied by longhouses; in this area, the first permanent Primary Neolithic sites appeared only during Lengyel times, several hundred years later.

Primary Neolithic settlements with large numbers of longhouses have long been presumed to represent "villages", with all of the socioeconomic implications of such a settlement form. Recently, however, some West German archaeologists have put forth the idea that not every Primary Neolithic settlement with longhouses was necessarily a village, but rather that many were either individual "farmsteads" or collections of farmsteads (Kuper and Lüning 1975; Lüning 1982a). As originally articulated some 10 years ago, this hypothesis stated that Linear Pottery houses were built and rebuilt over the course of several centuries (as indicated by the associated ceramics) within delimited parcels of land (*"Hofparzelle"*). This theory was based on the results of the excavation of the site of

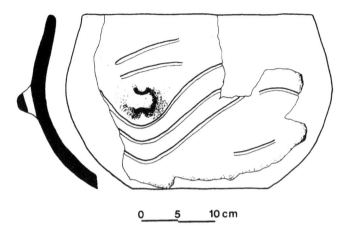

0   5   10 cm

Fig. 4.4 Linear Pottery vessel of the "earliest" phase from Eitzum (after Schwarz-Mackensen 1983: fig. 6).

Langweiler 9 (Kuper et al. 1977) on the Aldenhoven Plateau. At this site, two, later three, such farmstead-parcels were identified, two of which were occupied through four generations of houses. The average distance between houses in general at Langweiler 9 is 55 meters, but between coeval houses the average distance is 112 meters. Each parcel is estimated to have averaged about 1.1 hectares (Fig. 4.5).

Since then, this hypothesis has undergone some modification, based on the excavation of the neighboring settlement of Langweiler 8 (Lüning 1982b). Here, the average distance between all houses is 34 meters and that between coeval houses 66 meters, with an average of about 0.6 hectares per parcel (Fig. 4.6). The density of occupation at Langweiler 8 is similar to that found at other large Linear Pottery settlements such as Köln-Lindenthal, Sittard, and Elsloo, and it is questionable whether the model of individual farmsteads is still tenable in such cases. Instead, these appear to approximate more closely to the degree of nucleation that one would expect in a "village"-type settlement configuration. Lüning's conclusion (1982a: 32) is that there were three types of Linear Pottery residential bases: clusters of farmsteads (like Langweiler 9), small nucleated settlements (a good example outside the Rhineland would be Olszanica in Poland), and large nucleated settlements (like Langweiler 8 and Köln-Lindenthal.) I would agree with such a conclusion, for while it is difficult to ignore the fact that there are longhouses which occur either singly or separated by long distances from each other, there are also larger residential bases which must have had some greater degree of organizational complexity than just collections of discrete farmsteads.

As Primary Neolithic settlement developed in areas such as the Rhineland where permanent residential bases were established fairly early in the sequence, there was a tendency towards greater nucleation with time. The Rössen settlements of the Rhineland, exemplified by those at Inden 1 (Kuper and Piepers 1966), Aldenhoven (Jürgens 1979), Jülich-Welldorf (Dohrn-Ihmig 1983), and Deiringsen/Ruploh

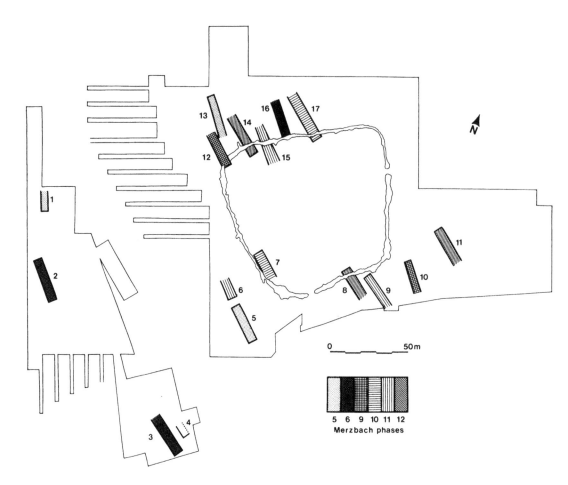

Fig. 4.5 Plan of the Linear Pottery settlement at Langweiler 9 (after Kuper et al. 1977). Phases are those of the Linear Pottery chronology developed for the Merzbach valley.

(Günther 1976), exhibit a degree of nucleation similar to that observed for the Linear Pottery nucleated settlements and a greater amount of organization in the alignment of the houses (usually all within a few degrees of each other), yet the overall spatial extent of these settlements is quite small, about that of Langweiler 9 (Fig. 4.7). Lüning (1982a: 25) interprets this as a reflection of the type of organizational coherence that one would expect of a true village, rather than a more or less nucleated collection of farmsteads.

The Lengyel residential bases of the North European Plain, on the other hand, show a diversity of form similar to that observed for the late Linear Pottery in the Rhineland. There are large nucleated residential bases, such as Brześć Kujawski 4 (Jażdżewski 1938; Bogucki 1982; Bogucki and Grygiel 1983), and smaller ones, such as Krusza Zamkowa (Czerniak 1980). In additon to these, there are many one- and two-longhouse settlements such as Brześć Kujawski 3, Dobre, Kościelec

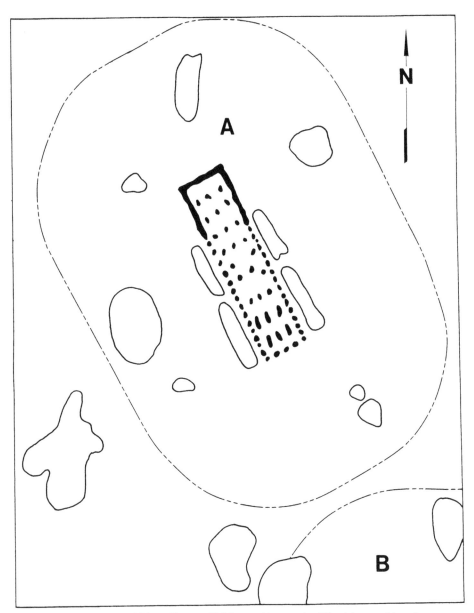

Fig. 4.6 Plan of an idealized Linear Pottery *Hofplatz* and its associated "activity zone" based on examples at Langweiler 8 (after Lüning 1982b: fig. 19). Radius of "activity zone" is approximately 25 meters.

Kujawski, Biskupin 18a, and Dobieszewice, which would appear to parallel the "farmsteads" of Langweiler 9. The difference is that one typically finds only one trapezoidal-plan longhouse at such a site, whereas at Langweiler 9 the parcels have up to four house outlines indicating successive rebuilding episodes. One possible reason for this difference is that the Lengyel houses have bedding trenches for their wall posts rather than individual postholes, and thus rebuilding and repair may not have necessitated the excavation of new postholes. The trapezoidal shape of the

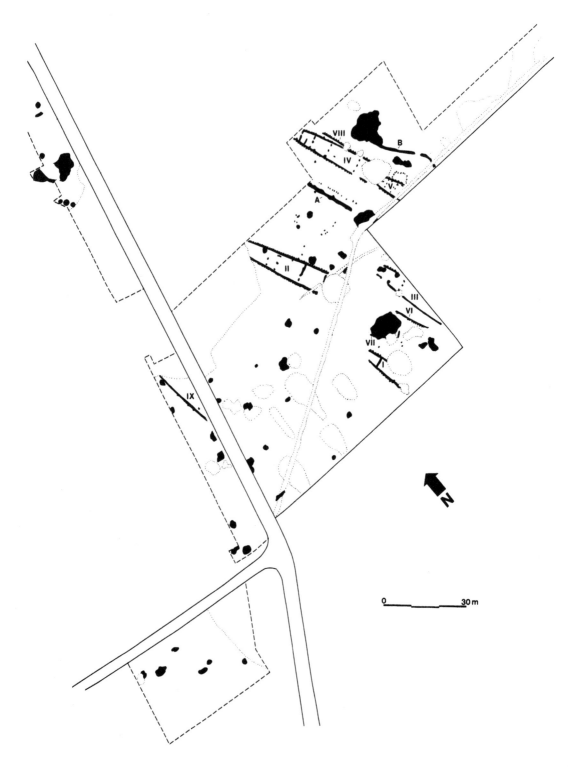

Fig. 4.7 Ground plan of the Rössen settlement at Aldenhoven (after Jürgens 1979: fig. 2). Key: I-IX – houses; A, B – ditches, interpreted as "boundaries".

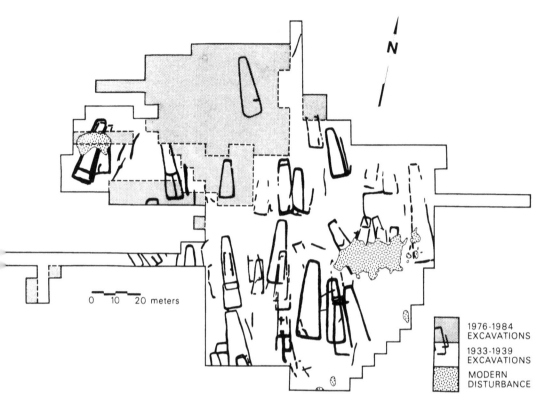

Fig. 4.8. Plan of Lengyel settlement at Brześć Kujawski 4 (after Grygiel and Bogucki 1986: fig. 3). (Reproduced with the permission of the *Journal of Field Archaeology* and the Trustees of Boston University.)

Lengyel structures would also have been more wind-resistant than the rectangular Linear Pottery structures (Bogucki and Grygiel 1983: 107), which would have added to the longevity of these buildings. It is therefore probable that the single Lengyel houses of the North European Plain correspond structurally to the Linear Pottery farmsteads of the loess belt, although there are differences in how they present themselves archaeologically.

Primary Neolithic longhouses, although basically similar in the details of their construction and dimensions across central Europe, nonetheless exhibit some variation across time and space. Almost every structure has some peculiarity that sets it apart from the others, although they can be grouped into broad typological schema, like that of Modderman (1972) for the Linear Pottery houses of the Netherlands. Modderman identified three types of Linear Pottery houses, all of which are rectangular-plan post structures. The categories are based on the number of segments in the houses as determined by the placement of interior partitions. Essentially, there are houses with one, two, and three segments. Common to all of the Linear Pottery houses of Dutch Limburg and the Rhineland is a segment which occupies the middle position in the three-segment houses and has a Y-pattern of internal posts. Further to the east and south, this regularity does not occur, however.

The relative numbers of the various Linear Pottery house types at sites in the Merzbach valley on the Aldenhoven Plateau have been reported by Lüning (1982a: 28). Of the 83 houses, 83% are three-segment houses, 12% two-segment, and 5% one-segment. Of the three-segment structures, the segment which characteristically occurs at the southeastern end of the house (almost all the houses are oriented NW-SE) has the most massive internal posts, leading to the hypothesis that this area supported a loft or some other complex structure in addition to a roof. Accordingly, Modderman has theorized that this area functioned as a granary. Lüning (1982b: 17) reports that the botanical samples from the three-segment structures have more chaff and weed seeds in them, suggesting a greater degree of crop processing activity around these houses.

Stroke-Ornamented Pottery, Rössen, and Lengyel houses share the broad characteristic that they all tend to be roughly trapezoidal in plan. This trait is most pronounced among the Lengyel houses, while Rössen and Stroke-Ornamented Pottery houses often have side walls which appear in plan to bulge outward and one end wall shorter than the other. Aside from this common trapezoidal plan, however, there is considerable variability in the architecture of the later Primary Neolithic houses which reflects the adaptation of house forms to local conditions in different parts of central Europe.

Stroke-Ornamented Pottery houses in Bavaria, Bohemia, and Saxo-Thuringia often have double rows of postholes along their side walls, usually with an inner row of smaller postholes and an outer row of larger postholes at greater intervals (Modderman 1977; Lička 1981). This may well represent the buttressing of the hips of the roof to support the heavier snow accumulation that may occur in the upland areas of central Europe. Lengyel houses, especially those of the North European Plain, are similarly sturdy, although they lack the double post rows. Instead, they were constructed with stout uprights set into deep bedding trenches, which appear to have reached a greater depth than the postholes on most Linear Pottery sites. On the flat North European Plain, the winds are strong in all directions, and the labor expended in sinking the bedding trenches deep would not have been wasted. Rössen houses often combine the two techniques, generally having an inner bedding trench and outer rows of posts close by, almost as though niches were dug into the walls of the trenches to accept the additional posts.

Stroke-Ornamented Pottery, Rössen, and Lengyel houses do not appear to have been divided into modules as were many Linear Pottery houses. The only real functional differentiation of space in these structures is the extension of the side walls of some Rössen houses beyond the wider of the end walls to form a sort of enclosed "porch". This configuration appears on the Lengyel house at Biskupin 18a as well. Whatever function this space served (stable? workshop?), it was delimited much more sharply than its functional counterpart, if it had one, in the Linear Pottery houses. In general, however, the interior areas of the later Primary Neolithic houses are not as cluttered with posts as the Linear Pottery structures are. There is generally a greater amount of open space, even allowing for the roof supports.

Rössen houses display considerable variation in size, ranging from stubby structures like House VII at Inden 1 (11 meters long) through the huge house at Bochum-Hiltrop (60 meters long – more than twice the length of the average Linear Pottery longhouse.) This degree of variability carries across to the Lengyel houses of Bohemia and southern Poland. Short houses, such as the ones at Březno (Czechoslovakia) which range from 10 to 15 m in length (Pleinerova 1981: 32), and long structures, such as the house at Niedzwiedz (Poland) which is 48 m long (Burchard 1973), both occur. On the North European Plain, however, Lengyel house forms are much more uniform. Lengths usually fall in the 15–25 m range, about the same as most Linear Pottery longhouses. Outbuildings also make their appearance late in the Primary Neolithic, at the Lengyel site of Dobre and the Rössen site of Inden 1 in particular. They generally take the form of small rectangular or oval structures adjacent to a longhouse.

The other architectural features of the Primary Neolithic landscape that deserve mention here are the earthworks with palisades, ditches, and banks (Whittle 1977; Kaufmann 1978). These appeared toward the end of the Linear Pottery culture and continued through Rössen times. Most of the Primary Neolithic enclosures that are known have been found in the Rhineland, for it is in this area that large areas have been stripped, revealing features not directly located within settlements. Another concentration is found north of the Harz mountains in the Hannover-Magdeburg region. Other examples are known from Bavaria and Bohemia (at Bylany – Soudský 1966), and recently a Linear Pottery ditch system not associated with a settlement has been reported from Vochov, also in Bohemia (Pavlů 1981). They assume a variety of shapes, both in plan and cross-section. Some appear to have been bank-and-ditch systems, some seem to have had palisades. Most are not fully circular but rather form semi-circular arcs, often with several concentric ditches.

The function of these earthworks is problematical. Habitation within the ditch systems appears to have taken place at some, but not all of the earthwork sites, including Köln-Lindenthal, Esbeck (Fansa and Thieme 1985), and Eilsleben (Kaufmann 1978) among them. Many others can be linked with one or more Primary Neolithic cultures only by the few sherds found in the filling of the ditches or their proximity to a settlement outside the enclosed area. Kaufmann (1978) has proposed a three-fold typology of Later (*"jüngere"*) Linear Pottery earthworks:

A. "fortified settlements" with an oval plan, e.g. Köln-Lindenthal, and Eilsleben (and now Esbeck);
B. "fortified locations" without interior habitation and with round (or approximately round) plan, e.g. Langweiler;
C. enclosed locations with a "ritual" character, e.g. the possible earthwork at Kothingeichendorf in Bavaria.

The position that the earthworks that surround settlements served a defensive purpose has been advanced. Fansa and Thieme (1985: 87) are of this opinion in the case of Esbeck with its two concentric ditches:

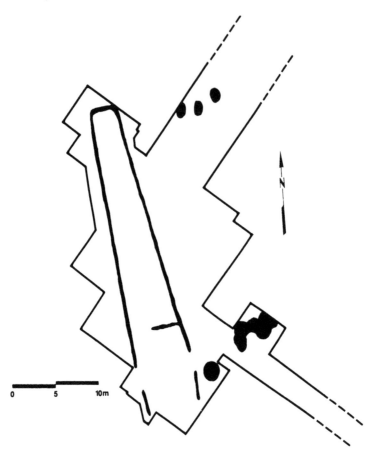

Fig. 4.9 Lengyel house at Biskupin 18a (after Grygiel 1986: fig. 156).

> The function of the earthwork appears...less as an occasionally visited refuge or as a cattle enclosure...but more as a defensive construction around the settlement itself. [PB translation]

At Eilsleben, two superimposed earthwork systems were found, the earlier dating to the Earliest Linear Pottery, while the later one was built several centuries later. The older earthwork at Eilsleben consists of a ditch, bank, and post-and-wattle palisade system, with fairly shallow ditches, while the later one has has a very deep ditch. Kaufmann (1978: 6) has suggested that the earlier enclosure would have been of little defensive value and rather may have served to keep livestock within the settlement precincts. The later ditch system, in Kaufmann's view, had a more defensive character, although it would have also served to restrain livestock. Other enclosures, especially the simpler Linear Pottery ones which do not surround settlements, are often located in low-lying areas and not on defensible positions such as promontories or hilltops. This would argue against a defensive function for this category of earthworks. The hypothesis has been advanced that the Vochov earthwork had a ritual function (Pavlů 1981: 23), and Whittle (1977:

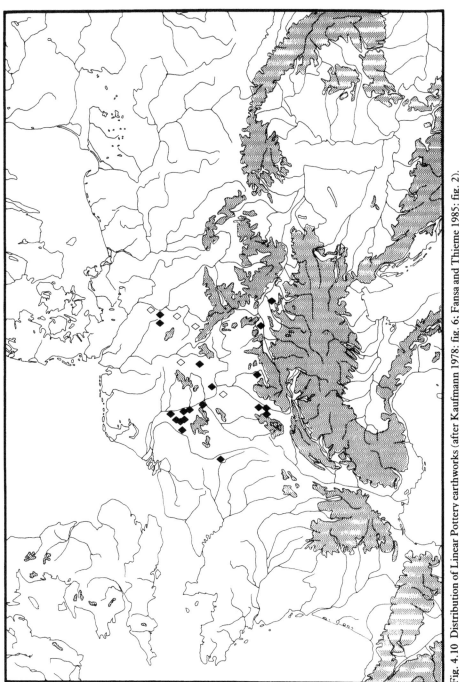

Fig. 4.10 Distribution of Linear Pottery earthworks (after Kaufmann 1978: fig. 6; Fansa and Thieme 1985: fig. 2). Key: open diamonds – possible earthworks; closed diamonds – definite earthworks.

345) has obliquely suggested a similar function for other such structures. I prefer
the more prosaic explanation that they either were for the confinement of domestic
stock or to protect fields from predation by wild herbivores, although this reflects
my own bias towards subsistence-related pursuits.

Primary Neolithic Settlement Patterns

Primary Neolithic settlement patterns in central Europe can be examined on
several different levels. The first is to view them on a continent-wide basis, looking
at broad geographical patterns over the entirety of central Europe. The second is
from a regional perspective, examining the patterns of Linear Pottery, Stroke-
Ornamented Pottery, Lengyel, and Rössen settlement within well-bounded geographical areas, such as the uplands of southern Poland, the middle Elbe basin, and
the loess plateaus of the Rhineland. Finally, Primary Neolithic settlement can be
studied on the local level, that of the "microregion" or "site catchment." Until 20
years ago, Primary Neolithic settlement patterns were discussed almost entirely
from the first perspective, tracing broad patterns of settlement across all of central
Europe. More recently, a number of regional studies have been undertaken, and
many of the advances in the study of Primary Neolithic adaptations in central
Europe have come from these. In general, local studies, in many cases involving
applications of site catchment analysis, have been undertaken only recently, and
then in only scattered instances (e.g. Jarman 1976; Bakels 1978; Linke 1976;
Jarman, Bailey, and Jarman 1982; Howell 1983).

From a continental perspective, two aspects of Primary Neolithic settlement are
readily apparent. These are the discontinuous nature of the areas settled by the first
farmers of central Europe and the general correlation between the settlements and
the loess soils of central Europe (Fig. 4.1). Distribution maps of Linear Pottery
settlements indicate that rather than being evenly and continuously spread across
central Europe, settlements of this culture show a distinct tendency to be clustered
in the basins among the central European mountains and hills and in the loess
"bays" along the southern edge of the North German Plain. Subsequent Primary
Neolithic settlements continued to occupy these same areas and to exhibit an even
greater degree of clustering on this scale of observation. To some degree, these
clusters are artifacts of the distribution of archaeological fieldwork, since they lie
generally in proximity to major archaeological research centers (see discussion in
Hamond 1980). For instance, in the Moravian Gate area on the Polish-Czech
border, there is a paucity of Neolithic sites known from the Polish side of frontier,
located over 100 km from the research centers in Kraków and Wroclaw, but a
number are known from the Czech side, which is closer to the cities of Opava and
Ostrava. Soils and topography are essentially the same on both sides of the border.

Over the last century, however, there has been sufficient archaeological research
in central Europe to permit the conclusion that these clusters are, for the most part,
real. In Germany and Bohemia, most occur in the basins surrounded by the
Hercynian hills and uplands. Such basins are commonly referred to as *Siedlungskammern* or "settlement cells." Elsewhere, they are found in areas less circums-

cribed by topography, such as the piedmont and upland regions along the upper Oder and Vistula valleys, the rolling hills of the Hesbaye in Belgium, and the river valleys of the Paris Basin. Finally, there are areas where no apparent topographical divisions exist, such as the lowlands of northern Poland, yet Primary Neolithic sites are clustered nonetheless in distinct areas along the lower Vistula and Oder.

The areas which separate these clusters of sites are generally those with soils of marginal fertility, either the thin hill and mountain soils of central Europe or the glacial outwash areas of the North European Plain. This observation leads to the other salient feature of Primary Neolithic settlement when viewed from a very broad perspective, namely a preference of these communities for the loess soils of central Europe. This phenomenon is usually explained by the assertion that it was the great fertility of these soils which attracted Primary Neolithic settlers interested in high crop yields. Such a facile explanation, although it may contain a large element of truth, loses some of its explanatory value when it is realized that the loess blanket in the *Siedlungskammern* of central Europe is so ubiquitous (especially when contrasted with the glacially derived soils of the North European Plain) that it would have been difficult to find alternative soils which would be of greater value agriculturally, save for marginally fertile sands and mountain soils, until the Primary Neolithic communities had reached the areas to the north and west of the loess belt. Even much of the alluvium of the river valleys of central Europe is loess-derived (*Schwemmlöss*), thus reducing the choices basically to loess, eroded loess, or non-arable soil. Differences in soil fertility would have been conditioned more by edaphic factors and plant cover than simply by soil type in this area. Clearly, loess was the soil of choice for the Primary Neolithic communities of central Europe, but whether it was chosen because of its fertility, because it was a familiar soil with which the Primary Neolithic communities were comfortable, or because the alternatives were fundamentally unacceptable remains uncertain, although it was probably a combination of these and other factors.

There are several areas where Primary Neolithic communities left the loess zone. One of these is in the Paris Basin, although in the Aisne valley the Primary Neolithic settlements are found on the *Schwemmlöss* washed down from loess deposits further upstream which covers gravel river terraces. In northern Poland and East Germany, Primary Neolithic (Linear and Stroke-Ornamented Pottery) sites are found along the lower Vistula and Oder rivers. These, too, fall into large clusters. One group is found in the triangle formed by the towns of Pyrzyce (Poland), Angermünde (DDR), and Prenzlau (DDR) along the lower Oder, while another occurs in the lake belt of the Kuyavia and Wielkopolska regions of Poland, with a few Linear Pottery sites lying on the east side of the Vistula river north of Toruń and near Warsaw. These two areas lie on the North European Plain, which was glaciated during the Weichsel glaciation, hence no loess is found. Instead, there is a mosaic of soils of varying fertility, based on both ground moraine and glacial outwash. Across other parts of the North European Plain, many stray Primary Neolithic ground stone tools, and even an occasional pottery vessel, are found (Richtofen 1930; Dieck 1977; Fischer 1982). Whether these represent traces of Primary Neolithic incursions into this area remains to be seen, but many are not found in association with either Mesolithic or Consequent Neolithic occupations (with some exceptions – see Fischer 1982). If Primary Neolithic groups did penetrate the North European Plain beyond the settlement clusters mentioned above, their settlements were so ephemeral as to leave no traces that are visible archaeologically.

It has only been within the last 20 years that researchers in central Europe have begun to study Neolithic settlement patterns from a regional perspective. In some cases, their efforts have taken the form of intensive survey and excavation projects (e.g. Kruk 1973, 1980; Kuper and Lüning 1975), while others have made use of distribution maps of previously discovered sites (e.g. Quitta 1970; Lenneis 1982; Starling 1983). Hamond (1980) has discussed the biases inherent in the use of archaeological distribution maps for the study of Neolithic settlement patterns which have resulted from uneven survey coverage and post-depositional erosion and site destruction. In many of the *Siedlungskammern*, however, there are so many Primary Neolithic sites that, although the maps may not accurately reflect site density, they do show broad distributions very well. After verifying distribution maps against "ground truth" in the Elbe-Saale area (DDR), Starling (1983) has concluded that when the sequence of settlement distribution is studied through time, it can be "accepted with a high degree of confidence as reflecting the real situation when sampling effects have been fully noted."

There is a remarkable similarity among the Primary Neolithic settlement patterns observed by researchers working in different parts of the loess belt in three salient aspects. The first of these is the primarily riverine orientation of the sites. Most strikingly, they rarely occur along the *major* rivers of central Europe such as the Danube, Rhine, Elbe, Oder, and Vistula, but rather are most common along rivers and streams of more moderate size, streams with names like Merzbach and Szreniawa (Fig. 4.11). In the valleys of these smaller rivers, there would have been relatively fresher deposits of alluvium and simpler floodplain/watershed configurations than on the alluvial terraces found along the major streams. Linear Pottery communities generally avoided the valleys of the smaller creeks and runs, although Kruk's studies indicate that some Early Lengyel and Stroke-Ornamented Pottery sites occur in such zones in southern Poland. The minor streams would have been generally lacking in alluvium and would have had relatively constricted valleys. In the dendritic drainage pattern of the loess belt, therefore, the specific order of *stream rank* was a major consideration of the Primary Neolithic settlers.

The second most important aspect of Primary Neolithic settlement patterns is that *within* the larger clusters of sites discussed above there are also smaller clusters. These generally include 5–8 sites within a five kilometer or so radius, separated from other sites both upstream and downstream by some distance. Hodder (Hodder and Orton 1976) and Starling (1983) have applied Clark and Evans' (1954) nearest-neighbor statistic to sites in southern Poland and the Elbe-Saale area respectively and have found that the degree of aggregation is statistically significant in both cases. Starling, in fact, notes that of the sites of different Primary Neolithic cultures, the Stroke-Ornamented Pottery sites,

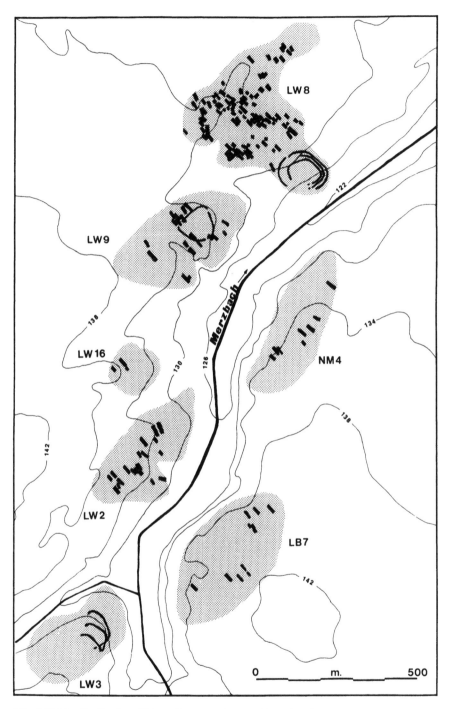

Fig. 4.11 The distribution of Linear Pottery settlements, house locations, and earthworks along the Merzbach valley near Cologne (after Lüning 1982b: fig. 15). Key: LB – Laurenzberg; LW – Langweiler; NM – Niedermerz.

although fewer in number, are even more clustered than Linear Pottery settlements, whereas Rössen/Gatersleben clusters are similar in their degree of aggregation to the Linear Pottery ones.

The third salient aspect of Primary Neolithic settlement in the loess belt is an overall decrease in settlement numbers over time in proportion to the duration of particular Primary Neolithic cultures. This phenomenon has been best documented by Lüning (1982a, 1982b) for the Aldenhoven Plateau in the Rhineland, but it has also been noted by Starling (1983) for the Elbe-Saale area and can be seen in the primary data presented by Kruk (1973, 1980). In general, there are many more Linear Pottery sites per year of duration of this culture in any given *Siedlungskammer* than there are of Stroke-Ornamented Pottery, Rössen, or Early Lengyel sites. Although many Linear Pottery sites continued to be occupied by later Primary Neolithic cultures, most contain Linear Pottery components only (or were re-occupied only much later in prehistory). In the case of the Rhineland, this phenomenon is most striking, but it could probably be readily documented in the other loess *Siedlungskammern* as well. The implications of this for Primary Neolithic demography will be discussed in Chapter 5.

When they are considered on the local level, some further regularities emerge among the Primary Neolithic loess belt settlements. These have been documented by Kruk (1973, 1980), Jarman (1976), Bakels (1978), Linke (1976), Modderman (1982), Howell (1982, 1983), and Starling (1983). The first of these is the preference for settlement on the border between the floodplain and the lower edges of the watersheds, a habitat found along the medium-sized rivers of central Europe. Settlement on the floodplain itself was generally avoided, as this zone would have been seasonally flooded and in many cases would have been covered by a thicket of alder carr (Bakels 1978). Settlement on the upper slopes and summits of the watersheds is also rare. The result is that within the small clusters of Primary Neolithic settlement, the sites are strung out parallel to the stream along the lower margins of the watershed slopes (Fig. 4.12). In some cases, the "sites" are often large belts of settlement debris stretching for several hundred meters along the edge of the floodplain, which leads to difficulties in the definition of discrete habitation areas.

One feature of Primary Neolithic settlement which has been documented only by the geographer Linke in north-central Germany (between Bochum and Göttingen) but which may well be the case in other areas as well is the predilection of the early farmers for relatively flat settlement locations even in areas of more rolling terrain (Linke 1976). Linke studied the terrain around a number of Primary Neolithic settlements and found that within 750 meters of the sites there were rarely any major slopes greater than 2% (with the exception of minor terrain features such as small gullies and stream banks). In general, then, Primary Neolithic settlements in this area are not found at the bases of steep interfluve slopes, but rather at points where there is a gradual transition from floodplain to watershed.

The tendency for Primary Neolithic sites in the central European uplands to be located within only a limited range of topographical situations (specifically, the

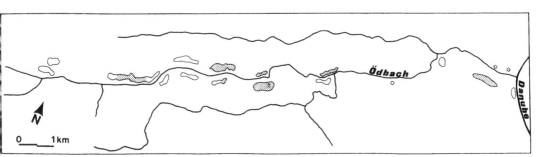

Fig. 4.12 Primary Neolithic settlements along the Ödbach, a tributary of the Danube in Bavaria (after Modderman 1982: fig. 2). Shaded areas indicate sites with Linear Pottery components.

floodplain-lower interfluve slope zone) has the result that within each site catchment, there is generally a good amount of both alluvium (on the floodplain) and uneroded loess (on the watershed), a fairly consistent pattern throughout central Europe. The actual proportion of soil types, such as chernozems and brown earths, within each site catchment is quite variable, and it is difficult to perceive any real regularities of pedological preference. The study of this aspect of Neolithic settlement is further complicated by the fact that today's soil types are not necessarily those of 6,000 years ago but have undergone considerable modification under many millennia of cultivation. It may be, however, that the primary determinant of Primary Neolithic settlement location in central European loess belt was *not* the distribution of specific soil types but rather the occurrence of the preferred floodplain-lower slope habitats. There are large areas of loess which do not have many traces of Primary Neolithic settlement, but which also lack the set of terrain features which characterize the areas of denser Primary Neolithic settlement. The fact that the preferred habitats were in loess areas was an additional payoff, but soil alone may not have been the determining factor.

The preceding discussion of Primary Neolithic settlement patterns has focused on the sites found in the loess belt of central Europe. As mentioned above, there are two areas where Primary Neolithic sites are found off the loess. One of these is the Paris Basin (Ilett et al. 1982; Boureux and Coudart 1978), while the other is on the North European Plain along the lower Oder and Vistula (Wiślański 1974, Bogucki 1982, Bogucki and Grygiel 1983). In the Paris Basin, Primary Neolithic sites are found in the usual linear distribution along major streams such as the Aisne. The clustering observed in the loess *Siedlungskammern* does not really occur, however. Rather, large sites are fairly evenly spaced at about five-kilometer intervals along the streams (Fig. 4.13). These sites are generally located on the lowermost gravel terraces, primarily in areas where there is a veneer of redeposited loess eroded from deposits upstream. As in the sites studied by Linke, there appears to be a preference for very flat settlement locations.

On the lowlands of northern Poland and East Germany, a different sort of Primary Neolithic settlement pattern is found. Here, the rivers do not form hierarchical dendritic patterns but either meander across broad outwash fans or cut

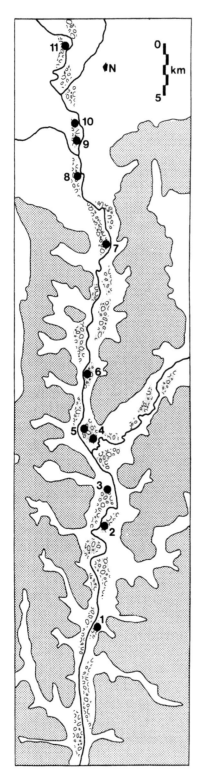

Fig. 4.13 Late Linear Pottery settlements along a
70-kilometer stretch of the Aisne river (after Ilett et al.
1982: fig. 3). Shading indicates limestone plateaux;
pebbly areas indicate gravel terraces. Key: 1 – Pernant; 2
– Villeneuve-Saint-Germain; 3 – Missy-sur-Aisne; 4 –
Chassemy; 5 – Vailly; 6 – Cys-la-Commune; 7 –
Cuiry-lès-Chaudardes; 8 – Pontavert; 9 – Berry-au-Bac
"Le Chemin de la Pêcherie"; 10 – Berry-au-Bac "La
Croix Maigret"; 11 – Menneville.

through sections of ground moraine. Minor streams connect glacial lakes and ponds and often intersect with each other in poorly defined drainage systems. The soil cover of the lowlands is also quite different from that of the loess belt. Rather than the relatively homogeneous blanket of loess and loess-derived soils of the upland zone, the lowlands have a patchy distribution of glacially deposited clays, gravels, and sands, as well as river-borne alluvium. The settlement patterns of the lowland sites contrast sharply with those of the loess belt. Although there are the large clusters of sites which are broadly analogous to the *Siedlungskammern*, which occur along the lower Oder and Vistula, the smaller localized clusters of Primary Neolithic sites do not occur in this area. Instead, settlement is more dispersed, with little apparent organization when viewed from a regional perspective. Moreover, settlements do not occupy analogous habitats to those of the loess belt, largely because the same sorts of floodplain-slope configurations do not exist in the lowland zone. Rather, Primary Neolithic communities often avoided the river valleys themselves and gravitated towards the kettle lakes and finger lakes found in the lowland areas of Primary Neolithic settlement. There is generally a relatively large lake, pond, or marsh within a kilometer of most lowland Primary Neolithic settlements (Fig. 4.14).

Wiślański (1969, 1980) has pointed out that Primary Neolithic sites in the lowland zone occur on or near the boundaries of soil types. This observation loses some of its explanatory value when it is realized that the soil cover of the lowlands is so varied that it is difficult to find locations *not* on or near the boundaries of soil and terrain types. More important appears to have been the avoidance of certain soil and terrain configurations, such as the sands of the larger glacial meltwater valleys (although the Linear Pottery settlement at Krzywosądz lies on a dune in a smaller meltwater channel) and the outwash areas south of the Baltic moraine belt across northern Poland.

Primary Neolithic Subsistence Systems

Although it has been close to 15 years since the idea was first questioned, the notion persists in general archaeological literature that the Primary Neolithic subsistence system in central Europe was based on slash-and-burn agriculture, which exhausted the soil and necessitated frequent settlement relocation (e.g. Fagan 1983: 175; Wallace 1983: 248). Such an agricultural regime had been proposed as the "prime mover" in the spread of food production in central Europe by generations of archaeologists starting with Childe (1929). Few specialists in the Neolithic of central Europe consider this to be a viable hypothesis today, however. In the hope that this myth will be put to rest once and for all, it would be useful to first review the development of this theory and the cogent argument against it.

The notion of Primary Neolithic shifting agriculture can be traced to the 1929 publication of V. Gordon Childe's *The Danube in Prehistory*. Childe noted the relatively shallow accumulations of settlement debris on Primary Neolithic sites in central Europe when compared with those of the Balkans and the relatively large numbers of Linear Pottery sites when compared with those of later cultures. He interpreted these data in light of his cultural-evolutionary perspective. To him, the

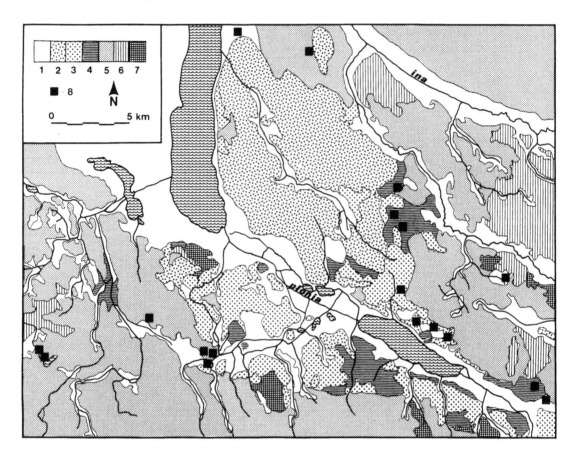

Fig. 4.14 The distribution of Primary Neolithic sites in the Płonia valley near Szczecin (after Wiślański 1980: fig. 2). Key: 1 – alluvium; 2 – marl-sand; 3 – clay-marl; 4 – sand; 5 – boulder clay; 6 – sand over boulder detritus; 7 – exposed underlying sand; 8 – Primary Neolithic sites.

Neolithic peoples of central Europe were "primitive agriculturalists", hence they should have practiced "primitive agriculture." What could be more primitive than a system in which "the peasant was free to shift his hut and break fresh ground as soon as his former fields showed signs of exhaustion" (Childe 1957: 105). After all, such extensive systems of slash-and-burn cultivation were practiced by modern "primitive agriculturalists", mostly in the tropics, people presumably at the same level of socioeconomic development as the Danubians. This hypothesis, of course, ignored the fact that the central European settlements had timber architecture, not the baked clay of the Balkan houses which leaves more residue. In 1929, the traces of the longhouses of Köln-Lindenthal and Bylany had yet to be found. Moreover, Childe assumed that the postglacial soils of central Europe were incapable of sustaining repeated cropping without fallowing. This model of Danubian shifting cultivation became engraved in the archaeological literature when Buttler, the excavator of Köln-Lindenthal, interpreted the apparent breaks in his ceramic sequence as the result of such an agricultural system. By the early 1950s, the theme of Primary Neolithic shifting agriculture had entered the archaeological literature as fact.

To many, this argument made sense, since the progression from extensive to intensive agriculture linked to population increases by Boserup 30 years later was already widely accepted intuitively. Additional support could be found in the pollen diagrams from Denmark and elsewhere in northern Europe, which seemed to indicate that widespread land clearance was coeval with the appearance of agricultural settlements (Iversen 1941). On this basis, J.G.D. Clark in *Prehistoric Europe: the Economic Basis* (1952) was able to say with some degree of confidence that shifting extensive agricultural techniques were the first used by the earliest farmers of central Europe, and the strength of his authoritative presentation led others to reiterate this hypothesis as having been proven conclusively.

In the 1960s, an offshoot of the shifting cultivation hypothesis appeared, although the basic theme is the same. This was the notion of "cyclical agriculture" advocated by Bohumil Soudský. On the basis of his excavations at Bylany in Bohemia, Soudský believed that the development of ceramic styles at the site was not a continuous process, but rather there were breaks similar to those identified by Buttler at Köln-Lindenthal. The result was the predictable argument of periodic settlement abandonment. The difference was that Soudský believed that he had located the other sites in the Bylany microregion where the ceramic inventories corresponded to the gaps in the sequence at the main site. Soudský proposed that the inhabitants of Bylany shifted their settlement in a regular pattern in order to allow the vegetation and ultimately the soil fertility at previous stops in the circuit to regenerate (Soudský 1966; Soudský and Pavlů 1972). In other words, the Primary Neolithic farmers essentially stayed in the same area but moved around nonetheless as a result of their extensive agricultural system. Soudský and Pavlů (1972) formulated this model in greater depth and arrived at the average duration of 60 years for each such cycle. The persuasiveness of such a model of Neolithic agriculture was such that it still forms the basic working hypothesis for a number of archaeologists working with these cultures (e.g. Czerniak and Piontek 1980).

The first cracks in the model of Primary Neolithic shifting agriculture came in the early 1970s, when it was questioned by Modderman (1970, 1971). Modderman based his argument on two lines of evidence. The first is that his excavation of large Linear Pottery sites in Dutch Limburg and the analysis of the structures and pottery showed that the settlements were continually occupied for periods ranging up to several hundred years instead of the intermittent occupation argued by Childe, Buttler, and Soudský. Modderman also pointed out the fundamental inappropriateness of the analogy between tropical slash-and-burn cultivators and the early central European farmers. Especially crucial to his argument was the difference between the thin tropical soils and the thick, nutrient-rich soils of the central European floodplain margins.

Modderman's argument has since been amplified and expanded by others (e.g. Kruk 1973, 1980; Jarman 1976; Lüning 1980; and Rowley-Conwy 1981). Kruk, in particular, has postulated that the Primary Neolithic communities of central Europe practiced intensive floodplain horticulture in gardens in and around their settlements (Kruk 1973: 156-75, 1980: 238). Rowley-Conwy (1981) has adduced an impressive amount of evidence to show that the continuous cropping of loess and similar soils would result in only slightly declining yields over a period of many decades. I am in considerable agreement with this position. It indicates, essential-ly, that there is no compelling reason to assume that in any ecological system the initial condition of any agricultural system will necessarily be the most extensive. It is, of course, a misnomer to call the Primary Neolithic agricultural system "intensive", for although it used a limited amount of land it did not require the constant and concerted labor that truly intensive systems such as rice farming and multi-cropping require. The clearance of sections of the Alno-Padion floodplain forest would have had large initial labor requirements, but the maintenance of soil fertility could have been easily accomplished through the alternating of grain and legumes and by the natural nutrient subsidy of the floodplain ecosystem. The natural productivity of such an "energy-subsidized" habitat (Odum 1971) makes it unsurprising that Primary Neolithic settlements were able to be occupied for such long periods.

Although the Primary Neolithic communities of central Europe occupied a habitat which was capable of producing sustained crop yields from year to year, one should not automatically assume that the agricultural system was uniformly productive from one year to the next. Soil fertility and the productivity of the floodplain habitat would have been just two of the factors regulating agricultural productivity. Others would have been beyond the control of the Neolithic farmers. A major problem would have been localized climatic variation, such as excessive rainfall or drought, windstorms, and hail. In the central European environment, these are frequent, localized, and unpredictable conditions. Another concern of the Neolithic farmers would have been predation by wild herbivores and insects on the growing crops. After harvesting, the grain would have needed to be preserved from microfauna and spoilage, and it is probable that storage losses were common. Despite the potential productivity of the floodplain habitats, Neolithic agriculture under such conditions still may have been a very risky proposition.

Gregg (1986) has examined the question of Neolithic harvests and whether it is realistic to assume that crop yields were consistent by means of a computer simulation which took into account a number of stochastic factors. Her simulation was based on a village of six households with a total of 30 individuals and ran for one hundred years. The results of Gregg's simulation suggest that it was impractical for grain to provide over 80% of the diet, since even with a half hectare per person under cultivation dietary minima were frequently not met and it was difficult to maintain emergency stores. More reasonable figures on field sizes and crop yields, between 0.35 and 0.45 ha/person, were obtained when wheat was taken to provide between 50 and 70% of the diet. Such proportions, Gregg concludes, could result in surpluses seven years out of every ten. The annual fluctuations in crop yields, however, would have been unpredictable. Increasing land under cultivation would have been impractical, for not only would labor requirements have been high, but in many years such a strategy of production maximization could have resulted in excessive surpluses that could not be absorbed through consumption or exchange.

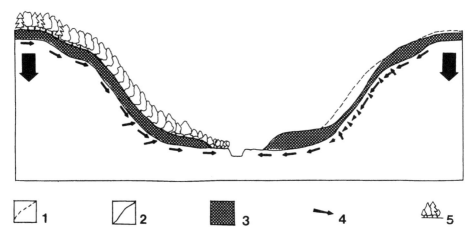

Fig. 4.15 Idealized cross-section of loess watershed in southern Poland showing "energy subsidy" of lower slopes and valley bottom (after Milisauskas and Kruk 1984: fig. 3). Key: 1 – original shape of slopes; 2 – present shape of slopes; 3 – soil profile; 4 – direction and intensity of groundwater movement; 5 – zones of primary vegetation.

A critical problem would have been the "window of unpredictability" between planting and harvest. Modern wheat can be sown in both the fall and spring. The common practice in Europe today is to sow in the fall, since many wheats require a period of cold (vernalization) before they can develop fully (J. Renfrew 1973: 66). One cannot tell from the morphology of the grain whether it belongs to a variety with a winter or spring habit, so it is not possible to say with certainty whether Neolithic wheat was winter or spring sown. Sherratt (1980: 319) is of the opinion that spring growing was practiced in Neolithic temperate Europe, with no definite indication of winter varieties of wheat until the first millennium bc. Among other crops, barley, in particular, is well adapted to a spring growing season. Bakels and Rousselle (1985), on the basis of weed contaminants in carbonized plant samples from Belgium and the Netherlands, also believe that spring sowing was practiced. With a spring growing season, there would have been little opportunity to re-plant a crop that had suffered damage during germination and sprouting (if, in fact, sufficient reserve seed grain was available). Once the crop was growing, it may not have been possible to tell until after the growing season was far along what percentage of the diet it could provide when figured against the other components of the subsistence system. Unpredictable total crop failures would have been difficult to foresee until well into the growing season, when it would have been impossible to replant or to plant additional crops. Clearly, such catastrophic failures were not frequent, for Neolithic communities survived and prospered, yet the potential for their occurrence was probably not far from the minds of the Neolithic farmers.

It appears probable, then, that although Neolithic agriculture was normally adequate to meet nutritional requirements, the margin by which these requirements would be met was uncertain from year to year. One possible response of Primary Neolithic communities would have been to expand crop production to offset the losses to predators, spoilage, and other "predictable" outtakes. There would have been considerable motivation to maximize the area of land under cultivation (given the limitations of time, labor, and seed supplies) in order to maximize the "potential harvest." The disincentives to maximizing crop production were mentioned above, most importantly the problem that if crop yields were unpredictable, a planting strategy based on a "worst case" model could lead to fluctuating surpluses in most years. It is possible, however, that Neolithic farmers did plan production on the assumption that each year would be a "bad" year. Forbes (1982), in his study of subsistence farmers in Greece, found that they usually produce a substantial surplus over their annual consumption needs and seed requirements by basing production on such an assumption. Another possible economic response would have been to diversify the subsistence base rather than to rely exclusively on grain crops. Unfortunately, the archaeological record does not provide adequate data on this. The best indication of the use of a broader range of resources comes from the faunal data, and I shall argue below that domestic animals, particularly cattle, played a greater role in Primary Neolithic subsistence than has been hitherto assumed. The hunting of wild animals does not appear to have been important, however. Several possible reasons for this are outlined below.

The real "wild card" in the subsistence deck is the role of gathered plants in the Primary Neolithic economy. There are hints that some seed-bearing plants, such as goosefoot (*Chenopodium album*), were gathered by Primary Neolithic communities even beyond the amount taken in as crop contaminants (J. Renfrew 1973: 170). Unfortunately, the bulk of the edible plants in the Central European ecosystem would not yield parts which would be prone to carbonization and preservation in the archaeological record. Nonetheless, they would have constituted a resource which would have been most available at a crucial time of the year. In the early spring, the floor of the forest, especially on the floodplain, would have been covered with sprouting vegetation in countless shades of bright green. The sunlight which penetrated the still-open tree canopy would have provoked the flowering of many species of shrubs, ferns, greens, rhizomes, tubers, and other wild plants, most of which had at least some edible parts. It is precisely these plants which do not appear archaeologically, and the record is biased towards the seed and nut plants which mature later in the year. The efflorescence of the forest floor would have coincided with a lean period which may have resulted from a poor harvest the preceding fall, when grain supplies would have been running low or lost to spoilage. The wild plants would have also supplied a number of vitamins and minerals which would not have been adequately provided by a meat- and grain-based diet, notably Vitamin C.

It is inconceivable that the Primary Neolithic inhabitants of temperate Europe would have ignored this potential source of nutrition, especially in light of its seasonal timing. The exploitation costs of the wild plants would have been relatively low, and they could have been easily collected. The limiting factor, of course, would have been the natural productivity of the environment. In the loess belt, the floodplain and lower slopes would have been the richest areas of wild plant growth, and given the location of the settlements in these zones, it would seem likely that these areas were exploited. Unfortunately, these would also have been the most circumscribed habitats, and in times of severe crop shortfalls, it may not have been possible to meet the entire dietary requirements of a whole Neolithic community with wild plants alone. The wild plant resources of the watersheds would have been sparser, and the exploitation costs of wild plants in this zone would have been markedly higher. On the North European Plain, the wild plants of the forest floor would have been profusely abundant during the period prior to the closing of the upper-story canopy, and it seems very unlikely that they would have been ignored by the Primary Neolithic communities that penetrated the lowlands. Here, the limiting factors in the exploitation of such resources would have been the economic costs of their collection and recovery.

Until now it has been assumed that stockherding played a relatively minor role in Primary Neolithic subsistence. This view was first articulated by Childe, who stated that:

> Only small herds of stock were kept; bones of sheep, Bezoar goats, oxen, and pigs turn up in settlements, but animal dung was never incorporated in hut walls, as is usual where the farmyards are well stocked. (Childe 1957:106)

The poor preservation of bone on many of the loess sites was the prime source for this idea, and the plant exploitation indicated by the impressions on pots and the carbonized remains assumed a great importance. Childe's view has been relatively unchallenged until now, and discussions of Primary Neolithic subsistence have focused almost exclusively on agricultural systems.

There is, however, evidence to suggest that stockherding for both meat and milk production played an important role in Primary Neolithic subsistence. The preponderance of cattle bones in the faunal samples is one indication of this. Since cattle give birth singly, have a gestation period of approximately 280 days, and have a prolonged period of immaturity before reaching their productive peak, the keeping of very small numbers of cattle by relatively self-sufficient communities would have been economically unsound. The management of a small herd of cattle requires a fine-tuned mixture of bulls, steers, mature cows, juveniles, and calves. If herd sizes were too small, the death of one or several cattle due to disease or predation would radically affect the structure of the herd, generally adversely, and it would take several years to recover. Even the reproduction dynamics of a too-small herd could have disastrous effects. For instance, if several male or several female calves were born in succession, the consequences for the composition of the herd several years ahead would be serious. In short, a self-sufficient community cannot keep domestic cattle like pets or as modern peasants may keep a single milch-cow. Rather, it needs to keep enough animals to make it economically feasible to extract products, both meat and milk, from the herd.

Determining the number of cattle needed to make keeping them economically viable, however, is not an easy task. To some degree, it is possible to make a start

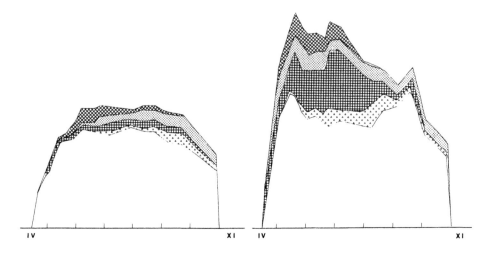

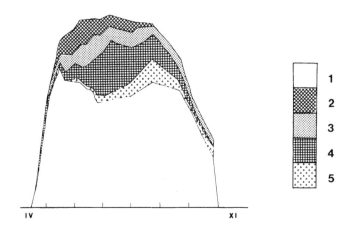

Fig. 4.16 The seasonal pattern of the flowering of the herb layer in various plant associations observed in Białowieża forest, Poland (after Falinska 1973: fig. 6). Key: 1 – vegetative phase; 2 – phase of flowering buds; 3 – blooming phase; 4 – phase of unripe fruits; 5 – phase of ripe fruits and dissemination of seeds. Plant associations: top left – *Querco-Piceetum*, top right – *Tilio-Carpinetum stachyetosum*, lower left – *Circao-Alnetum*.

on this by examining the herds kept by modern subsistence herders such as the Karimojong (Dyson-Hudson and Dyson-Hudson 1970) who also have an agricultural component to their economies. The aim would be not to compare absolute herd sizes, but rather the proportions of bulls, cows, and other classes of stock in their herds. It is not possible, of course, to determine the absolute sizes of Primary Neolithic cattle herds, but rather to get an idea of the minimum herd sizes which would have made cattle-keeping worth the while.

Since cattle take such a long time to reach maturity, a large portion of a self-reproducing herd (i.e. one not maintained through the acquisition of outside stock) will be composed of individuals at various pre-adult stages of development, such as calves, heifers, and young bulls and steers. Only one or two mature bulls are necessary to father the calves of a small herd. To these can be added several immature bulls who will replace the older males in time as the progenitors of the herd. The remainder of the male calves would be castrated to speed their attainment of their maximum meat weight. (On the basis of his East German faunal samples, Müller (1964) believes that Primary Neolithic communities practiced castration.) Since the female cattle are productive, in terms of both milk and calf production, well beyond the point at which they mature physically, there would be many more mature cows in the herd than bulls. They would be kept until they ceased to be productive and then slaughtered. The number of female calves and heifers would be expected to approximately equal the number of immature bulls and steers (which would be slaughtered at or before maturity) although in very small herds there would be considerable variation in their numbers. The balancing of such "equations" has resulted in the hypothetical herd compositions given in Table 4.2, which gives some approximate idealized compositions by sex and age of herds of 10, 20, 30, 40, and 50 cattle when used for subsistence herding. Interestingly, these figures approximate the percentage compositions of 11 herds of Ugandan subsistence herders reported by Dyson-Hudson and Dyson-Hudson (1970: 112), but were not actually based on the Ugandan data.

Several points emerge from Table 4.2. The first is that in 10- and 20-head herds, it would be difficult to maintain herd sizes, much less to increase them, unless there were an external source of new stock. If several male calves were born in succession, for instance, the future of the herd would be endangered, since there would ultimately be a lack of females to succeed the current calf-bearers. The second point is that the smaller herds would be very vulnerable to disease and predation by wild animals. The death of a few calves, especially female ones, would

Table 4.2. *Hypothetical "ideal" compositions of small herds being used for subsistence herding*

Figures indicate the approximate "best" quantities of each category needed to sustain the herd as a self-reproducing unit.

mature males ·	2	2	2	1	1
immature males	4	3	3	2	2
castrates	11	8	5	4	2
mature females	19	16	11	7	3
immature females	14	11	9	6	2
totals	50	40	30	20	10

constitute a major impediment to herd survival in the long run, again because of the gaps it would create in the succession of the adult members of the herd.

In light of such considerations, it would appear that the minimal size required to buffer a herd against the effects of disease, predation, escape, and meat production would be in the order of 30-50 head. Only on such a scale could it be relatively certain that there would be enough cows, female calves, and bulls in the proper proportions to ensure the maintenance of the herd.

The above calculations do not consider the *optimal* herd sizes required to provide enough products to make it worth keeping the animals or to permit herd enlargement. A herd of 10 or 20 cattle would not provide enough meat or dairy products to make it worth keeping the animals even as a supplemental source of nutrition, since of these cattle, only a small percentage would be productive females or steers which could be slaughtered. Almost half of the herd would be bulls (needed for herd maintenance but not directly producing subsistence products) and immature females (not yet producing milk and calves but who ultimately will). If milk production was one reason behind Primary Neolithic cattle herding (and there are ample indications that it was – see below), it would have been necessary to keep more than the number of females contained in the hypothetical 50-head herd described above. The Ugandan data presented by Dyson-Hudson and Dyson-Hudson (1970: 111-13) indicate that only about half of the potential milk cows are giving milk at any one time. Of these, only about half are giving milk beyond the needs of their calves. Therefore, if there are twenty mature females in a small herd, only about five may be giving surplus milk for human consumption. If the steers which may compose 14-20% of the herd are added to this, then only about 30% of a small herd of cattle may be producing subsistence products for humans, although the other 70% cannot be considered to be surplus animals for they are needed for herd maintenance.

The foregoing discussion of herd sizes has been based, in part, on the assumption that milk was a product exploited by Primary Neolithic communities. This suggestion may raise some eyebrows, for such a possibility has been hitherto thought unlikely. A frequent reason given for this is that the ability to ingest lactose, or milk sugar, without ill effects, is a relatively late advance in human evolution on the part of some populations, most importantly the inhabitants of central Europe (and their descendants in America and Australia) and pastoral tribes of East Africa. Most of the world's peoples cannot ingest lactose without suffering cramps, flatulence, and diarrhea, and it has been presumed that the Primary Neolithic populations of central Europe had this condition as well. Sherratt (1983), however, has recently suggested that there would have been a selective advantage for the Neolithic populations of temperate Europe to have had the ability to consume milk, since the cereal-based diet of Neolithic populations, with little vitamin D from fish and liver, would have left them prone to rickets. Such a hypothesis has yet to be investigated more fully, but it militates against the presumption of lactose intolerance on the part of Neolithic peoples in central Europe.

The conversion of milk into cheese, however, would mitigate the potential difficulties posed by lactose intolerance, if it was in fact prevalent in Neolithic populations. Most of the lactose is drained off with the whey in the course of cheese production and what remains is broken down into simpler sugars. There is considerable artifactual evidence to indicate that at least some Primary Neolithic communities did practice some form of cheese-making. Fragments of ceramic sieves have been found at many Primary Neolithic sites across central Europe (Jażdżewski 1981; Jürgens 1978/9; Bogucki 1984). These sherds, although usually too small to permit the reconstruction of vessel forms, are generally perforated all over with small holes 2–3 mm in diameter about 10 mm apart (Fig. 4.17). Such vessels have been interpreted variously as braziers (Jażdżewski 1981) and honey-strainers (Clark 1952) as well as cheese-strainers (Wiślański 1974; Jürgens 1978/9; and Bogucki 1984 among others). It seems unlikely that they were anything but cheese-strainers, for they have numerous similarities with documented cheese-strainers from Apennine Bronze Age (Barker 1981), Roman (Brothwell and Brothwell 1969), and historical European and American contexts (Kerkhoff-Hader 1980, Beaudry et al. 1983).

The relative paucity of wild animals, particularly red deer and roe deer, on Primary Neolithic sites in the central European loess belt reflects the relatively low population densities of these animals in the loess *Siedlungskammern* and the relatively circumscribed exploitation ranges of Primary Neolithic settlements. The low overall natural productivity of the loess watersheds would have probably led to a concentration of wildlife along the valley slopes and bottoms. Thus, wild animal populations would have had a riverine distribution similar to that of the Primary Neolithic settlements. The difference would have been that the animals would not have had a nucleated distribution as did the humans but would have been fairly regularly distributed along the streams and their tributaries, with a low overall density per unit of stream length. The exploitation ranges of the Primary Neolithic settlements would have probably overlapped with the home ranges of a few of each wild species. The result would have been that the costs of foraging for wild herbivores and other game would have been relatively high in proportion to the returns, since it would have necessitated an expansion of the exploitation ranges of each settlement cluster in a linear fashion, upstream and downstream, instead of in a compact radius around the settlements. For this reason, it can be argued that the red deer and other large herbivores whose bones appear in Primary Neolithic faunal samples were animals whose chance encounter with Primary Neolithic farmers resulted in their deaths. This impression is reinforced by the fact that the meager remains of these animals from Primary Neolithic sites betray no signs of the deliberate culling of any particular age-grade. Another possible pathway for these animals to have reached the farming communities would have been through exchange with local hunter-gatherer populations (see Chapter 5).

It is quite interesting that where Primary Neolithic sites are not clustered but rather are strung out along valley bottoms, such as in the Aisne valley in France, there is a relatively higher proportion of wild herbivore bones in the faunal samples, particularly of red deer and the smaller fur-bearing animals (Desse 1976; Meniel 1984). In such a situation, the exploitation ranges of the spaced settlements may have more nearly approximated the home ranges of some animal populations, allowing for greater opportunities to encounter game and thus reducing the costs of

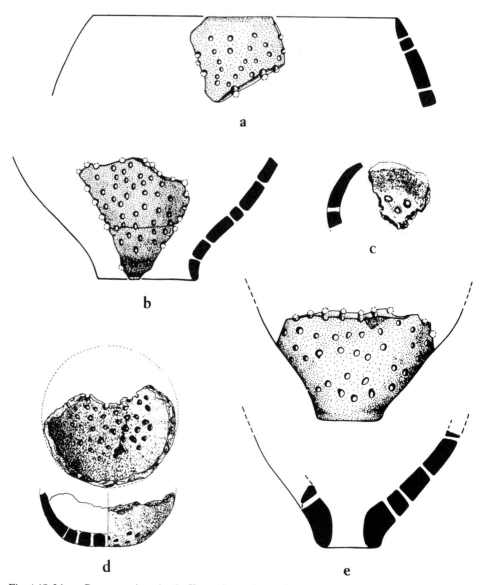

Fig. 4.17 Linear Pottery strainer sherds. Key: a, b, e, – Brześć Kujawski, Poland; c – Murr, West Germany; d – Ditzingen-Schöckingen, West Germany (after Bogucki 1984: fig 1).

deliberately pursuing wild animals. Such a spaced settlement pattern would also have not led to the rapid depression of resource yields in the immediate vicinity of a settlement as would be expected in areas of more clustered occupation.

Coping with risk in Primary Neolithic subsistence
The Primary Neolithic subsistence base was centered on two procurement systems with markedly different logistical requirements. On one hand, the maintenance of

grain crops necessitated the establishment of stable residential bases which are represented by the farmsteads and villages with longhouses. On the other, the relatively large numbers of cattle demanded some degree of mobility due to their forage and fodder requirements. To understand why such conflicting logistical requirements were tolerated by Primary Neolithic communities it is necessary to understand the risks involved in each of these procurement systems.

Agricultural resources are relatively concentrated and predictable in time and space. In other words, they grow where they are planted and ripen at known times. Most systems of subsistence farming also have an unpredictable aspect in that crop yields can vary greatly from year to year depending on the vagaries of weather, crop-robbing, plant diseases, and similar factors. The storing of subsistence resources in the form of live animals has the effect of ameliorating the unpredictability of crop yields on the human population, since barring unforeseen calamities such as epizootic disease, the trends in animal yields can be predicted some time in advance (especially if milk, rather than meat, is the primary product). Browsing resources to feed the livestock, however, are extremely unpredictable as to when and where they will be at their best, or even at acceptable levels. Gregg (1986: 123) points out that persistent browsing can cause changes in the composition of understory vegetation, as preferred species are removed from the community and less preferred taxa are left with little competition.

It could be argued that the most frequent and ubiquitous worry in the lives of the early central European farmers was the margin of agricultural success and the risk of subsistence shortfall or even complete failure. As I noted above, both cultivated plants and domestic stock were vulnerable to disease and predators, not to mention the vicissitudes of climate. Although some degree of shortfall may have been common from year to year, resulting in a seasonal period of undernutrition in some settlements, there were probably also years in which the crops or animals in particular regions were devastated by predators, pathogens, or the weather, resulting in serious nutritional deficiencies on the local, microregional, or regional scale. Such deficiencies would have occasioned social responses which would have had implications for social organization.

To some degree, the Primary Neolithic subsistence system contained internal buffers against seasonal undernutrition. Such a season could be anticipated from year to year, most probably coming at the end of winter and the onset of the growing season when the previous year's supplies were running short and the wild plants had not yet begun to mature. A decision could then be made whether the period of undernutrition could be weathered without special preparations or whether measures such as food conservation and storage were needed. Such decisions would have been based on the yield of the previous harvest and the projected productivity of alternative resources during this period. Severe nutritional deficiency caused by complete crop failure or animal disease, however, would have caused severe perturbations throughout the total cultural system. Such major shortfalls in subsistence resources would have been difficult to anticipate and could necessitate the exploitation of subsistence alternatives beyond the ability of the ecosystem to provide them. Nonetheless, alternatives still would have been available, although perhaps not in sufficient quantities to meet all of a community's dietary requirements. The longevity and survival of Primary Neolithic communities indicates that shortfalls which affected the ability of communities to survive were rare, yet if there was a difficulty in generating surplus crops as a buffer, the options in the event of their occurrence would have been limited.

No subsistence system is so perfectly calibrated that resource yields can be taken for granted. The establishment of a system based on exogenous cultigens and domestic animals in a novel environment would have magnified the degree to which crop yields, while normally adequate, were prone to fluctuation. Unlike many familiar human colonizations of new habitats, Neolithic communities of the central European loess belt did not have a wide range of subsistence options in the event of problems with crops or herds. Rather, their survival was predicated on the development of social options to offset the lack of predictability in the subsistence system. The next chapter represents an attempt to develop some hypotheses about the forms that these social options may have taken.

5

Population, ecology, and Primary Neolithic society

The conditions of subsistence shortfalls described at the end of the previous chapter may represent the exceptional situation, rather than the usual condition of Neolithic life, one would hope. Yet the threat of such conditions was very real each year, and Neolithic farmers never could be absolutely sure that the crops they planted in the spring would be available for consumption the next fall and winter. The possibility of subsistence shortfall or failure must have been such a perennial feature of Neolithic life that it can be inferred to have affected other organizational aspects of society. If risk and uncertainty concerning subsistence are presumed to have permeated Neolithic life, then a number of other cultural systems can be investigated in the context of the response and adjustment to the potential for subsistence shortfalls. Demography, trade, interaction with indigenous peoples, and even social organization can all be viewed as mechanisms for providing a support system for Primary Neolithic communities to buffer them from the risks inherent in the establishment of a new economy in the central European forests, for all of these represent ways by which Primary Neolithic society affected and altered its relationship to its environment.

This is not to imply that all activities of the Primary Neolithic communities were singlemindedly directed towards coping with subsistence shortfalls. It can, however, be argued that the ever-present possibility of food shortage necessitated configurations of social forms which presented an effective limitation on the options which were available to the Primary Neolithic community. In the most general terms, it required a degree of flexibility and diversity among the agriculturalists which would have suppressed the development of specialized social and economic forms, such as rigidly unilineal descent systems. There would have been a constant tension between the need to have ever larger populations to meet agricultural labor demands and the ever scarcer land and personal opportunity within individual microregions. In short, once one realizes that the Primary Neolithic subsistence system in central Europe was at once capable of high crop yields yet also capable of falling short of meeting subsistence demands, one can view many aspects of Neolithic life in a different light.

The preceding chapter discussed the habitat occupied by the Primary Neolithic farmers and some of the basic subsistence practices through which they exploited that habitat. This chapter will attempt to characterize the *ecological niche* occupied by the Primary Neolithic communities more closely. As defined in Chapter 1, the ecological niche of a human population represents the sum total of the exchanges made by that population with its operational environment. These exchanges include not only energy but also both material and social resources, and the position of the human population in this web of interaction constitutes its niche. Such a definition of "ecological niche" is somewhat broader than that used by some ecological anthropologists (e.g. Hardesty 1975: 109) but it is still in keeping with recent discussions of the topic in anthropological literature. Love (1977: 32) defines the niche of a human group as "an aggregate representation of the relations of its members to income generating resources at a point in space and time." In Love's view, the critical resources in the ecological niche of a human group are land, water, labor, capital, space, and time. To this list can be added "information", for any organization must be able to predict the outcome of its behavior under certain conditions as well as to optimize its use of time and energy.

If the Neolithic colonization of central Europe can be characterized as the occupation of a new ecological niche, then there are several aspects which must be considered on a more theoretical level first, for there are a number of general issues that may apply to many populations in similar situations. These aspects include the demography of pioneering populations, the perceptions of the new environment by the incoming populations, and the results of the potential failure of the subsistence system. A number of cultural elements of the ecological niche can then be considered in light of the relationship of the Neolithic population to its social and physical environment. Such elements include the relations with indigenous foraging populations, exchange systems and "wealth", and social organization. Since this chapter is based on theory and interpretation, it clearly must be considered as an attempt to build models of Primary Neolithic society, not as a series of conclusions based exclusively on empirical data.

The demography of the Neolithic frontier
The Neolithic colonization of central Europe is in many respects a demographic issue. Any human population must ensure that there is a sufficient labor pool to acquire resources and enough individuals for the population to survive as a biological entity. The Primary Neolithic communities of central Europe exhibit high rates of population growth and large-scale movements of peoples, issues that can be addressed through the study of the size and structure of the populations involved. Unfortunately, the demographic study of the archaeological record is hampered by the lack of hard empirical data on population size and structure. Estimates of size can be reached through the density and duration of the settlements, but the age and sex structure is very difficult to apprehend. Mortuary data may be of use in the study of population structure, but the Primary Neolithic cemeteries are few and far between, and it is possible that they may not reflect complete populations. For instance, there is a scarcity of infantile skeletons, presumably due to preservation conditions, a fact that frustrates any understanding of infant mortality and survivorship. The discussion here will explore some theoretical issues of frontier demography, a relatively new topic of study by demographers, to see if any correlates of their observations can be identified in the Primary Neolithic archaeological record.

An early attempt at the demographic analysis of Primary Neolithic settlement in central Europe was that of Ammerman and Cavalli-Sforza (1971, 1973, 1984), who plotted the distribution of 106 radiocarbon dates across Europe and measured their distance from centers of domestication in the Near East. They found a remarkable consistency in the rate of spread of Neolithic cultures, both in central Europe and beyond, with the "frontier" moving at an average of 25 kilometers every generation (Ammerman and Cavalli-Sforza 1984: 61). Ammerman and Cavalli-Sforza interpreted these results as an indication of situation in which a frontier with exceptionally high levels of population growth rolled across Europe like a wave. In their model, population growth was logistic, with a high initial rate of growth which subsequently leveled off. Behind the frontier, in areas already settled, the rate of population growth would have been steady. In the zone of high population growth at the leading edge of the frontier, settlements would have reached a critical threshold very quickly, whereupon they fissioned and established daughter settlements nearby (Ammerman and Cavalli-Sforza 1973: 13).

The wave-of-advance model of the expansion of food production assumes that Primary Neolithic settlement was continuous across central Europe, which it certainly was not. It also obscures the very real differences in the adaptations of the Primary Neolithic and Consequent Neolithic populations which are documented in this chapter and the one which follows. Once the differences in topography, soils, and natural productivity of the different central European habitats are taken into account, such a model loses much of its utility in all but the most abstract sense. Moreover, there are conceptual difficulties with the isochronous interpretation of radiocarbon dates due to the fact that radiocarbon dates are not absolute values but statements of statistical probability (Wilke and Taylor 1971).

Some of these considerations were taken into account by Hamond (1978, 1981) in his simulation of Primary Neolithic settlement processes in the Lower Rhine Basin. Within the ecological context of the Aldenhoven Plateau, Hamond modeled the development of the Linear Pottery settlement system. One of his fundamental assumptions was that there would be a net annual growth rate of the Primary Neolithic population of 3 ± 1%. Such a figure, while phenomenally large, is not entirely unreasonable, for there are ethnographically documented migrations where the growth rate has been in this range (e.g. Lefferts 1977: 41). At such a growth rate, the combination of in-migration and fertility would have resulted in the saturation of the *Siedlungskammer* within 50-100 years. Such a situation clearly did not take place, and Hamond's simulation suggests that the out-migration from a *Siedlungskammer* was prompted by factors other than simple population pressure. In the view of some, however, Hamond's simulation was flawed by his assumption of an exponential rate of growth (Ammerman and Cavalli-Sforza 1984: 157).

The demographic analyses of the Primary Neolithic colonization of central Europe discussed so far have addressed one aspect of the demography of these cultures, namely population size and growth. The other aspect of demography, that of the structure of the Primary Neolithic populations and their fertility, has been generally bypassed, simply because of the difficulty in obtaining empirical data. It is, however, possible to discuss this aspect theoretically and then to investigate whether any archaeological correlates can be found.

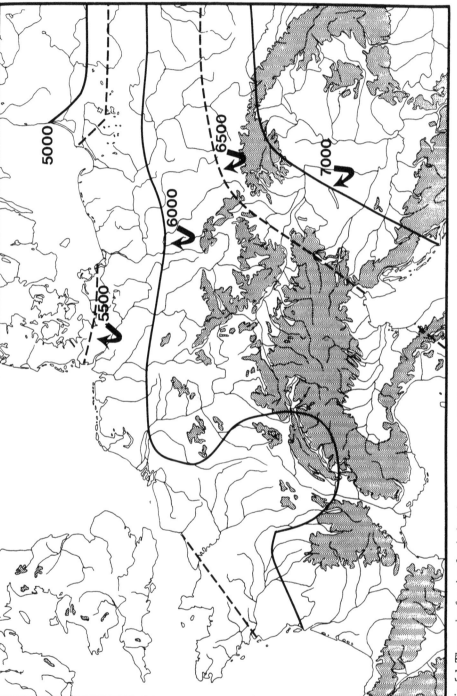

Fig. 5.1 The moving frontier of agricultural expansion (in years BP) in temperate Europe proposed by Ammerman and Cavalli-Sforza as their

Lefferts (1977) has called attention to the unique dynamics of population structure in areas undergoing colonization. He discusses two case studies in pioneer demography, one drawn from his own fieldwork in Thailand, the other from the historical demography of Simkins and Wernstedt (1971) in Davao, Philippines. In the latter case, the researchers concentrated on the study of the migrants into a valley and their points of origin, while Lefferts' own work focused on a particular village which was established through migration and which in turn was sending out migrants. In the Philippine case, the initial migrants into the valley (ca. 1918) were predominantly male (209 males per 100 females), while by 1939 the sex ratio was down to 135 and heading towards parity. The further away from the valley the migrant originated, the greater the likelihood the migrant was a male. The age structure of the initial migrant population was heavily weighted towards young adults. With the increase in settlements, however, the median age rose, even though fertility also increased as more women were brought in. In general, Simkins and Wernstedt observed that the median age of the population showed significant decreases closer to the fringes of settlement (1971: 84).

Lefferts' demographic study of a Thai village documented trends similar to those observed by Simkins and Wernstedt. His study also had a considerable amount of time depth, covering the period 1922–72. Although Lefferts did not document the initial phase noted by Simkins and Wernstedt in which single males identified the site as a good settlement location, the subsequent out-migration from this village followed such a pattern, in which single males were sent out and then followed by households. The age structure of this village and its changes over time also paralleled that of the Philippine valley discussed above. Prior to 1947, the age distribution was skewed heavily towards the 20–40 year age group. In 1937, only 5.1% of the population was over 40, and Lefferts reports that the 20-year age categories obscure the fact that most of the individuals in the 20–40 age group were in the younger part of that range.

On the basis of these studies, Lefferts has defined several general relationships among demographic variables in frontier contexts, which are summarized graphically in Figure 5.2. Curve A represents the changes in the variability of several key population characteristics: growth rate, sex ratio, and the contribution of in-migration to population sizes. The growth rate is expected to move from high to low, the sex ratio from male-biased to relative parity, and in-migration from being the major cause of population growth to a minor component. Curve B is the logistical curve depicting population growth in absolute numbers. Curves C1 and C2 represent the broadening of the age structure. Curve C1, the lower one, shows the effects of the changing sex ratios and the concomitant rise in fertility, while C2, the upper curve, moves upward more slowly, since it represents indigenous aging and may be affected by heightened mortality during the earlier stages of colonization.

Curve D represents the most dynamic aspect of frontier demography: human fertility. This is perhaps also the most important, for it reflects the inherent ability of a population to produce enough labor for immediate survival and enough offspring for long-term survival. Lefferts, on the basis of his own research and the

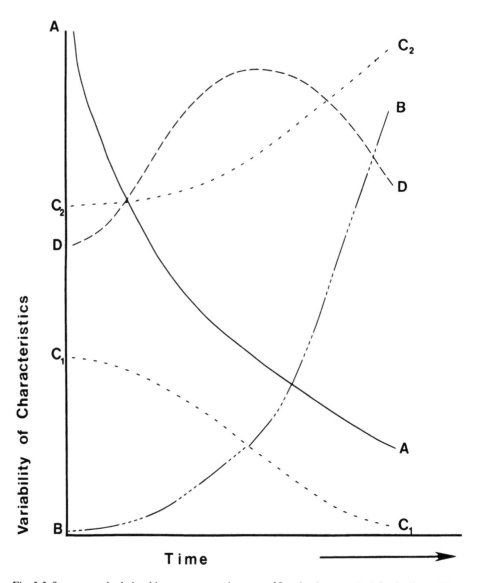

Fig. 5.2 Some general relationships among several aspects of frontier demography (after Lefferts 1977: fig. 4). Key: A – growth rate, sex ratio, contribution of in-migration; B – population numbers; C – age structure; D – marital fertility.

historical studies of Easterlin (1976) on North American settlers, suggests that there may be some regular and predictable patterns in human fertility over time in a frontier context. Easterlin observed that with increasing distance behind the frontier, fertility rates dropped off. The exception to this generalization is in the communities along the *leading edge* of the frontier. In these areas, average fertility, while still higher than that in areas well to the rear of the frontier, was 5 to 10% lower than in the areas just behind the frontier. Easterlin found that as the population of a given area moved through successive generations of settlers, marital fertility rose between the second and third generations, then declined as the third generation became the reproductive unit. The highest fertility levels occur in the second generation, the first group of residents native to a particular region. Easterlin concluded that this phenomenon is not the result of any special pro-fertility conditions on the frontier but rather as a cumulative effect of factors which work against fertility, problems which are not apparent to the first native-born inhabitants of an area but which become more obvious to the members of succeeding generations. Many of these problems revolve around the fact that there is a decreasing amount of land available per individual in any particular area and the relative decrease of economic opportunities.

Among small-scale agriculturalists there are reasons for high fertility levels that may not have occurred in the populations studied by Easterlin. Handwerker (1983) suggests that the high fertility levels associated with agricultural populations stem from a very high demand for children. In many agricultural communities children contribute to productive activity from childhood and can open up additional avenues of support for their parents by providing alliances with other corporate groups through marriage, pawning, wardship, and ritual coparenthood (which is not to imply that all these took place in Primary Neolithic Europe!). Moreover, the settled nature of agricultural communities means that the energy cost of child care is generally lower than in mobile hunting-gathering societies. Finally, in most agrarian societies, parental obligations to their children are decidedly less impor-tant than the obligations of the offspring to their parents. The underlying economic rationale is that as parents age, the size of their support network will be proportional to the number of surviving offspring (Caldwell 1977). It is therefore in the agriculturalists' interest to have as close a birth spacing as possible in the hope that a reasonable number of offspring will survive to adulthood.

At the same time, there are a number of factors which work against the desire for high numbers of offspring among agriculturalists (Handwerker 1983). Primary among these is that among settled societies there appears to be a lessened chance that a given pregnancy will yield a live birth or that the live birth will survive to adulthood. This fact stems from the anthropogenic degradation of the environment around agricultural settlements and the enhanced conditions for the transmission of airborne and feces-borne disease vectors. The implications of this observation, when combined with those of Easterlin, are that for a period after the establish-ment of a settlement there should be a relatively high rate of population increase, whereupon it would be offset by increased morbidity and mortality, particularly among infants. The environmental degradation of the immediate habitation area and its observed effects on fertility would have been a strong impetus for settlement reconstruction and relocation.

The generalizations about frontier demography summarized in Figure 5.2 may not be testable against the central European archaeological record as it now stands. It is impossible to determine sex and age ratios from Primary Neolithic burial data, as none exist for the very earliest Linear Pottery phases and the data from later cemeteries do not appear to represent complete samples of entire populations (infants and children are especially lacking, and given the considerations of infant mortality noted above, they should be a relatively large proportion of the burials).

The one area where it may be possible to make a link between theory and the archaeological record may be in the discussion of fertility. If the density of Primary Neolithic settlement in a particular region can be assumed to reflect relative population levels over time, it may thus be possible use this as proxy evidence to trace fertility (although it will not be possible to filter out the contribution of continued in-migration and out-migration to the settlement data).

The changing density of Primary Neolithic settlement in the Rhineland has been documented by Lüning (1982a). In this region, the intensity of archaeological research over the last 20 years has ensured that there is a representative sample of sites for each Primary Neolithic culture, although the distribution maps do contain some spatial biases (Hamond 1980). Lüning has compared the total number of Linear Pottery settlements known in the Rhineland with those of later Primary Neolithic cultures and groups (Grossgartach, Rössen, Bischheim) and graphed the settlement numbers against the approximate temporal duration of each culture or group (Fig. 5.3). Whereas 98 Linear Pottery settlements were occupied over a 450-year time span, only 34 Rössen settlements can be found from the 230-year duration of this culture, and of these just 26 were in the same part of the Rhineland as the 98 Linear Pottery settlements (i.e. the Aldenhoven Plateau). The Grossgartach and Bischheim groups have similarly low numbers of settlements in proportion to their temporal duration. Moreover, the settlements at the end of the Primary Neolithic sequence appear distinctly smaller than those of the middle and late Linear Pottery culture.

The data presented by Lüning may reflect the substantial population growth which occurred on the Linear Pottery frontier, with population levels of succeeding cultures being substantially lower. It is possible that this observation parallels the findings of Easterlin, in which the fertility levels of pioneer populations decline as the frontier moves on. It should also be noted that most of the 98 Linear Pottery sites have their primary occupations during the *late* phases of this culture, so that the actual curve of site numbers over time would conform approximately to the fertility curve in Figure 5.2. The fundamental difference between the recent examples of pioneer demography which contributed to Figure 5.2 and the case of Primary Neolithic Europe is that the former processes took place over a few generations, while the latter occurred over the course of a millennium. Nonetheless, I think that the parallels are real and represent similar processes, with the Neolithic case taking place over more time due to the overall low population levels and the checks on unrestrained population growth such as infant mortality.

Perception of the Primary Neolithic habitat
The establishment of a population in a new ecological niche involves the initiation of exchanges with many elements of the ecosystem. Besides the exchanges of material resources with the physical environment and other human populations, there is a need to exchange information within a community and with other human groups. The exchange and flow of information in small-scale cultural systems has been exceedingly difficult to document both archaeologically and ethnographically, due to their ephemeral and intangible nature. Prehistoric societies in particular are

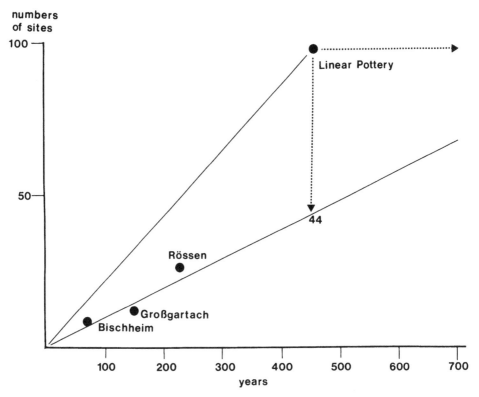

Fig. 5.3 A graph of settlement numbers by culture against the time-span of each Primary Neolithic culture in the Rhineland (after Lüning 1982a: fig. 5).

often presumed to have been fully informed about their environment. Ignorance, misconception, and error are very real characteristics of the human condition, however, and it would be wrong not to consider them in the context of Primary Neolithic adaptations in central Europe.

The earliest Primary Neolithic populations of central Europe entered an environment which was unlike anything they or their ancestors had previously encountered. Deciduous forests, different species of wild plants and animals, new soil types, new climatic characteristics, new landforms, and indigenous foraging bands were encountered and incorporated into the "mental map" of the particular *Siedlungskammer* or microregion where a Primary Neolithic community had chosen to settle. The cognitive ability of the Primary Neolithic colonists to process the information on these environmental variables was affected by several factors. The first was that they did not have the benefit of a body of knowledge accumulated over many generations, a condition especially true of the earliest Primary Neolithic communities in a given area. Secondly, the deciduous forests made exploration difficult and masked a considerable degree of environmental diversity. Then, there would have been the variable central European climate, so that it would have been several years at least before the full range of possibilities was encountered. Finally, the initial population densities would have been so low that there would have been little opportunity for the sharing of information among a large number of households and communities.

The Neolithic colonization of Europe can be viewed as a continual feedback process in which new information was continually gathered from the environment and added to a community's accumulated store of data concerning the central European ecosystem. There would have been a continuous refining of the cognitive models of the environment held by individuals, households, and communities until those models drew closer and closer to the actual characteristics of the ecosystem. It can be inferred that there was "a dynamic of constant assessment, evaluation, and choice among alternative attempts to achieve subsistence goals from environmental possibilities ... in which changes in the range of possibilities [could] be quickly incorporated into the actors' cognitive framework" (Britan and Denich 1976: 69). In this way, the ecosystem would have been made more *predictable*, a characteristic highly valued by agrarian communities that are tethered to specific locations by virtue of their subsistence system.

The environment about which the Primary Neolithic communities had to procure information consisted of all the other elements of the ecosystem: geophysical elements such as soil types, biological elements such as wild plants and animals, and social elements – other human populations, both foragers and agriculturalists, living in the same area. There are two ways of examining the problem: from the point of view of the observer or that of the participant, the "interpretative" or the "cognized" models (Rappaport 1968: 237). Obviously, when one is dealing with archaeological data, it is quite difficult, almost impossible, to apprehend the cognized model of the environment held by prehistoric communities. Nonetheless, Ellen (1982: 229–30) has suggested that it may be possible to examine cognitive models of the ecosystem through the study of the "end-states" of decision-making processes, such as settlement patterns. The discussion below will be an attempt in this direction.

Social scientists dealing with the behavior of organizations (and it can be argued that the Neolithic household was an "organization" in the sociological sense) have defined a typology of "system environments" as viewed from the perspective of the organization which is adapting to them (Emery and Trist 1965; Aldrich 1979: 70–4). Emery and Trist used three dimensions – stability, concentration, and turbulence – to describe four types of environments, which they called "causal textures". Of these four environments, two are relevant to this discussion given the level of organizational complexity in Neolithic societies.

The most elementary environmental type defined by Emery and Trist (Type I) is what they call "placid-randomized" and to which Aldrich (1979: 71) refers as "stable, dispersed." In this type of system environment, resources are effectively randomly distributed, and therefore, the causal laws which connect the various elements of the environment are unknown to the organization. The environment is unchanging, but this stability is of little consequence because the organization does not yet know where the relevant "goods and bads" are. From the point of view of the organization, these are randomly distributed in space and time because the organization has not been able to map the variability.

The second sort of environmental type recognized by Emery and Trist (Type II) is what they call "placid-clustered" or, in Aldrich's terminology (1979: 72) "stable, concentrated." In this type of environment, the environmental goods and bads are effectively clustered in space and time or at least the organization has sufficiently mapped the localities where they occur. Resources are no longer randomly distributed from the point of view of the organization but rather they are more predictable both spatially and temporally as the organization becomes increasingly familiar with its surroundings.

Organizations respond in different ways to Type I and Type II environments. An organization faced with a Type I (placid-randomized) environment will respond *tactically*. This entails making short-term maneuvers to respond to the exigencies of the situation – "it does its best on a local level" (Emery and Trist 1965). There is a shifting relationship between the organization and its surroundings as increasing familiarity with the resources in the environment develops. Organizations faced with Type II (placid-clustered) environments, on the other hand, respond *strategically* by locating their centers of activity cognizant of optimal positions on a broader scale. Strategic activities are those which exercise a degree of planning and foresight rather than simply trying to make the best of a local situation.

The behavioral correlates of such perceptions of the environment should be expected to appear in certain archaeological "end-states", especially the settlement pattern. According to Clay (1976), who has applied the Emery and Trist model to Mississippian sites in the southeastern United States, settlements in a placid-randomized environment can be expected to be of relatively uniform size and duration (generally short) with a low density of sites in the region as a whole. There is a relatively rapid cycle of use-abandonment-reuse of the site area, reflecting decisions made for short-term advantage based on limited information. Settlements in a placid-clustered environment, on the other hand, should be of longer duration (reflecting the greater investment of time and labor in a particular location) and there should be continued rebuilding (not just re-occupation) on the site over time. There should also be a greater diversity of site sizes and (possibly) functions.

The Primary Neolithic settlements of central Europe appear to reflect such a two-stage process of cognitive mapping. In the loess belt, the earliest Primary Neolithic settlements are usually *not* characterized by the presence of multiple longhouses. Rather, there are few traces of permanent architecture at settlements with "Earliest" Linear Pottery with the exception of Schwanfeld and perhaps Eitzum and Eilsleben. Instead, most large settlements with multiple longhouses appear to have been constructed only after the initial Linear Pottery entry into a *Siedlungskammer* in the middle and late stages of this culture. The sizes of the earliest sites are generally small, and only later is there the differentiation of sites into the single- longhouse "farmsteads" and the small and large nucleated settlements, the so-called "villages". In the lowlands of the North European Plain, a parallel process took place except that it was much more drawn out (Bogucki 1979). Here, Linear Pottery sites are striking for the regularity of their sizes and artifact content, especially in the ratio of pottery to animal bone density in individual features and the consistent recurrence of one or a few sherds of ceramic sieves on each site (Bogucki 1984). There are no traces of *permanent* Linear Pottery structures in this region, particularly not of longhouses. Such settlements could be argued to represent "tactical" responses to the poorly known environment of this area, markedly different from that of the loess belt. The later Primary Neolithic settlements of the North European Plain, particularly the Lengyel settlements like Brześć Kujawski and Krusza Zamkowa, can be argued to represent "strategic" responses to an increasingly better mapped environment. The relative slowness of the mapping process on the North European Plain can be possibly attributed to the fact that while the various *Siedlungskammern* of the loess belt share many common characteristics, the lowland zone would have presented a completely novel (and much more varied) environment at first. Moreover, the larger indigenous foraging populations of the lowlands would have added greater complexity to the operational environment.

While it seems reasonable to suppose that such a two-stage mapping process occurred during the Neolithic colonization of Europe, the question then arises as to the mechanisms by which the cognitive maps of the central European habitats held by the Primary Neolithic farmers progressed from one stage to the next. One must assume that scouting and exploration played a role, at least in the initial investigation of an area. Although one can infer the use of descriptive terms, assessments of distance, and notions of direction that could be "stored" by a Neolithic community, the superficial images obtained during a single passage through an area may not have provided all the information needed by Primary Neolithic farmers to commit the time and energy to locate a settlement in a new area.

Behavioral geographers have emphasized the importance of repetitive travel, particularly travel to and from work, in the formation of cognitive maps (Pipkin 1981). While most considerations of this have been in the context of modern industrialized society, the role of repetitive travel may be equally relevant for Neolithic society. The most common sort of repetitive travel for Neolithic farmers would have been to and from their fields. Assuming that fields were located as close to settlements as possible (which seems reasonable given the floodplain locations of the settlements), the opportunities for the cognitive mapping of a wide area in this way would have been limited. There would have been other contexts in which repetitive travel would have been undertaken to points more distant from settlements. One of these would have been the procurement of flint and other stone raw materials, the sources of which usually lay outside the loess belt, or at least beyond the immediate catchment of an individual settlement. In addition, there would have been other resources, such as timber, clay, and antler, whose procurement would have required regular trips away from the immediate environs of the settlement.

Another important context for repetitive travel in Primary Neolithic life would have been cattle herding. If this activity was as significant as I have argued in Chapter 4, it probably would have played a major role in the identification of optimal settlement locations by Primary Neolithic communities. While fields are concentrated and fixed in space and crops ripen at predictable times, grazing resources are dispersed and unpredictable as to when they will be at their peak. There is therefore a mobile component in any subsistence system in which one finds this degree of livestock herding, and the low density of browse and grazing for cattle in the primeval European forests would have made it necessary to range some distance from the settlement. Areas with high-quality grazing, such as beaver meadows, would have been revisited often in the course of a year and would have had the added advantage of being near water sources. As herding parties moved about in search of good grazing, optimal settlement locations could thus be identified and mentally filed for future reference. In such a way, areas more remote from the residential base could be included in the cognitive maps developed by a Primary Neolithic community.

Figure 5.4 depicts the development of a cognitive map of a region by its Primary Neolithic colonists. 5.4a represents the initial stage, in which the environmental goods and bads are more or less randomly located, save for the small area through which the initial entry into the area took place. In 5.4b, the area originally identified as promising has turned out to be acceptable, and it has become a node of activity. Nearby, other optimal areas are starting to be identified, but beyond them, the region is still essentially unknown. Finally, in Figure 5.4c, several further nodes of activity have emerged, and other outlying areas have been determined to have potential for activity of one kind or another.

The role of cognitive mapping must be taken into consideration when the Primary Neolithic colonization of central Europe is discussed. It can account for many phenomena, including the relatively long time-lag between the colonization of the loess belt and the establishment of farming communities on the North European Plain. It also accounts for the fact that most of the large Linear Pottery settlements with longhouses come from the later stages of this culture, since they arguably represent "strategic" responses to a better known environment. Finally, the role of repetitive travel in the formation of such cognitive maps cannot be overemphasized, and the frequent movement of herds in search of grazing would have been an ideal context for such travel.

Mesolithic – Primary Neolithic interaction

The Primary Neolithic colonists of central Europe were not entering entirely uninhabited territory. Although the actual density of indigenous hunter-gatherer populations of the loess belt was low, such groups were, in fact, present and would have been encountered by the agriculturalists. The model of a Neolithic wave-of-advance across central Europe supposes that the Mesolithic populations retreated before it, but if the Neolithic expansion is perceived as a more sporadic, open, and fragmented process, then a more dynamic relationship between indigenous hunter-gatherers and Primary Neolithic communities can be proposed.

Moore (1981, 1985) has simulated the effect of agricultural expansion on foraging populations. The decrease in the number of potential foraging territories would increase the probability of unsuccessful searches for such areas, which in turn would increase the seasonal movement costs for a foraging group. The increased costs would result in a decrease in the optimal number of hunter-gatherer

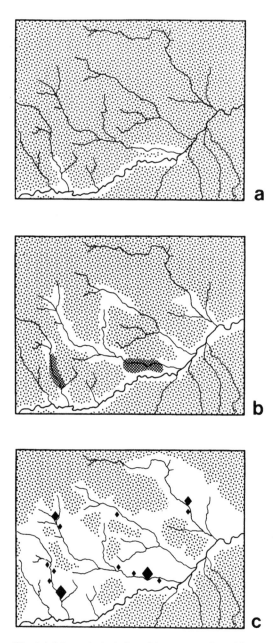

Fig. 5.4 Schematic depiction of the process of cognitive mapping in Primary Neolithic central Europe (see explanation in text).

seasonal camps in any particular region. Moore argues that there will thus be an advantage to any foraging strategy under such conditions which (1) reduces the number of hunter-gatherer settlements; (2) reduces the seasonal mobility of the foragers; and (3) increases information-sharing among the foragers (Moore 1981: 211). On the basis of his simulation, Moore concludes that there would have been no direct displacement of hunter-gatherers by agriculturalists, for most of any particular region would still remain unutilized. Rather, Moore's simulation suggests that there would have been a rapid decrease in the archaeological "visibility" of foraging bands through the reduction in settlement numbers. The implication of this is that models of agricultural expansion which postulate that indigenous European foragers were pushed into marginal areas along the fringes of the continent may not reflect the real dynamics of interaction between the two populations.

The main areas of contact between Mesolithic and Primary Neolithic populations would have occurred in the upper reaches of the main river systems of central Europe. In particular, large numbers of Mesolithic sites are known from the upper Danube, Rhine, and Vistula basins (Taute 1980; Jochim 1979a; Milisauskas 1977), where their inhabitants would have been primarily attracted by the plentiful anadromous fish resources. Both populations would have had an essentially riverine focus, but while the agriculturalists were tethered to their garden plots, the hunter-gatherers would have had much wider exploitation territories. In southern Poland, for instance, Mesolithic sites have been found on the loess watersheds in addition to the river valleys themselves (Milisauskas 1977).

The more mobile Mesolithic communities would have had access to a wider range of wild resources than would have had the agriculturalists. Moreover, they would have been much more familiar with the local topography, flora, and fauna than the newly arrived farmers. It would have been in the best interests of the farming communities to ensure good relations with the Mesolithic groups, rather than simply to displace them. The Mesolithic groups of the loess belt would have been rather small, given the relatively low productivity of wild resources in this zone, and may have had fairly broad exploitation territories. The arrival of agriculturalists within these territories probably did not have an immediate impact on the hunter-gatherer exploitation patterns, but ultimately may have led to a reduction in the numbers of Mesolithic settlements on a regional scale.

There is a growing ethnographic literature on hunter-gatherer/farmer interaction (reviewed by Peterson 1978a, b) and much of it focuses on exchange. A recurring theme is the exchange of wild protein obtained by hunting populations for domestic carbohydrates produced by farmers. In the Philippines, Agta hunters exchange deer, boar, and fish for the grain provided by the Palanan farmers (Peterson 1978b: 337–44). These transactions generally take place on the household level, in which one Agta (typically married and male) develops a "special relationship" with a Palanan counterpart. These friends have a mutual commitment to provide foodstuffs for each other, and each produces a small surplus, generally between 10 and 30% above the needs of their household, to exchange. The complementary subsistence practices effectively provide both populations with a much-widened food web and permit the "double exploitation" of essentially the same ecosystem. Other reported instances of hunter-gatherer/farmer interaction often follow a similar pattern, and Peterson (1978b: 347–8) suggests that such intercultural exchanges were widespread in prehistory.

It is thus clearly possible for hunter-gatherers and agriculturalists to coexist in both congruent and overlapping habitats. Whether or not this happened in

Primary Neolithic central Europe is difficult to say, of course, given the lack of the archaeological correlates of such interpersonal dealings. Gregg (1986) has established the theoretical rationale for some form of forager-farmer interaction in Neolithic temperate Europe through her simulation of Neolithic exploitation patterns, which considers both subsistence and non-subsistence variables. The simulation indicates that it would not be unreasonable to expect that agriculturalists and indigenous foragers entered into "facultative" relationships, in which each population provided the other with resources that may not have been absolutely crucial for the other's survival but which did allow it to live at a level of abundance and security that would not otherwise be possible. Gregg argues that non-agricultural resources – labor, building materials, firewood, and collected forest foods from the hunter-gatherers and dairy products and meat surpluses from the farmers – would have been crucial elements in such a pattern.

A suggestion of close ties between hunter-gatherers and farmers in Neolithic central Europe is given by the relative speed with which the former disappeared as distinct, "archaeologically visible" entities after the appearance of the agricultural communities. If an antagonistic relationship existed, one might expect that the hunter-gatherer populations would have been forced into marginal areas not exploited by the agriculturalists, such as the smaller mountain systems of central Europe (e.g. the Taunus, Harz, Ore, and Vosges) or other areas of low arable potential (such as the *karst* area northwest of Kraków in southern Poland.) This does not appear to have happened. Instead, the sparse Mesolithic communities of the loess belt seem to have been absorbed fairly quickly by the Linear Pottery culture and its successors. There are several different mechanisms by which this might have taken place. One likely possibility is that the Linear Pottery communities regarded their Mesolithic neighbors as a source of potential mates, an important consideration in a labor-intensive agricultural system. Such a situation would have also benefited the Mesolithic communities, for it would have plugged them into the kinship structure of the Neolithic communities and would have cemented the exchange relationships hypothesized above. Another possibility is that hunter-gatherers were engaged to help in periods of high labor requirements by Primary Neolithic communities, such as field preparation, planting, and harvesting, and were thus integrated into the Neolithic communities in a sort of *Gastarbeiter* status.

As Primary Neolithic communities moved off the loess, the situation was potentially more complex. The earliest Primary Neolithic settlements of the North European Plain were small and ephemeral, and whatever contacts were made with local Mesolithic populations were probably similarly fleeting. As permanent residential bases were established, such as in the Polish lowlands, contact must have been more frequent. There are hints, and only hints, of such contacts from the finding of bone armlets in Ertebølle/Ellerbek contexts along the south Baltic coast which are virtually identical to those found at many Lengyel sites in the Polish Lowlands (Czerniak 1980) as well as the finding of ground stone celts very similar to Primary Neolithic axes in Ertebølle contexts in Denmark, which would have been coeval with late Lengyel and Rössen (Fischer 1982). In the Paris Basin, late Linear Pottery communities established permanent settlements along major streams such as the Aisne. These Primary Neolithic settlements were located at about five-kilometer intervals, a settlement distribution that would have been imposed on a productive resource zone for the late Mesolithic groups of this area.

The question of relations between indigenous populations and Primary Neolithic communities around the northwestern fringe of Primary Neolithic settlement is bound up with the problem of the so-called "Limburg pottery" (Cahen et al. 1981). Limburg pottery is completely different from Linear Pottery ware in its technique of manufacture, especially in its heavy tempering with organic material and its tan or brown color. Its decoration (Fig. 5.5) consists of incised lines and crosshatchings, often covering the entire surface of the vessel. The incised nature of the decoration echoes that of Linear Pottery, but the baroque patterns do not directly copy Linear Pottery motifs. Limburg pottery was first found at Köln-Lindenthal in the 1930s, where the excavators recognized its unusual characteristics and termed it *Importgruppe I* (Buttler and Haberey 1936: 106). In the 1960s and 1970s, Modderman noted the occurrence of sherds of this ware at Linear Pottery sites in Dutch Limburg and presented it as a regional group centered on this area, as this was where the earliest dated finds were (Modderman 1970: 141). Although these early finds occurred as rare elements on larger Linear Pottery sites, Limburg pottery was subsequently found at Kesselyk on the middle Limburg coversands, outside the zone of Linear Pottery settlement (Modderman 1974). Since then, Limburg pottery has been found at many sites further west in the Hesbaye and Hainaut regions of Belgium (Constantin and Demarez 1981) and the Aisne valley of France (Constantin, Coudart, and Boureux 1981). The term "Limburg pottery" is therefore a misnomer, for this ware has a considerably wider distribution, and Limburg is really on the eastern fringe of its range.

The occurrence of Limburg pottery both at sites with Linear Pottery and independently has led many to the conclusion that it represents a separate pottery-using culture in this region (Modderman 1974; Louwe Kooijmans 1976), probably derived from an indigenous Mesolithic culture such as the late Oldesloe or Tardenoisian. Unfortunately, few materials other than the pottery are known, hence it is very difficult to make an accurate assessment of the derivation of its makers. The proximity of Primary Neolithic settlement in Limburg and the Paris Basin to the sands and gravels of northeastern France and Belgium would have brought agriculturalists into contact with indigenous hunter-gatherer populations. The situation here was somewhat different from that elsewhere on the North European Plain (save for the region around the much-later Lengyel settlements of the Brześć Kujawski Group in the Polish Lowlands), since in Limburg and in the Paris Basin large long-term Primary Neolithic settlements were established, affording an opportunity for prolonged interaction between the two populations.

It is possible that the interaction took the form of the exchange of protein for carbohydrates described above, and in this connection it is perhaps also significant that some sites in the Aisne valley have a relatively higher proportion of wild mammals in their faunal samples when compared with those of the Linear Pottery culture as a whole (Desse 1976; Meniel 1984). Alternatively, the exchange of labor

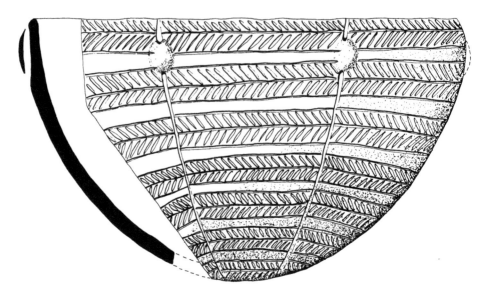

Fig. 5.5 A Limburg vessel from Aubechies (after Constantin and Demarez 1981: fig. 1).

and non-agricultural products, along the lines of that proposed by Gregg (1986) may have occurred. The indigenous foragers of central Europe could have also served as attractive sources of mates unencumbered by the kinship structure of the incoming agriculturalists. It is not inconceivable that this accounted for their rapid integration into Neolithic populations, especially if some sort of economic symbiosis also existed. It is a short step from providing protein and labor to providing sons and daughters as mates. When this possibility is considered, the rapid disappearance of Mesolithic communities in areas settled by Primary Neolithic peoples becomes less surprising. The phenomenon of the Limburg pottery at Linear Pottery settlements in Holland, Belgium, and France may well have been related to this sort of activity.

Social responses to food shortage

The overall productivity of the central European floodplain habitats should not lead one to conclude that the Primary Neolithic communities were assured of consistently meeting their nutritional requirements. The small size of the Primary Neolithic fields, the rigors of clearing land and maintaining an agricultural system in the central European forests, the predations of granivorous birds and herbivorous mammals, losses in crop productivity due to soil bacteria and nematodes, losses in crop processing and storage, and the vagaries of the Central European climate all led to the probability that the harvest of one year often barely lasted to the next, and occasionally did not. Although total catastrophic subsistence failure may have been an unusual occurrence, the argument was presented in Chapter 4 (pp. 90-2) that the options in the event of unpredictable shortfalls were very limited. The need to offset the potential effects of such shortfalls as well as to diversify the subsistence "portfolio" would have led to the elaboration of the stockherding and wild plant-gathering procurement systems.

It would have been a fairly straightforward matter for a Primary Neolithic community to cope with seasonal undernutrition. The Central European biome, particularly the ecosystem of the North European Plain, would have contained sufficient diversity to make it unlikely that all food resources would have been equally affected simultaneously. Stored resources would have become more important, perhaps a factor underlying the manufacture of cheese by Primary Neolithic communities and the increasing use of pigs by later Primary Neolithic cultures (particularly Lengyel and Rössen). It is also possible that social activities were reduced during such lean periods, as they are in most areas which suffer regular lean seasons today. In central Europe, such a hungry season, probably in the late winter/early spring, would have been mitigated by the activation of the natural vegetation in the late spring and ultimately by the harvest season, which probably then would have been a time of heightened social activity.

Seasonal shortages would have been of predictable severity and intensity, and it would have been possible to develop a number of social mechanisms for actively coping with such risk, some of which are discussed later in this chapter. A worse situation, however, would have been precipitated by the simultaneous failure of several subsistence resources. The question is one of the degree to which these would be anticipated. Whereas expected shortages can be institutionalized and dealt with, unpredicted failures can have dire and serious consequences, especially when they involve the agricultural sector. In some instances, it might have been possible to foresee the potential for food shortage early in the growing season, which may have led to attempts to resow crops or to plant reserve "famine foods". Hoarding of food is another possibility, and in central Europe some varieties of wild plants might have lent themselves to this sort of activity. Dietary requirements could be revised downward, either by a reduction in the number of meals consumed or by the dilution of food with water to obtain a feeling of satiation.

Occasionally, however, a crop shortfall would have been impossible to foresee, in particular one resulting from either climatic conditions just before or at harvest time or the destruction or spoilage of large amounts of stored crops. In such a case, a Primary Neolithic community would have been severely limited in the range of economic responses open to it. Rather, there would have been a variety of social responses depending on the severity of the deficit. Such social responses would not have necessarily improved conditions in the community, but they would have provided a means by which households and individuals could cope (or feel as if they were coping) with progressively scarcer food supplies.

Dirks (1980) has discussed the effects of food shortages on human populations, and borrowing Selye's "adaptation syndrome" in response to stress (Selye 1956), he proposes a three-stage reaction of a community experiencing some degree of nutritional stress. These stages, which Dirks argues are almost universal cross-culturally, include an alarm stage, a resistance stage, and an exhaustion stage. Each successive stage is brought about by longer durations of famine conditions.

According to Dirks, the alarm stage is characterized initially by "general hyperactivation and intensified interaction in virtually every institutional sphere" (Dirks 1980: 27). Not only is there a hyperactivation in subsistence activities, but

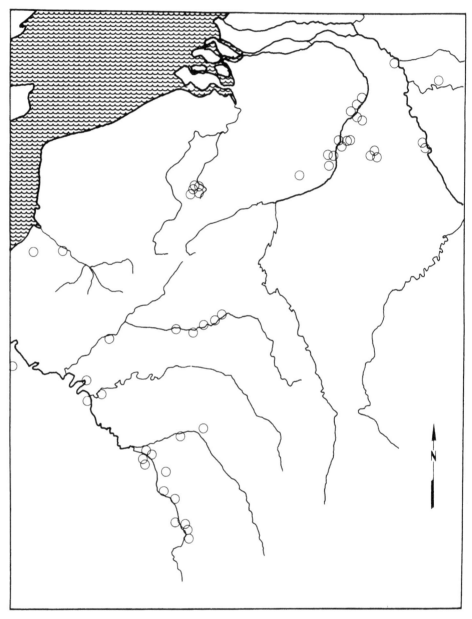

Fig. 5.6 Distribution of non-Linear Pottery ceramics at sites around the western fringe of Linear Pottery distribution (after map in Cahen et al. 1981).

there is also a heightened exploitation of kin and friendship ties to alleviate regional or local shortages. Ritual activities increase as an attempt to forestall further hunger. The cooperative social interaction which characterized the beginning of the alarm stage soon gives way to an increasing amount of agonistic interaction. Human foraging populations exploiting dispersed resources can break up into smaller groups, but agricultural populations are "tethered" to permanent settle-

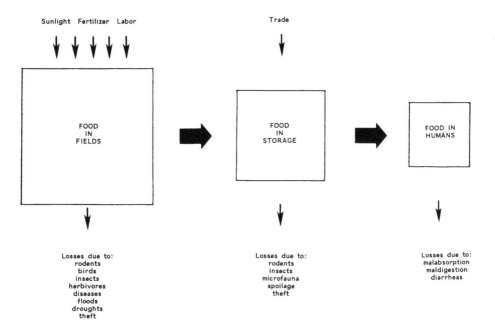

Fig. 5.7 Potential avenues of loss of cultivated crops between planting and nutritional gain.

ments and concentrated, sometimes scarce, food resources. This clustering of irritable and excitable individuals creates a potentially volatile situation.

The resistance stage in response to food shortage is characterized by a downward adjustment in activity levels caused by the increasing shortfall in energy (Dirks 1980: 28). From the hyperactivity of the alarm stage, a population moves into a state of hypoactivity, producing markedly less social interaction among communities, families, and individuals. Individuals begin to drop extended kin and friends from food-sharing networks and hoarding of food by individuals and residential groups increases. Human foraging groups will atomize even further during the stage, but in agricultural communities, aggression is increased as hungry neighbors begin to covet each others' food. Fields and gardens are guarded closely. In such a context, institutions tend to break down. Chiefs and headmen lose authority (in Tikopia, Firth (1959: 92) observed that their gardens were pilfered as much as anyone else's), and rituals are postponed or reduced in scale and complexity.

The final stage, exhaustion, occurs when the family ceases to function as a redistributive, protective entity and individuals begin to fend for themselves. As exhaustion sets in, people become immobilized both physically and socially. Markedly fewer activities are initiated and less is accomplished in those that are undertaken.

Although it is possible that some Primary Neolithic communities suffered all the way through the exhaustion stage of Dirks' sequence and disintegrated, it is probable that the consequences of most food shortages did not last past the alarm or resistance stages. The central European environment, in contrast to marginal ecosystems such as the Ogaden or Kalahari, has sufficient diversity and seasonality to ameliorate all but the most severe crop or livestock failures in the long run. The trick would have been maintaining the ability of either whole communities or individual households to plant the following year's crops and to procure food via exchange and sharing networks. The natural seasonality of the European environment could have prevented the utter breakdown of society which characterizes the final stage of famine. However, the failure of a crop or the devastation of the herds could conceivably precipitate the initial hyperactive phase in the late summer or fall, which, depending on the severity and spatial extent of the shortfall, could either grade into the resistance phase before the onset of the next growing season or be ameliorated by either intercommunity exchange or the exploitation of distant resource zones unaffected by the shortfall. Given the concentrated nature of Primary Neolithic settlement in much of central Europe, such social hyperactivation and possible agonistic behavior – as well as the desire to forestall these unpleasant consequences of food shortage – may have had marked social effects and have been responsible for a number of archaeological phenomena, particularly in the area of settlement geography and exchange.

Primary Neolithic settlement fissioning
There seems to be little doubt that Primary Neolithic communities in central Europe fissioned when their population levels reached certain critical thresholds. The real question lies in the determinants of these thresholds. Conventional wisdom has usually attributed the division of Primary Neolithic settlements to their having exceeded the ability of their catchments to produce sufficient food. In other words, population pressure on primary subsistence resources has been traditionally viewed as the "prime mover" in the fissioning of Primary Neolithic settlements.

The fact that Linear Pottery communities appear to have spread across central Europe in several spurts rather than in a single, uniform "wave-of-advance", yet at the same time dispersed across the continent fairly rapidly, suggests that something more than simple population pressure is involved. If communities routinely increased in size and spun off "daughter" settlements, the process of the Neolithic colonization of Europe probably would have been much smoother, with a greater infilling of areas to the rear of the "wave". One would also expect the overall size of the larger Linear Pottery village sites to have been more uniform, if the notion of such an automatic "threshold" prevailed. The discussion of Primary Neolithic subsistence and settlement in Chapter 4, however, suggests that these communities did not really come close to exceeding the carrying capacity of their catchments, much less that of the surrounding microregions and *Siedlungskammern*. Moreover, one would expect that the daughter settlements would have been routinely established fairly close by, rather than in distant *Siedlungskammern*. Consequently, if population pressure were the sole "prime mover" behind the Neolithic colonization of Europe, one would expect that the overall dispersal of Neolithic communities would have been slower and more gradual.

Another indication that population pressure on resources played a minor role in the spread of Primary Neolithic communities is that there is not an increasing spatial concentration of settlements over time in areas which were circumscribed by topography and soils. For instance, along the *Lössgrenze* near Hannover and Hildesheim, where the loess boundary is topographically almost imperceptible yet pedologically well defined, Linear Pottery settlements do not extend beyond the north fringe of the loess, yet there is little "packing" of settlements along the loess fringe, as might be expected if demographic pressure were a prime factor in Neolithic expansion in this area. Rather, the Primary Neolithic communities in this area apparently still found it possible to locate settlements on the basis of their usual preference for loess rather than being driven off it by population pressure.

Rather than invoking a constant "bumping up" of Primary Neolithic populations against a resource "ceiling", the reasons for the rapid expansion of agricultural communities across Europe must be sought in the motives and behavior of individuals and kin groups. In the absence of evidence for unrestrained Primary Neolithic populations and pressure in subsistence resources, it must be recognized that these communities were prone to localized, ephemeral phenomena, some of which derived from the problems of obtaining a *constant* diet, and which led to segments of a community budding off and moving elsewhere.

The high fertility levels of frontier populations as new ecological zones are exploited for the first time were discussed above. In the case of Primary Neolithic Europe, there also would have been the assimilation of indigenous foraging groups into the Neolithic population, further raising the already high population gradient along the leading edge of the frontier. A social correlate of such high population levels may often have been a high degree of interpersonal conflict and aggression as a result of competition for unappropriated resources on a local scale. There conceivably would have been situations along the Primary Neolithic frontier where certain individuals or kin groups would have found themselves frustrated in their efforts to obtain adequate living space, agricultural land, grazing areas, or any of a number of spatially defined resources. It should be emphasized that such resources in Neolithic central Europe were not limited in any absolute sense. Rather, within the catchments of individual settlements, the demand for such resources might have often exceeded their supply. In addition, the increased amount of social interaction in populous settlements would have led to greater opportunities for disputes over social and economic matters. These social stresses would have been additionally affected by the generally imperfect knowledge of the environment on the part of the Primary Neolithic colonists. Things might have looked worse at times than they actually were. The actual geographical scope of such confrontations and disputes might have been very limited, confined to isolated settlements or microregions, yet if these disputes resulted in out-migration to another area, the cumulative effect would have been the pushing forward of the frontier.

The buildup of social stresses which takes place during the initial stage of food shortage may also have played a role in the fissioning of Primary Neolithic settlements. To some degree, this is also a function of population levels, but it is more difficult to relate it directly to resource abundance or scarcity over a long term. Rather, it might have been the product of short-term nutritional stress which

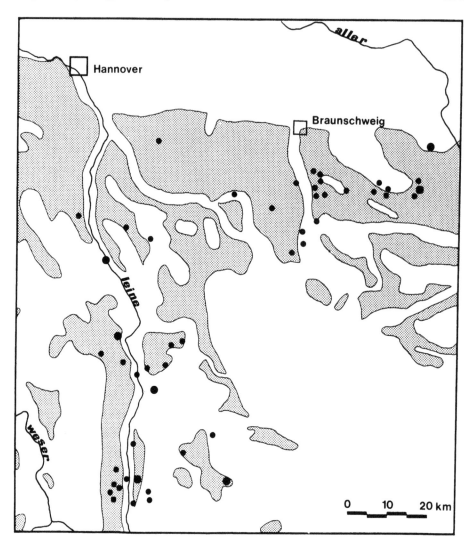

Fig. 5.8. The distribution of Linear Pottery sites and loess soils (shaded) in the *Siedlungskammer* just south of Hannover and Braunschweig in West Cermany (after Schwarz-Mackensen 1982).

might ultimately have been ameliorated but only after out-migration took place. If community fissioning were linked in this way to human behavior, rather than directly to the lack of resources, and if agonistic behavior was the trigger to population dispersal, one would expect to find the sort of punctuated, yet rapid, dispersal of Primary Neolithic communities across central Europe which appears in the archaeological record. The different stages of the spread of the Linear Pottery culture, for instance, may well have been correlated with with widespread yet short-lived ecological phenomena, such as droughts and epizoötic diseases, which would have had the potential for causing food shortages that might have produced the agonistic social responses postulated here. If this was the case, then it might be proposed as an alternative hypothesis to explain the rapid spread of agricultural communities across central Europe.

If the underlying reason for the dispersal of food-producing communities across central Europe is to be sought in behavioral reactions to stress, why did this process stop before the agriculturalists reached much of the North European Plain, Normandy, and Brittany? One possible answer is that there was a continual readjustment of the land-labor-consumer relationships in Primary Neolithic communities, first through out-migration, then through the decline in human fertility suggested above for Rössen and Lengyel communities. The fact that the optimal resource areas of the lowland zone are not as locally concentrated as they are in the valley bottoms of the loess belt may also have been a major factor in arresting the rapid dispersal of Primary Neolithic communities. Ultimately, though, there was a fundamental transformation of the social landscape as the central European environment became better mapped, as attachments to particular tracts of land grew, and as crops and animals became better adapted to the central European biome, thus possibly alleviating local pressure on the food supply to some degree.

Primary Neolithic social organization
The question of Primary Neolithic social organization, with its many ramifications, has generally been a neglected aspect of these cultures, given the current emphasis on subsistence and settlement systems. Sporadic attempts have been made to draw analogies between Linear Pottery social organization and that of the Iroquois, based on the similar types of houses found in both cultures. Such analogies do not work particularly well, for even the similarities in house forms are superficial at best. Another, and perhaps the most ambitious, attempt to study Primary Neolithic social organization has been made by van de Velde (1979a, 1979b), who studied Linear Pottery cemeteries in Dutch Limburg. Van de Velde reached a number of conclusions about Primary Neolithic society, including that Linear Pottery villagers practiced virilocal postmarital residence and matrilineal descent. He also postulated that there was an incipient degree of stratification in Primary Neolithic society based on the variation among the grave goods found at Elsloo.

Van de Velde's conclusions have been criticized by Milisauskas (1982) and others, and in general, they require a greater degree of analytical manipulation and more assumptions than feel comfortable. The focus on the rules of postmarital residence and descent may well be the wrong route to take, for such aspects of culture are frustratingly difficult to apprehend archaeologically. Moreover, they are not mechanistic and standardized even within individual cultural groups, and many configurations are possible depending on the circumstances of individual communities and households. Rather, it may be more productive to operate at a different level of analysis, one which does not identify specific rules but which treats social systems as fitting broad categories such as "unilineal" and "bilateral", "egalitarian" and "ranked", without worrying especially about the standard configurations of social relations in greater detail. Such an approach will be taken here.

In general, farming communities do not normally resort to mobility to alter the

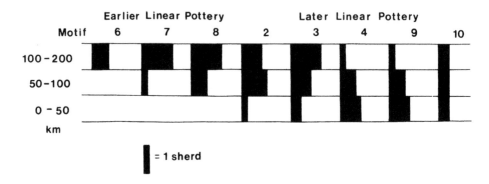

Fig. 5.9 Linear Pottery ceramic motifs at Schladen and the distance to their nearest parallels at other sites, showing changes over time (after Schwarz-Mackensen 1975: fig. 4). A possible interpretation of these data is that they reflect increased integration of social interrelationships within an increasingly-smaller radius over time.

relationships between them and their resources (excluding, for the moment, the question of out-migration from over-populated site catchments and microregions). Rather, they develop social structures which permit adjustments in these relationships without the need to relocate or fission on an annual or seasonal basis. There is, then, a link between agrarian social organization and the relative abundance of resources (Jochim 1981: 161). The position taken here is that most, if not all, social situations revolve around decisions about the allocation of resources, which fall under three broad headings: land, labor, and capital. The formal aspects of social organization can be viewed as rules for controlling and adjusting the relationships among these categories of resources and their consumers in the face of unpredictability and scarcity. Harner (1975: 121), in fact, has proposed that "scarcity is essential to any social situation."

The Primary Neolithic archaeological record indicates a relatively low degree of capital accumulation (what little there might have been is discussed below), so the crucial issues would have been the relationships among the supply of land, the supply of labor, and their consumers. In absolute terms of unoccupied space, land in central Europe was effectively unlimited. It is true that the preferred floodplain habitats were circumscribed, but nonetheless, they were apparently sufficient to accommodate the whole Primary Neolithic population of central Europe at any one moment. At the same time, there may have been situations in which local populations were quite large, and it is at this level that there were probably situations of *apparent* land scarcity. Again, it is not a question of the *absolute* amount of land available, but rather the degree to which a local population would permit its numbers to increase in proportion to the size of a particular tract of floodplain before making an adjustment. So long as land was relatively abundant on a regional scale, out-migration would have been a convenient method of making such adjustments. In general, however, the supply of land in Primary Neolithic central Europe probably exceeded the demand for it, especially on a regional scale.

The issue, then, is one of labor. The establishment of an agrarian economy in the forests of temperate Europe required that communities and households be able to mobilize the labor needed for a wide range of essential tasks. Not only did land have to be cleared, crops planted and harvested, and livestock herded, but settlements had to be built, raw materials procured, and other necessary tasks performed. If land was effectively unlimited, the amount of available labor then became a major constraining factor on agricultural production. Harner (1975: 126) points out that such a situation represents a condition of labor scarcity, a condition that would have been felt by whole communities but more so by individual households.

It is increasingly apparent that the household was the primary economic and social unit in Neolithic Europe. What actually constituted a household remains a bit ambiguous, but it can be assumed that it would correspond to the residential group that occupied one structure. Such is the case in almost all small-scale agrarian societies, and production activities are carried out around the structure in which the household members reside. At Brześć Kujawski, the archaeological correlates of a Primary Neolithic household consist of a complex of storage pits, trash pits, and graves which occur within 15 meters of a longhouse (Bogucki and Grygiel 1981; Grygiel 1986). The trash pits contain a variety of workshop and consumption debris which indicate that virtually all productive activity took place in the individual households. This point is echoed by Lüning (1982a: 28) in connection with Linear Pottery households in the Rhineland. He notes that there are no common granaries or barns on Primary Neolithic settlements, and that the residential groups that occupied individual longhouses were discrete economic units. The only features which may have served more than one household were the enclosures, if they indeed had the function of cattle corrals.

The identification of the household as the primary productive unit in Primary Neolithic society carries with it the implication that individual residential units were responsible for the cultivation of particular plots as well. Whether or not there was a notion of "ownership" attached to a particular tract of land is impossible to determine, but one can infer that the household had exclusive rights to the crops produced by its plot. The amount of land that a household could successfully cultivate would have been, of course, finite, subject primarily to the constraints of its "time-energy budget" (Carlstein 1982). One can assume that fields were located as close to the houses of their cultivators as possible in order to minimize the time and energy spent going to and from them. In the Linear Pottery, Rössen, and Lengyel farmsteads, the fields were probably located within a few meters of the houses, whereas in the larger nucleated settlements, they were probably located somewhat further from the settled area.

The major limitation on how much land a household could bring under cultivation was the time-energy budget for that household. Land, for an individual household, would have been effectively limitless, even though its members might have had to walk a bit further to the fields or have a plot in a less productive area. Since each household would have had the same opportunities to acquire land, the sheer "ownership" of land would have meant little in terms of personal wealth if it were impossible to cultivate it. The question would have been how much land a household could effectively cultivate, which would have been a function of its time-energy budget. The energy resources of a household could be expanded up to a certain point, but its time would have been very limited. The only way for a household to expand its time budget would have been through the addition of more people to its labor pool. Essentially, this would have been the motivation behind the high fertility levels arguably maintained by Primary Neolithic communities, particularly those of the Linear Pottery culture.

The condition of labor scarcity in Primary Neolithic communities would have been a relatively constant problem with which a household had to cope as best it could. The seasonal shortfalls of subsistence resources presented a similar chronic problem, and the essential tension in Primary Neolithic subsistence strategies resulted from the need to balance the supply of labor with the need to produce and to collect as much as possible to tide the household through lean periods. The addition of adults to the labor pool of a household probably would have had little effect on this equation if they were able to contribute their share of productive labor. Children, on the other hand, would have posed a problem. On one hand, they were necessary to assure the continuity of the household and to support its adults in their old age. Yet, although they could contribute to the labor pool at an early age, children would have been a drain on the subsistence resources of the household both during their mothers' pregnancies (when caloric requirements increase markedly) and during early childhood before they could contribute significantly to subsistence activity. The Primary Neolithic household would have had to deal with the same problem of juggling fertility levels and subsistence production that confronts all agrarian societies of similar levels of complexity.

The real problem would have arisen if there were lean periods following crop shortfalls. During such periods, the strategy of maintaining high fertility levels would effectively backfire, and the Primary Neolithic household would have had difficulty providing for its own subsistence needs. The degree to which a household could weather such periods would have been determined by the extent to which it could mobilize assistance in return for delayed reciprocity. If the subsistence failure was confined to the fields of a particular household, it might have been possible to obtain help from other members of the same community (who possibly would have been kin of some sort). If just one community were affected, then assistance could be sought from others in the same microregion. The real test of the support network of a Primary Neolithic household or community would have been the degree to which it could mobilize help beyond the confines of a particular microregion or *Siedlungskammer*.

It therefore would have been in the interest of a Primary Neolithic household to maintain linkages with other households, both close at hand and relatively far away. The inherent uncertainty of establishing a food-producing economy in the central European forests would have necessitated a support network of some sort. The fissioning of Primary Neolithic communities, then, would have had a real adaptive value in that there would have been communities linked by kinship bonds in different microregions or even in different *Siedlungskammern*. The daughter settlements, in one sense, could be considered as "colonies" of their parent settlements, except that they, too, may have periodically been in need of aid.

The intercommunity ties generated through settlement fissioning would not have been the only way by which a household could develop its support system. The other way would have been through using the widest possible definition of what constituted "kin" and extending that definition to include members of households in widely dispersed areas. The inherent exogamy of the Primary Neolithic community had an adaptive value similar to that of settlement fissioning, in that it forced people to look for mates in relatively distant microregions or *Siedlungskammern*. Many modern agrarian societies recognize the value of maintaining ties beyond the catchments of their settlements and of formalizing those ties in their kinship and descent systems. Netting (1974: 31–2) notes that where land is abundant and where there is some leeway in adjusting land-labor-consumer relationships, bilateral systems of kinship are common. The focus of such kinship systems is the individual household, from which a network of social ties radiates. This network facilitates adjustments to "microdifferentials in environmental conditions and economic difficulties" (Netting 1974: 32). Given the environmental conditions which prevailed in Primary Neolithic central Europe, it is not unreasonable to propose that similar bilateral kinship systems were the norm as well, rather than rigid unilineal descent systems which tightly defined the range of kinship ties.

As the offspring of the initial household in a particular microregion budded off to establish their own households nearby, the resulting daughter settlements would have been tightly integrated by kin bonds. Such communities should have been exogamous, since each household would have been established by the descendants of the founding household(s). Their offspring would have had to seek mates outside the community, resulting in further links to nearby settlements. Given the low population densities of each local microregion, however, this would have resulted in a progressive decline over time in the number of acceptable mates in any one region as the individual communities became increasingly interrelated. The fissioning of parent settlements would have exacerbated this condition, if the daughter settlements were located within the same region. The potential result would have been a kind of "intermarriage gridlock" which would have frustrated the finding of mates locally for a large segment of the population. There must have been a very strong impetus, then, to develop and maintain strong intercommunity ties *not* based on kinship beyond the confines of a particular region, possibly even to adjacent *Siedlungskammern*, in order to obtain suitable mates.

The household as an adaptive unit in Primary Neolithic central Europe thus served two related purposes. The first was as the organization to which labor was added in the form of additional mates and children, both through the maintenance of high fertility levels and by the recruitment of individuals from other households by virtue of the inherent exogamy of these units. Secondly, the household served as a node in an interlocking network of kinship and social ties both within the microregion and beyond. It seems unlikely that rigid unilineal descent rules existed in Primary Neolithic society. Rather, the goal would have been to create a web of kinship ties among households, communities, and microregions strong enough so that no one community or household would have been in danger of economic collapse yet loose enough so that it was still possible to find unrelated or marginally related potential mates close at hand.

Primary Neolithic political economy

The issue of limiting resources raised in the preceding section leads to the consideration of the institutions that organized the acquisition and control of these resources in Primary Neolithic communities. I have suggested that land and labor were the key resources in Primary Neolithic society, as they are for any agricultural group. If one accepts the position that land for a Primary Neolithic community was not effectively limited (although there may have been logistical constraints on its ability to occupy additional land), labor, then, emerges as the crucial resource. Just as the labor supply was argued to have been a central element in determining the nature of Primary Neolithic social organization, it may be similarly argued that it played a role in the Primary Neolithic political economy as well. "Political economy" refers here to the sociopolitical processes involved in the management and acquisition of resources, including the emergence of individuals and factions who are in a position to control more resources than others, with the accompanying social prestige and power.

Leaving aside the question of "capital" for a moment, it can be proposed that the access to and control over labor would have been a basic element of social inequality in Primary Neolithic society. The key question, however, is whether it would have been possible for individuals who were able somehow to control labor resources to emerge in Primary Neolithic communities. The notion that this was possible has at least been implicit in the central operating hypothesis of a number of discussions of Primary Neolithic political economy (e.g. Milisauskas 1977, 1978). These discussions have focused on drawing an analogy between the Primary Neolithic archaeological record and the "Big Man" form of political economy found in highland New Guinea, where particular individuals provide nodes of leadership and redistribution (Sahlins 1963). Archaeological correlates of this system in Primary Neolithic Europe have been sought in the fact that on many Linear Pottery, Lengyel, and Rössen sites, one longhouse differs from the others by its large size, and it has been argued that these are residences of high-status individuals.

At first glance, it would appear that a "Big Man" political economy could be a very plausible method of integrating Primary Neolithic communities, for it is specifically based on the control of labor as opposed to other resources. Basically, it is an artificial device to link atomized social units which are self-sufficient and which are scattered across the landscape. Each of these spatially separated segments has its own hierarchical organization. At their core are individuals who can convince others to produce over and above their own subsistence needs in order to support the massive feasts and redistribution which ultimately lead to their achieving status as "Big Men." An individual does not become a "Big Man" overnight, but rather he develops into one over a number of years as he is able to convince more and more households to overproduce in his name.

When viewed in the ecological context of Primary Neolithic Europe, however, the "Big Man" model appears to have difficulties as an organizational principle for early farming communities. "Big Man" systems at present function in environments where there is a relatively low risk of subsistence failure. While the swidden agriculturalists of highland New Guinea live in a stable environment (save for those in high, marginal areas such as the Fringe Enga – Waddell 1975) which is tremendously productive, the central European biome has marked seasonal and annual variability. The social issues posed by the risk and uncertainty in the Primary Neolithic subsistence system may have damped the tendencies for individuals to develop the cumulative status that New Guinea "Big Men" have. It would have been difficult enough for a Primary Neolithic household to meet its own subsistence needs, much less to accommodate the overproduction required to drive a "Big Man" system. The subsistence shortfalls and failures which, I have argued, were a central feature of Primary Neolithic life may have cut short any sort of aggrandizing behavior involving labor control before it got too far.

The fact that certain Primary Neolithic communities would have been in a position to assist other settlements suffering from crop failures and other subsistence problems would have potentially created situations in which social differentiation at the community level could arise. Such situations would lead to two categories of people: those experiencing short-term hunger and those who were not. Such conditions, however, probably would have been ephemeral, and rather than being attributes of particular individuals they would have been ascribed more to communities and regions. The following year, it would have been possible for the situation to be reversed, depending on the vagaries of the central European climate. The net effect over time would have been the damping of long-term tendencies towards intercommunity differentiation based on subsistence production, for no one habitat in central Europe could be guaranteed of stable productivity.

The other force working against the development of Primary Neolithic social stratification was the fact that settlements fissioned at a point well below the carrying capacity of the surrounding microregion. As Primary Neolithic communities fissioned, the net effect was the redistribution of labor within the region. Since the goal of "Big Man" systems and similar forms of political economy is to control labor resources first in a single location, then on a more regional scale, the redistribution of labor by settlement fissioning would have probably arrested local tendencies towards hierarchical social organization. As a result, even though labor was the key resource for a Primary Neolithic community, and the activities of individual households were largely directed towards increasing their share of the labor pool, it seems quite unlikely that single individuals would have been able to mobilize and coerce the labor resources required to sustain the development of political economies based on household overproduction.

There may actually be some support for this argument in the ethnographic record from highland New Guinea. The most powerful "Big Men" and most marked social differentiation are found in the Western Highlands, among groups such as the Chimbu and Enga. These communities live in dispersed hamlets and farmsteads which are reasonably permanent over time. In the Eastern Highlands, among groups such as the Tairora, there are nucleated settlements that often fission (Watson 1983). Here, the degree of social differentiation appears to be less marked and leaders emerge on a more or less ad hoc basis. Although it may be premature to draw a conclusion from the New Guinea situation, the parallels between the settlement systems in the Eastern Highlands and Primary Neolithic Europe are indeed striking.

I have put off the question of "capital", in the sense of accumulated goods, in Primary Neolithic society. In the absence of evidence to the contrary, the overall level of accumulation of material goods in the Primary Neolithic household appears to have been quite low. There are few domestic caches of flint blades or obsidian cores, for example, known from Primary Neolithic sites. Goods seem to have been used expediently and discarded. There are few decidedly non-functional artifacts, which might have represented some medium of exchange. Primary Neolithic graves are relatively bare. Normally, essentially utilitarian items such as ceramic vessels and axes are included as grave goods. The only exceptions are the sporadic appearance of artifacts made from the Aegean mussel, *Spondylus gaederopus,* and the rich burials of the Brześć Kujawski Group of the Lengyel culture (very late in the Primary Neolithic sequence), where bone, shell, and copper ornaments occur in certain graves.

It could be argued that livestock would have constituted "capital" of sorts for a Primary Neolithic household. Yet there would have been a ceiling on the number of animals that a household could manage, again a function of its labor resources. Only so many cattle, sheep, and goats could be managed by one individual, so the household with greater labor resources may well have had access to greater numbers of livestock. It would not have been simply a matter of leading livestock to food and water, but of milking them and then processing the milk into dairy products. Livestock and the labor needed to control them would have been subject to the same effects of settlement fissioning described above. If the effect of such fissioning was that the numbers of livestock kept by individual households were relatively equal, the role of animals as the object of aggrandizing behavior would have been minimized.

There remains, however, the question of the existence of regional and interregional exchange systems in Primary Neolithic central Europe. The presence of ornaments of *Spondylus* shell, clearly of Mediterranean or Aegean origin, on central European sites was noted above. Hungarian obsidian is found on sites in southern Poland (204 pieces in the case of Olszanica – Milisauskas 1983), which represents contacts across the Carpathian mountains. The amphibolite at Rhenish and Dutch Linear Pottery sites, first believed to come from a Silesian source (Frechen 1965), has been argued to have originated at a much closer source in central Germany (Bakels and Arps 1979), yet still well beyond the immediate catchment of the sites at a distance of at least 250 km. Basalt implements, on the other hand, appear to be derived from sources much nearer at hand. Analysis of amphibolite and hornblende implements from the Harz Foreland indicates probable sources in the Western Carpathians or even in the Balkans (Schwarz-Mackensen and Schneider 1983). There is no doubt that there was long-distance movement of raw materials

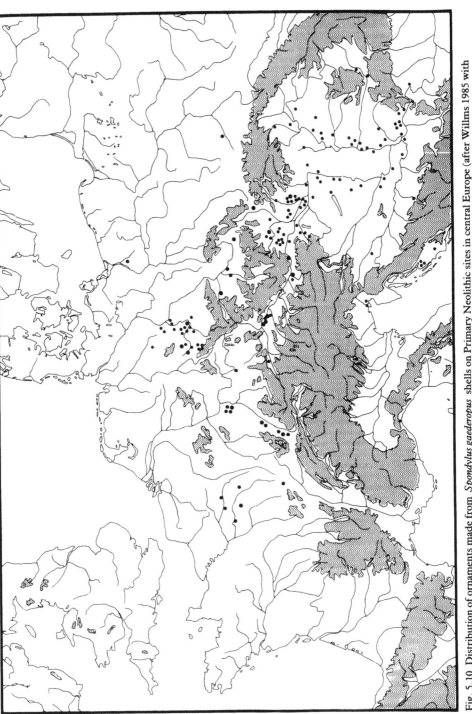

Fig. 5.10 Distribution of ornaments made from *Spondylus gaederopus* shells on Primary Neolithic sites in central Europe (after Willms 1985 with modifications – at certain sites in north-central Poland, ordinary *Unio* beads have been sometimes mis-identified as *Spondylus*).

in Primary Neolithic Europe. The question is whether this was in the context of formal exchange systems driven by aggrandizing motivations for the accumulation of "wealth" by certain individuals or communities or whether it was a less formal, largely ad hoc, set of transactions.

There have been attempts to ascribe a relatively high degree of complexity to Primary Neolithic resource acquisition. For instance, in order to explain the presence of *Spondylus* shells in central Europe, Shackleton and Renfrew (1970) proposed a model of prestige-item exchange patterned loosely on the *kula* trade of the Trobriand Islands. One exotic type of artifact, however, does not make a *kula* ring or necessarily indicate the existence of *any* formal exchange system. In the Melanesian exchange systems where shells play a major role, a prime factor in the maintenance of the demand for these exotic artifacts is the control exercised by certain individuals over the supply of shells, thus making them inaccessible to segments of the population. The further one gets from the source area, the tighter this control gets, further constricting the supply of shells. The archaeological correlate of such a system would be a progressive drop-off in the number of shells in the archaeological record. No such drop-off appears in the distribution map of *Spondylus* shells in central Europe, but rather they are spottily distributed across the whole area. No one appears to have been constricting their supply. Moreover, *Spondylus* are primarily found as grave goods. Such a pattern suggests that the Primary Neolithic peoples regarded them as luxury items rather than an economic necessity, either for practical use or for prestige, for their burial would effectively take the shells out of the trading network.

A distinction therefore needs to be made between luxury items, prestige items, and materials which were scarce but necessary for daily life. Aside from the *Spondylus* shells, most of the evidence for Primary Neolithic "exchange" falls into the last category. Linear Pottery utilization of distant resources is readily attributable to the fact that many of the essential raw materials for daily activities were lacking in the loess belt itself, especially flint. When the distribution of flint artifacts is examined, however, it can be seen that the Linear Pottery communities almost always utilized the best and nearest available resources. For instance, Linear Pottery communities in the Kraków area of southern Poland utilized the Jurassic flint from the *karst* area north of the city, lying within 20 kilometers of many major sites (Lech and Leligdowicz 1980). Linear Pottery settlements in Silesia, over 100 kilometers away, also used the Jurassic flint, for it was still the best material that was realistically available to them. The settlements in the Polish lowlands utilized both the erratic glacial pebble flint from the North European Plain or the "chocolate" flint from the Radom area, 200 airline kilometers away but still the nearest source of high-quality flint. "Chocolate" flint, although of excellent quality, appears in very low frequencies at those sites nearer to the sources of Jurassic flint. In the Rhineland, flint was acquired from the nearby chalk areas of Belgium and the Netherlands, close at hand. Among Linear Pottery communities in *Siedlungskammern* located some distance from good flint, such as the Münster Bay area and along the Saale, it appears that Linear Pottery communities contented themselves with the utilization of readily available local flint sources.

If complex and formal exchange networks were common in Primary Neolithic Europe, one would expect a much greater dispersal of high-quality resources from their source areas, rather than a sharp drop-off not far from their sources with little distant distribution. It would be expected that the Linear Pottery communities far from the highest quality resources would have taken measures to obtain them, presumably through participation in some sort of exchange system. Rather, many Linear Pottery settlements were content with the exploitation, almost exclusively, of local resources. The large Linear Pottery settlements of Dutch Limburg utilized Rijkholt flint probably from within 30 kilometers. A similar situation prevailed at Hienheim in Bavaria, where there was a marked lack of "imported" lithic material (de Grooth 1977, Bakels 1978: 105). The acquisition of raw materials by Linear Pottery communities appears instead to have taken the form of expeditions to source areas on an ad hoc basis when the need arose. There is no evidence to suggest that individual communities *controlled* source areas until several hundred years later at the end of the Primary Neolithic, when workshop and manufacturing settlements begin to be found (e.g. Dzieduszycka-Machnikowa and Lech 1976). The acquisition of raw materials by Primary Neolithic communities appears to have been a relatively free and informal affair, at least at the start.

To argue that no formal exchange networks existed in Primary Neolithic central Europe is not to deny that informal exchanges could have taken place between individuals, households, and communities. There are several likely contexts for such small-scale exchange. One would have been in the alleviation of temporary subsistence shortfalls, in which non-subsistence resources might have been bartered for food. To some degree, the interconnected kinship networks which resulted from settlement fission and subsequent intermarriage would have removed some of the "trading" element from such transactions, but there were almost certainly times when it was necessary to go beyond this network and offer hard goods in exchange. Another context for the small-scale movement of "exotic" materials in central Europe would have been through bridewealth and/or brideprice. The practice of one or the other is an almost universal trait of agricultural peoples, in which the sealing of the marriage contract necessitates some transfer of goods in addition to the bride. While it is impossible to demonstrate the such a practice existed in Neolithic Europe, it provides a much more plausible explanation for the patterns and level of Primary Neolithic "exchange" than do *kula* rings and formalized trading networks.

Conclusion

In the foregoing discussion, I have attempted to characterize the web of relationships which constituted the ecological niche of the first farming cultures of central Europe. My goal has been to try to move away from considerations of subsistence and settlement patterns only and to explore the forces which would have shaped the social relationships among Primary Neolithic communities and between these communities and the indigenous foraging bands of central Europe.

The major theme of this chapter is that in an imperfectly known environment where the risk of failure was great, the stakes would have been high. I have tried to point out possible institutional mechanisms by which the Primary Neolithic communities could minimize the impact of wrong decisions and environmental phenomena beyond their control, thus ensuring their survival.

The support network of a Primary Neolithic community took the form of exchanges of various resources with its environment. Parties to such exchanges would have included the geophysical and biotic components of the ecosystem, indigenous foraging bands, and the Primary Neolithic communities themselves. The resources exchanged would have been both tangible and intangible, and raw materials, food, labor, and information would have been the key items. Primary Neolithic groups needed as wide a network as possible to ensure that in the event of difficulty they could mobilize enough support to tide them through. It is therefore possible to suggest, much as Flannery (1976) has done for Formative villages in Mesoamerica, that a settlement's catchment area is not just a single radius but rather a series of circles of increasing radius and decreasing exclusivity. The external linkages of a Primary Neolithic community would have been strongest in its immediate microregion, but it would have been wise to have links with distant settlements as well.

I have attempted to characterize these linkages as a web rather than a hierarchy. Primary Neolithic society, despite some arguments to the contrary, was basically egalitarian. This idea is not particularly new or earthshaking. Perhaps, though, it is now possible to understand *why* Primary Neolithic society *should* have been egalitarian. Given the ecological constraints on subsistence productivity and security, it simply would not have made much sense for an individual, a household, or a community to establish its exclusivity. No social unit could have been so sure of its resource base that it could afford to set itself apart.

The process of adaptation to the new ecosystem in central Europe was not finished when the Primary Neolithic came to a close, however. As crops and animals became better adapted to the central European environment, and as the environment became better understood, Primary Neolithic communities would have been able to develop a greater degree of confidence and security in their subsistence system. They would have been much better equipped to alter the ecosystem to their own needs. Concurrently, there would have been a constant testing of the usefulness of the earlier social and behavioral patterns. Institutions would have been retained, modified, or rejected depending on the needs of the descendants of the Primary Neolithic colonists.

6

Continuity and change, 3500–2500 bc

6.1 Introduction

By the second half of the fourth millennium bc, the area of central Europe where agriculture was practiced had been expanded markedly beyond that penetrated by the Linear Pottery colonists a millennium previously. Many different developments were taking place. In north-central Poland, the very late Primary Neolithic settlements at Brześć Kujawski and Krusza Zamkowa were still flourishing. On the Dümmersee in northern Germany, some foragers appear to have settled down at quite an early date. In the Rhine-Maas delta, smaller agrarian settlements appeared, such as those at Hazendonk and the Swifterbant sites. The Dutch and German sites, while yielding charred grain and the bones of domestic animals, are closely related in their material culture to the late Ertebølle/Ellerbek culture of Denmark and northern Germany, which appears to have maintained its foraging economy until close to 3000 bc.

This expansion of an agricultural economy into areas where large and vigorous foraging populations previously existed has been mistakenly characterized by some as a continuation of the Primary Neolithic colonization, and by others as an "acculturation" of indigenous Mesolithic folk who saw the promise of the agricultural economy. In reality, it was neither, but rather an insinuation of alien cultigens and animals, with their keepers, into the system refined over several millennia of Mesolithic occupation for the efficient exploitation of these habitats.

The loess belt itself, the scene of the large Linear Pottery, Stroke-Ornamented Pottery, Lengyel, and Rössen longhouse "villages", was occupied by a large number of smaller, regional groups living in settlements whose remains are somewhat less impressive than those of the Primary Neolithic communities that preceded them. Small sites abound, often with minimal settlement remains, and they reach into ecological zones which were previously unexploited. This phenomenon has been interpreted as the result of an "extensification" of the agricultural regime (Kruk 1973, 1980) which resulted in smaller, less permanent sites. Such an interpretation has met with wide acceptance among specialists in this area, but alternative models are also possible. Within some loess *Siedlungskammern*, there is a distinct break in the continuity of occupation of specific settlement locations that characterized the Primary Neolithic (e.g. in the Elbe-Saale area – Starling 1983). In the well-surveyed loess uplands northeast of Kraków, Kruk found an increase in the number of Funnel Beaker sites over that of the preceding cultures (Kruk 1973, Milisauskas and Kruk 1984), but in other areas, there appears to have been a decline in the number of settlements. At the same time, the loess regions often exhibit a greater diversity of site sizes than those of the earlier Neolithic cultures. In short, the second half of the fourth millennium and the first half of the third millennium bc witnessed a major ecological reorientation of Neolithic settlement in the loess belt.

Empirical data on Consequent Neolithic subsistence

In considering data on Consequent Neolithic subsistence, it will be necessary to emphasize the regional variation in both faunal and botanical samples. The discussion below, then, will be organized somewhat differently from that of the Primary Neolithic situation in Chapter 5. In the Primary Neolithic case, the only major habitat under discussion was the loess belt. Even within this habitat, the subsistence data, particularly the botanical remains, displayed some degree of regional variability. Once food production had penetrated additional habitats in central Europe, particularly the North European Plain and the Alpine Foreland, the regional variability became somewhat more pronounced. More than ever, it seems inappropriate to speak of a Neolithic "package deal" in which developments in the lowlands of northern Poland and Germany are directly comparable with those in the loess belt.

The empirical data on subsistence for the Consequent Neolithic are somewhat more difficult to synthesize than those for the Primary Neolithic. Although many sites have yielded botanical and faunal remains, there are very few regional syntheses of these data which draw them together in a coherent way. There are, of course, some exceptions to this generalization (e.g. Lüttschwager 1967; Kruk 1980), but in general they are more limited in scope and quantity of data than those for the earlier Neolithic phases. There appears to be a general assumption that trends in subsistence which began during the Primary Neolithic simply continued a millennium later. In the loess belt, this observation appears to be supported by the evidence to some degree, but on the North European Plain, different patterns appear.

The loess belt

The botanical remains from Consequent Neolithic sites in the loess belt are primarily macroscopic finds rather than imprints on sherds and wall daub. The evenness of the archaeological coverage is much poorer than in the Primary Neolithic, however. Perhaps the most extensively reported plant remains from this period come from the loess in southern Poland (Klichowska 1976; Kruk 1980). Even here, the most important samples are from a handful of sites, such as Ćmielów and Ksjżnice Wielkie. In these samples, it is quite clear that emmer, *Triticum dicoccum*, is the most significant variety of grain. This pattern is even more pronounced than in the Primary Neolithic, when there was considerable variation from site to site and from region to region in the types of grain represented. One sample from Ćmielów is quite pure, suggesting that the seed grain had been carefully selected and that different grain types were sown separately.

The most striking aspect of the Consequent Neolithic grain samples from the loess belt of southern Poland is the virtual absence of barley. Towards the end of the Primary Neolithic, this grain was quite prevalent, both in southern Poland and in a number of other areas, such as at the Rössen site of Ur-Fulerum and in the Rhineland. A number of sites in southern Poland have absolutely no barley in evidence. Slightly to the west, however, in Silesia, barley does occur at Consequent Neolithic sites in some quantity (Wojciechowski 1973: 51).

There appears to have been a significant increase in the amount of non-grain cultivated plants during the Consequent Neolithic. Two plants which are of particular importance are peas, *Pisum sativum,* and flax, *Linum usitatissimum* (Kruk 1980: 203; Klichowska 1976: 59). Moreover, a deposit of *Lithospermum* seeds at Ćmielów has been interpreted as having been collected for their medicinal value (Zabłocki and Żurowski 1934: 20-1).

It is important to note that Consequent Neolithic botanical samples have not been collected and analyzed in the same consistent fashion which permitted Knörzer to identify segetal associations in the Primary Neolithic samples from the Rhineland. Although virtually all of the component taxa of Knörzer's weed association have been identified at Consequent Neolithic sites, it is impossible to say whether they have the same implications for field size and organization. Kruk (1980: 225) notes that in Funnel Beaker samples from southern Poland, forest taxa are more abundant than synanthropic species among the wild species. He interprets this observation as the result of the penetration of new ecological zones, specifically the open woodlands of the loess watersheds.

The most comprehensive tabulation of faunal data from Consequent Neolithic sites in the loess belt has been that of Kruk (1980, summarized graphically in his fig. 33), and data recovered since 1980 have not substantially altered the pattern. As was the case in the Primary Neolithic, domestic cattle constitute the major component of virtually all of the loess belt faunal assemblages of this period, but now usually on the order of between 50 and 70% of the identified specimens. The relative decrease in the proportion of cattle bones in the entire assemblage is due to the perceptible increase in the number of bones from smaller domestic stock, particularly pigs. While pig bones are scarce in Primary Neolithic faunal samples, and probably not for reasons of poor preservation or recovery, they are more frequent in Consequent Neolithic assemblages. The greater proportion of pig bones is most apparent in Czech and Polish samples, usually constituting in the vicinity of 15–20% of the number of identified specimens.

There are several Consequent Neolithic faunal assemblages in which sheep and goat are more abundant than pig as the second major taxon behind domestic cattle. These include the large samples from the Funnel Beaker component at Bronocice (Milisauskas and Kruk 1984; Hensel and Milisauskas 1985) and the Michelsberg site of Hetzenberg near Heilbronn (Beyer 1972). It is difficult to make regional generalizations on the basis of these isolated samples, however. For example, the Bronocice assemblage (with a relatively constant 28% sheep/goat throughout the Funnel Beaker occupation) differs in this respect from samples from other Funnel Beaker sites in the vicinity (where pig bones are more abundant) and from the Lublin-Volynian component at Bronocice itself (Kruk and Milisauskas 1985). The Hetzenberg faunal sample contrasts with that from the roughly coeval Schussen-

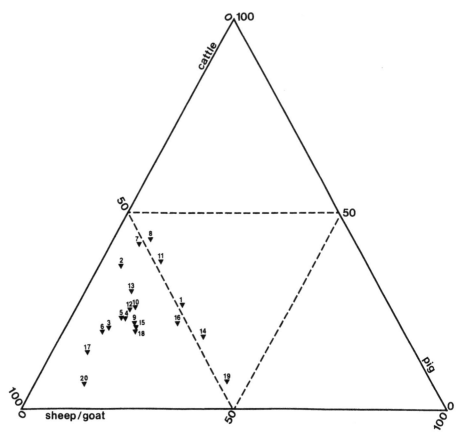

Fig. 6.1 Relative percentages of cattle, sheep/goat, and pig bones from 20 Consequent Neolithic upland assemblages, based on numbers of specimens attributed to *Bos taurus, Ovis aries/Capra hircus,* and *Sus scrofa.* Key: 1 – Nosocice (n=778); 2 – Janówek (n=87); 3 – Tomice (n=468); 4 – Gródek Nadbużzny (n=1970); 5 – Ćmielów (n=2480); 6 – Zawarza (n=682); 7 – Klementowice (n=123); 8 – Ksiaznice Wielkie (n=312); 9 – Kamien tukawski (n=2661); 10 – Gniechowice (n=189); 11 – Ludwigsburg "im Schlösslesfeld" (n=666); 12 – Reusten (Michelsberg component) (n=103); 13 – Reusten (Schussenreid component) (n=66); 14 – Bronocice (Funnel Beaker component) (n=850); 15 – Bronocice (Lublin-Volhynian component) (n=440); 16 – Niedzwiedz (n=1338); 17 – Makotřasy (n=2206); 18 – Zawichost (n=1867); 19 – Heilbronn (n=3344); 20 – Weissenfels (n=357).

reid settlement at Ludwigsburg "Im Schlösslesfeld" (Nobis 1977), also in the Neckar valley, where pig bones account for 36% of the faunal assemblage (compared with 46% cattle and 11% sheep/goat).

The decrease in the relative numbers of cattle bones in Consequent Neolithic contexts must not be interpreted as a decrease in the number of animals in living herds or a decrease in the economic importance of cattle. It does, however, indicate a greater role in the economy for the smaller domestic animals, particularly pigs. Pigs, of course, have no major economic function other than as rapid-growing meat producers, and their increase in Consequent Neolithic contexts reflects a greater diversification in the sources of animal protein in the agrarian economy. Sheep and goats, on the other hand, also yield "secondary products" – milk and wool – and thus add yet another economic dimension.

Age and sex data for domestic stock are frustratingly rare in the published analyses of faunal samples from Consequent Neolithic loess sites. Some basic data are available for the Lublin-Volhynian component at Bronocice (Kruk and Milisauskas 1985: 91) which suggest that the pattern for cattle is similar to that found at Primary Neolithic loess sites. The majority of the aged cattle specimens (68%) were from individuals older than 30 months. Unfortunately, the use of a 2½-year age as a division between subadult and adult categories is not useful in assessing kill-off patterns, for cattle are still growing until they reach 42-48 months when they attain their maximum meat weight. The data from Bronocice are thus ambiguous about the extent that meat production played a role in herd management. At Ludwigsburg "Im Schlösslesfeld", although the actual number of individuals in the sample is not reported, there are a greater number of immature specimens, including a number of bones from calves aged 5-6 months (Nobis 1977: 83).

An interesting feature of the Bronocice pig bone sample is that 76% of the aged specimens were older than 24 months, which suggests that the kill-off rate for this species was not as rapid as that often found in pig bones samples from prehistoric sites. The Bronocice age data (as hitherto published) are not fine-grained enough to permit the detailed study of kill-off rates, however, and until such studies are available for this and other Consequent Neolithic faunal samples, it will be difficult to draw further conclusions about slaughter patterns and their economic implications. At Ludwigsburg "Im Schlösslesfeld", by contrast, pigs were generally killed at 9-10 months (Nobis 1977: 84).

In the loess belt samples, relatively few bones of wild animals are found, continuing a pattern first seen in the Primary Neolithic of this area. In fact, if one considers only loess belt samples, there appears to be no significant difference in the relative proportions of wild and domestic bones between the Primary and Consequent Neolithic samples. Again, this relative scarcity of wild animal bones may reflect the ecological constraints of the loess-belt habitat and the fact that even a minimal amount of hunting in the vicinity of a settlement may have depressed populations of wild herbivores to the extent that this activity was not worthwhile. The relative absence of bones of birds, reptiles, amphibians, and fish from loess belt sites, on the other hand, may be due more to preservation conditions and to recovery methods, since the lighter bones of these taxa would be more prone to decomposition in a decalcified loess matrix. Valves of freshwater molluscs (*Unio* sp.) have been found on a number of sites (Wiślański 1979: 217).

The North European Plain

The North European Plain represents a habitat which had not yet seen the successful establishment of an agrarian economy prior to 3600 bc. There had been a number of settlements of the Linear Pottery culture in the lowlands of northern Poland and Germany about 4300–4000 bc, but these appear to represent a special sort of short-term adaptation based largely on cattle-herding in the lowland forests rather than settled, long-term agrarian communities (Bogucki 1982). Most importantly, the lowland forests were inhabited by indigenous foragers who exploited a broad range of forest resources. The tremendous productivity of the lowland ecosystem was discussed in Chapter 2, and it is difficult to imagine that the earliest agrarian communities would not continue to exploit the wild resources found in this zone. Nonetheless, the settlements of the earliest agrarian communities of the lowlands have also yielded data on their use of domestic plants and animals.

In assessing the Consequent Neolithic botanical remains from the North European Plain, it is important to distinguish between two general sorts of finds. One type is the usual occurrence of small amounts of carbonized botanical material in settlements, recovered either during troweling or sieving. The other is a new phenomenon during the Consequent Neolithic, the discovery of large caches of up to several kilograms of carbonized grain, often in large vessels. At least two such caches from northern Poland, at Radziejów and Opatowice, have been extensively reported (Gabałówna 1970, Grygiel 1980). One of the samples from Sarup (Jørgensen 1977) appears to have come from a similar sort of cache.

It is difficult to discuss the range and proportions of identified taxa at Funnel Beaker sites that have yielded carbonized grain in great detail. At many Polish sites such as Zarębowo (Klichowska 1976), emmer *(Triticum dicoccum)* is the major wheat species. At Sarup in Denmark (Jørgensen 1982) emmer is also the primary cultigen during this period, comprising up to 99% of the volume of some samples. Other Danish Funnel Beaker sites, where the data consist largely of imprints in pottery, have also provided indications that emmer was the major domestic plant, although einkorn and naked barley were also present (Jørgensen 1977: 61, 1982: 229). After about 2500 bc, however, it appears that there was a shift to a greater diversity of crops, with naked barley playing the major role in the economy.

Consequent Neolithic caches of grain, which somehow became carbonized, have been found in the lowlands of north-central Poland and in Denmark. Two major Polish caches are known, Radziejów (Klichowska 1970) and Opatowice (Grygiel 1980), and one from Sarup in Denmark (Jørgensen 1977). All three have been radiocarbon dated to the mid-third millennium bc. Emmer has been the primary constituent of the three samples: 99.5% of the Radziejów sample (over 150,000 grains), 99% of the Opatowice sample, and 94% of the Sarup sample. The remainder of the Sarup cache consisted of einkorn, club/bread wheat, and barley. These caches of carbonized grain are difficult to interpret, since they are contained in vessels and do not appear to have been casually discarded. Grygiel (1980: 48) has interpreted the Radziejów and Opatowice finds as ritual offerings, while they may also represent large amounts of accidentally carbonized grain or even stored grain which was slowly carbonized through the heat generated by its rotting in the vessel. Although the special nature of these grain finds means that they cannot be taken as a direct reflection of the percentages of cereal types actually grown, they do reflect the heavy use of emmer wheat in parts of the North European Plain during this period. In north-central Poland, this practice dates to the settlements of the Brześć Kujawski Group at the very end of the Primary Neolithic, where emmer is the main cereal found (Bogucki 1982; Grygiel and Bogucki 1986).

Two general observations can be made concerning the faunal remains from Consequent Neolithic sites on the North European Plain. The first is that in contrast to the samples from the loess belt, there is a much higher proportion of wild species represented in the lowland faunal assemblages. This is true across the entire plain, particularly in northern Poland and Germany (Lüttschwager 1967; Wiślański 1979; F. Johansson 1979). One caveat, however, is that the percentage of wild animal bones varies with the type of site. Table 6.1 presents the relative proportions of wild and domestic taxa from a number of Consequent Neolithic faunal samples from northern Poland, Germany and Denmark.

A dimension of the higher percentages of wild animal bones found at these sites is the number of pig bones in the samples. There is a great degree of ambiguity over what constitutes domestic and and wild pigs from an osteological standpoint. The usual procedure is to establish a threshold based on overall size of the specimen above which a bone is classified as wild and below which it is domestic, assuming that with domestication comes a diminution in size. The problem is that this procedure may obscure other factors which can account for size variation, such as sexual dimorphism. It is not unlikely that in many faunal samples with pig bones, some large "domesticated" males may be classed as "wild" and some small "wild" females are considered to be "domesticated." The question that needs to be asked is whether there is any sense in making such a distinction in the first place. In light of the fact that "domesticated" pigs probably would have been permitted to forage rather widely in the forests of the North European Plain, there would have been ample opportunity for them to encounter and mate with their conspecific counterparts, with relatively little human control over their breeding.

It would seem more appropriate, then, to consider these faunal samples as having three categories of mammalian bones: domestic (including cattle and sheep/goat), wild (all hunted mammal species except for pigs), and pigs (both wild and domestic). When considered from this perspective, they take on a character markedly different from both the Primary Neolithic and Consequent Neolithic faunal samples from the loess belt in which the overall numbers of pig and wild mammal bones were quite low. The question is not just one of the relative proportions of hunting versus stockherding, but rather of a quite different approach to the management of the animal component of the economy.

Along with the broad spectra of taxa represented in the mammalian samples, the lowland Consequent Neolithic sites have yielded significant numbers of bird bones, although well-analyzed assemblages are relatively rare. At Bistoft LA 11, one of the better studied sites, the majority of the bird bones were from mallards (*Anas platyrynchos*) and other waterfowl (F. Johansson 1979: 105). Fish bones have also been recovered at most sites, but they are generally not analyzed in any degree of detail. It must be noted that in virtually all cases, the deposits have not been sieved, and thus the chances for the recovery of small specimens such as fish and bird bones are minimized (Meadow 1976). In spite of this, several Consequent Neolithic sites in northern Germany have yielded large assemblages of fish bones which have been analyzed recently. At Bistoft LA 11 (Heinrich and Lepiksaar 1979), 71% of the identified fish specimens belonged to pike (*Esox lucius*), while

Table 6.1 *Percentages of wild and domestic taxa in identified faunal specimens from Neolithic settlements in Poland, northern Germany, and Denmark.*

Chronological designations are those conventionally used in the respective regions. EN – Early Neolithic (ca. 3100–2600 bc); MN – Middle Neolithic (ca. 2600 – 2400 bc). Data from F. Johansson (1979: 100) and Wiślański (1979: 217).

settlement	period/phase	specimens	wild%	domestic%
Rosenhof	Mesolithic/EN	358	87	13
Koustrup	EN/MN	118	87	13
Stinthorst	Mesolithic/EN	312	84	16
Sølager	EN/MN	854	82	18
Heidmoor	EN	6427	66	34
Szlachcin	Wiórek	213	60	40
Wolkenwehe	EN	7469	57	43
Bistoft	EN	518	52	48
Neustadt/ Marienbad	Mesolithic/EN	168	42	58
Ustowo	Luboń	1173	35	65
Fuchsberg/ Südensee	EN	925	15	85
Süssau	MN	790	5	95
Bundsø	MN	10000+	2	98
Lodsø	MN	938	2	98

the remainder came from members of the carp family, including perch *(Perca fluviatilis)*, bream *(Abramis brama)*, and tench *(Tinca tinca)*. The fish bone assemblage from Heidmoor (Mueller 1983) yielded an almost identical percentage of pike bones (68%), but of the remainder, a significant proportion (16.9%) belonged to the European giant catfish *(Siluris glanis)*. At Wolkenwehe (Mueller 1983), a similar percentage (66.8%) of the assemblage belonged to pike, but pike perch *(Lucioperca lucioperca)* with 18.3% and catfish with 10.6% were also major components of the assemblage.

The consistent appearance of pike as a major component of these assemblages appears significant. Heinrich and Lepiksaar (1979: 113) have identified two patterns of pike utilization at Bistoft LA 11. In the part of the settlement along the lake shore, the unburnt bones of very large pike were found. They estimate that these fish ranged in length from 53 to 96 cm, possibly longer, and believe that they were butchered upon landing. In hearths in the interior of the settlement, however, burnt bones of smaller pike, most under 50 cm in length, were found. These fish were apparently cooked whole. With the exploitation of the pike and large catfish, there was a clear focus on large species which would yield the most meat rather than the smaller members of the carp family.

Configurations of Consequent Neolithic settlement
As in the case of the subsistence data, it is important to draw distinctions between the North European Plain and the loess belt when discussing the types, sizes and

configurations of Consequent Neolithic settlement. The purpose of doing so is not to set up false dichotomies but rather to point out that the markedly different trajectories of Neolithic development in each of these areas is reflected in the physical remains of prehistoric settlements as well as in the patterns which emerge from those remains.

The loess belt

The *Siedlungskammern* occupied during the Primary Neolithic continue to be the foci of Consequent Neolithic settlement in the loess belt as well. In two of these areas, the configurations of Consequent Neolithic settlement have been particularly well studied – the loess uplands of southern Poland (Kruk 1973; Milisauskas and Kruk 1984) and the Elbe-Saale area of central Germany (Starling 1983, 1984, 1985, in press). In other areas, there have been isolated settlements and groups of settlements investigated, but not on the same scale. Surprisingly, the Aldenhoven Plateau, rich in Primary Neolithic settlement, has yielded relatively little Consequent Neolithic settlement.

Perhaps the most striking aspect of the Consequent Neolithic settlements of the loess belt is the greater diversity of site sizes and types in addition to great variability in the relative numbers of Primary Neolithic and Consequent Neolithic settlements in different regions. A simple classification of Consequent Neolithic settlements would be very difficult. It may therefore be more productive to consider the various elements of the differences between the Primary and Consequent Neolithic settlements individually, starting with the question of the differences in relative site numbers.

There are a number of factors which enter into the question of relative site numbers, including both the nature of the archaeological record and the patterns of fieldwork and survey. The large Linear Pottery settlements with their valley-bottom locations tend to be rather "obtrusive" elements in the archaeological record wherever they occur. The duration and spatial focus of these sites has resulted in a high level of archaeological visibility. It is difficult to place most of the Funnel Beaker and Michelsberg settlements of the loess belt in the same category, for there tends to be a much greater range of site sizes (meaning that small sites abound) and the occupation spans of these sites appear to have been generally shorter. Moreover, the massive construction requirements of the Linear Pottery settlements resulted in the formation of large pits which preserve archaeological data *in situ,* whereas the structures on Funnel Beaker and Michelsberg sites did not lead to the degree of subsurface excavation found on the earlier sites. Finally, the distinctive Linear Pottery ceramics have made these sites quite easy to identify and report, whereas there is often less decoration on Consequent Neolithic household wares. One sherd of Linear Pottery can mark a site of this culture, but it may require a whole assemblage of pottery before a Consequent Neolithic site is recognized and dated. The overall picture, then, is one of a Consequent Neolithic which is much less visible in the archaeological record than the preceding period.

To this can be added the differences in regional survey coverage (Hamond 1980). The variation in the archaeological record noted above will be reflected more strongly in areas where the data base consists of sites which have been recorded and documented in an accretional fashion over the last 100 years as opposed to having been discovered during surveys designed to spot and recognize sites of a particular period. One must address these issues before drawing significant interregional comparisons or contrasts.

The question of relative numbers of Primary versus Consequent Neolithic sites on a regional scale is of interest even in light of the above considerations. For instance, in the Elbe-Saale area of East Germany, there was a progressive decrease in site numbers over the course of the Primary Neolithic, but the beginning of the Consequent Neolithic saw an apparent break in this trend (Starling 1983, 1985). The net result is that the total number of Primary Neolithic sites is about twice that of the Consequent Neolithic, but there is little evidence for the continuity of occupation that marked many of the Primary Neolithic sites. On the loess uplands of southern Poland, in the microregion around Bronocice, however, the situation is just the reverse. There is approximately a 2.5:1 ratio of Funnel Beaker to Linear Pottery sites (Milisauskas and Kruk 1984: 11). One possibility is that in the Elbe-Saale area Starling is dealing with sites that have been discovered in an accretional manner, with the more "obtrusive" Primary Neolithic sites being favored, while Milisauskas and Kruk have systematically searched for Funnel Beaker sites with intensive surveys. On the other hand, on the Aldenhoven Plateau, where there has been an intensity of archaeological research probably unparalleled in Europe, very few Consequent Neolithic sites are in evidence.

Another aspect of the differences between Primary and Consequent Neolithic settlements of the loess belt is in the range of variation of site sizes. Milisauskas and Kruk (1984: 14) have identified a range of Funnel Beaker site sizes in the Bronocice region from 1.2 to 18 hectares, with most falling between 1.2 and 6 hectares. This range contrasts with the Linear Pottery size range in the same area, which lies between 1.1 and 5.3 hectares, with most between 1 and 4 hectares. In the Elbe-Saale region, Starling (1983, 1987) reports a similar broadening of the range of site sizes, as well as of site complexity. A number of the smaller sites could be called "generic" Consequent Neolithic settlements, consisting of a collection of pits, postholes, and other features reflecting traces of habitation. Besides the "generic" Consequent Neolithic settlements (which themselves exhibit a wide range of variation in size and content), there are a variety of sites in prominent topographical locations, often enclosed by ditches and banks. Known as *Höhensied-lungen*, a number of such sites are known from the Elbe-Saale region, and perhaps the best-known in southern Poland is Bronocice itself. These sites are clearly functionally differentiated from the "generic" Consequent Neolithic settlements and show a considerable degree of internal variation as well.

There are a few general observations that can be made about the *Höhensiedlungen* of the loess belt (for a more detailed discussion of the ones in central Germany, see Starling 1987). The first is that the internal structure of these settlements is often very difficult to apprehend, if one exists, to the point where it is often impossible to identify individual structures. Much of this difficulty, to be sure, is due to the fact that many of these sites are located on the higher interfluve margins, rather than the valley floors, and therefore have been subject to a greater degree of erosion than the floodplain Primary Neolithic sites. Moreover, large areas of these sites have generally not been excavated. The distribution of surface finds often covers such a large area that it is probably often difficult to decide where to excavate to most effectivly examine their internal patterning. Even supposing, however, that the traces of houses have been eradicated by erosion, it still seems doubtful that the *Höhensiedlungen* represent the same degree of population aggregation as the larger Primary Neolithic sites. At Bronocice, for instance, Funnel Beaker settlement debris is spread over a 52-hectare area (three discrete areas datable to different occupations with a maximum extent of 18 hectares). The archaeological remains are sufficiently concentrated on a regional scale to indicate that this was a single site, yet sufficiently distributed over the 52 hectares as to betray no clear organizational pattern.

The other salient feature of the *Höhensiedlungen* is their frequent demarcation by ditch systems and palisades. In contrast to the equivocal Linear Pottery earthworks described in Chapter 4, the Funnel Beaker and Michelsberg hilltop sites have a definite "monumental" character. Although it may be possible to propose the alternative hypothesis that they functioned as enclosures for livestock, this argument loses force in light of the hilltop locations of these sites, especially since cattle and other stock would find it difficult to negotiate the slopes of these sites after a day of grazing. The construction and siting of these earthworks suggests that instead of being designed to keep something inside, they were primarily intended to either keep something or someone out or to have some sort of symbolic significance.

Perhaps the two best-known Consequent Neolithic hilltop enclosed sites are the Dölauer Heide in central Germany (Behrens and Schröter 1980) and Bronocice in southern Poland (Kruk and Milisauskas 1981; Milisauskas and Kruk 1984). In addition, a number of other enclosed sites are known from Germany and elsewhere (Starling 1987; Lüning 1968; Howell 1983). The Dölauer Heide is a very prominent site with a total enclosure of 25 hectares. The enclosed area is divided into two parts, and in places there are six parallel banks and ditches. The enclosure at the Dölauer Heide appears to have been constructed early in the Consequent Neolithic, although the main domestic occupation is towards the end of this period (Behrens 1981), which Starling (1987) suggests represents a change in the function of the site. At Bronocice, the earthworks enclose a relatively small area, but there are three consecutive construction episodes. In the BR II Phase, about 2900 bc (uncalibrated) the first earthwork was constructed, enclosing 2.3 hectares. The settlement remains within this earthwork are those of the non-Funnel Beaker Lublin-Volhynian Group, a poorly-known cultural entity which appears to be related to the Lengyel-Polgar Primary Neolithic cultures of this area, but it is coeval with the major Consequent Neolithic occupation at Bronocice. Close by, another earthwork was constructed somewhat later, enclosing 4.6 hectares. Finally, towards the end of the Consequent Neolithic occupation at Bronocice, additional earthworks were built further down the slopes of the promontory, although it is unclear how large an area they enclosed or if they were enclosures at

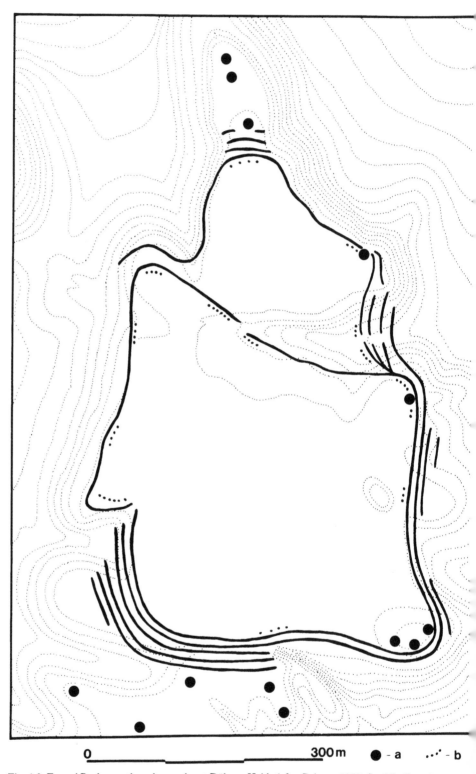

Fig. 6.2 Funnel Beaker earthwork complex at Dölauer Heide (after Behrens 1973: fig. 83). Key: A – barrows; B – palisade traces.

all. The striking aspect of Bronocice, in contrast to the Dölauer Heide, is that the occupation remains are spread over an area both inside and outside the earthworks. The difference, of course, is that the enclosed area at the Dölauer Heide is so large that it encompassed the settled areas, while at Bronocice the actual enclosures are smaller.

The term "generic" to describe the smaller, non-enclosed Consequent Neolithic settlements is perhaps somewhat misleading, for these sites display a much greater range of individual characteristics than do the Primary Neolithic settlements. In fact, there is such diversity that it is impossible to discuss more than a few cases here which reflect the general trends in settlement development in the loess belt. Their "generic" quality is more a reflection of the fact that they do not appear to have any marked degree of functional differentiation except in a few cases noted below, and their artifact and feature content is very similar. The distinguishing characteristics of these settlements are more their size and topographical siting.

The sizes of the "generic" non-enclosed Consequent Neolithic settlements tend to vary, but they usually fall between 1 and 5 hectares. In terms of content and structure, however, there seems to be relatively little difference between the sites on the smaller end of this range and the larger, except possibly that the larger sites may have a longer period of occupation. To a large extent, these site sizes are inexact, and often depend on the dimensions of excavated areas and the area covered by surface finds. The topographical locations of the Consequent Neolithic non-enclosed settlements are also variable, but in some cases there seems to be consistency within particular regions and microregions. For instance, in the loess uplands of southern Poland, there is the well-known shift in settlement locations from the valley bottoms to the interfluve margins between the Primary and Consequent Neolithic, and the later settlements tend to be consistently located on the higher points in the terrain. In the Elbe-Saale area of central Germany, on the other hand, there is relatively little difference between the settlement zones of the Primary Neolithic and the Consequent Neolithic. There is little continuity of occupation between the two periods at individual sites, but the preferred settlement locations on the lower slopes and valley bottoms are generally similar. In the Oder drainage, there are a number of cases of the use of the same settlement locations in both periods, for instance at Pietrowice Wielkie (Bukowska-Gedigowa 1980), Tomice (Romanow, Wąchowski, and Miszkiewicz 1973), and Nosocice (Wiślański 1979). Further west, however, Michelsberg sites do not tend to be associated with Primary Neolithic settlement locations, but there has not been a systematic regional study of their settlement patterns.

The choice of settlement locations by Consequent Neolithic groups in the loess belt sometimes was not identical within a single microregion. A good example of this is found in Lower Silesia, where the essentially coeval sites of Janówek and Tomice are located 800 m apart on opposite sides of a small river. Janówek (Wojciechowski 1973) is located on a promontory whose slopes steeply descend to the river, while Tomice (Romanow, Wąchowski, and Miszkiewicz 1973) is on lower, flatter terrain. The direct-line distance from the river is about the same in both cases (100 m), but the choice of site location was different. Instances of the

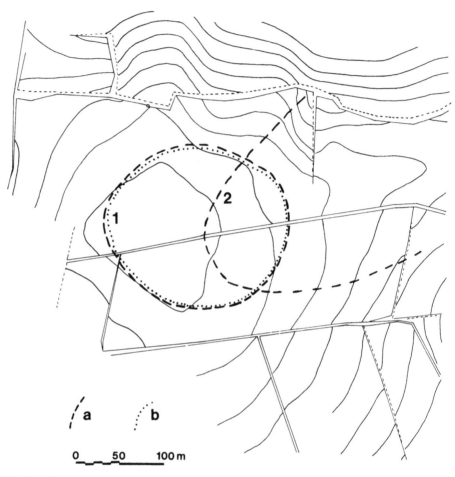

Fig. 6.3 Consequent Neolithic earthworks at Bronocice (after Kruk and Milisauskas 1979: fig. 2). Key: a – ditch systems; b – palisade traces; 1 – Lublin-Volhynian earthwork; 2 – Funnel Beaker earthwork.

pairing or the clustering of these smaller Funnel Beaker sites are common. In addition to the Tomice-Janówek pair, there are a number of similar pairs in Lower Silesia (Wiślański 1979: 204). An examination of the distribution of Funnel Beaker sites around Bronocice suggests a similar tendency.

The identification of structural remains on the smaller non-enclosed Funnel Beaker sites is much more difficult than on the Linear Pottery residential bases of the loess belt. In a number of instances, large pits, sometimes with associated postholes, have been identified as subterranean dwellings (e.g. at Janówek, Tomice, and Nosocice in Silesia). The believability of these as subterranean houses depends on one's approach to the issue of site formation processes. At Tomice and Janówek, the large pits are generally very shallow, and rather than being subterranean houses, they may instead be the remains of intensively used domestic areas. The actual houses have presumably left no trace, except in the form of the scattered postholes in the vicinity of the pits. Some credibility is lent to this argument, since the smaller, deeper pits at both sites tend to cluster around these

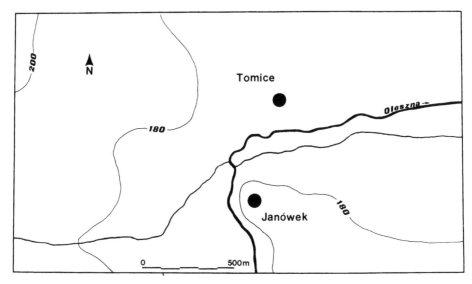

Fig. 6.4 Location of Funnel Beaker settlements at Janówek and Tomice in Silesia.

broad, shallow pits, giving the impression of a "household cluster" of different sorts of domestic features. At Niedzwiedz, in southern Poland near Kraków, there are actual traces of an above-ground post structure, 16 m by 6 m, with associated pits and features (Burchard 1973). Wallendorf/Hutberg, located in the Elbe-Saale region of central Germany, appears to have nine similar structures (Behrens 1973: 199) separated by distances of between 10 and 35 m across an area about 100 by 200 m. Several of these houses appear to be situated in pairs.

Elsewhere in the loess belt, the settlement data are rather meager. Near Münster, two Michelsberg sites yielded large oval pits reminiscent of some of the Polish upland Funnel Beaker sites (Willms 1982). A large Schussenreid site at Ludwigsburg "Im Schlösslesfeld" in the Neckar valley is characterized by a large number of features which do not reflect any functional differentiation (Lüning and Zürn 1977). The burnt daub in the Ludwigsburg pits indicates wood construction using fairly complicated joinery (Fig. 6.6).

The North European Plain
Across the North European Plain, one finds a number of different Consequent Neolithic settlement forms. Unlike the Primary Neolithic settlements of central Europe with their longhouses and much like the Consequent Neolithic settlements of the loess belt, it is not easy to develop a typology of settlement forms for the Consequent Neolithic of the North European Plain. One problem is the general lack of preserved structural remains on these sites, so they cannot be grouped on the basis of the presence or absence of structures. The other problem is one of site definition. The structural remains and other subsurface features on Primary Neolithic sites result in reasonably clear boundaries to settled areas. On the Consequent Neolithic sites of the North European Plain, one most often finds scatters of artifacts which vary in density but which may also result from different occupations of the same site. It is often difficult to determine whether scatters 100

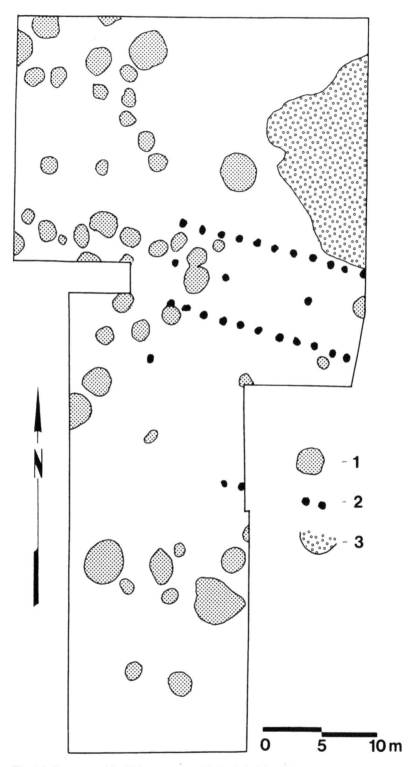

Fig. 6.5 Consequent Neolithic structure at Niedzwiedz (after Hensel and Milisauskas 1985: fig 37). Key: 1 – Funnel Beaker pits; 2 – postholes; 3 – natural depression.

meters apart are coeval or represent entirely different occupations. As a result, many maps of Funnel Beaker site distributions in particular microregions consist of a number of small locations scattered across the landscape.

The problem of site definition is the greatest for sites on sandy soils, where various aeolian processes have occurred and where the occupations were frequently short. Such sites pose a problem for the excavator, for control of both the horizontal and vertical stratigraphy is difficult to maintain. These are also areas which are still forested or only recently deforested, and as a result there is often considerable disturbance from the roots of coniferous trees. It is possible, however, to distinguish two *VERY* broad categories of Consequent Neolithic settlement on the North European Plain: smaller, dispersed sand dune sites and larger lacustrine and riverine settlements. Within both of these categories there is considerable variation both in the spatial extent of settlement remains and in the density of archaeological material. Each Consequent Neolithic settlement in the lowlands seems to have its own distinctive character.

The sand sites have the broadest range of variation, from a few sherds and flint flakes to dense concentrations of artifacts. The smaller ones rarely find their way into archaeological literature, while the ones which are noted are of the order of 100 m^2 in surface area and over. Not infrequently, one finds Consequent Neolithic sand sites which have an area of 500 m^2 or more, consisting of a number of smaller concentrations of archaeological material. Here, the problem of site definition is most severe, for the reasons noted above. The knowledge of structural remains on these sand sites is very limited. At some, pieces of burnt wall-daub are found, suggesting somewhat solid structures (Wiślański 1979: 202). The sand, however, does not lend itself to the preservation of distinct postholes in the same way that loess or clay do. In additon, erosion and deflation of many of these sites have obscured traces of construction.

Such sand sites occur frequently in areas of glacial outwash in central and northern Poland and Germany (Wiślański 1969, 1979). The author has direct familiarity with such a Funnel Beaker site at Nowy Młyn, located approximately 5 km NW of Brześć Kujawski in a zone of sandy outwash and dating to between 3200 and 3000 bc. Nowy Młyn has poorly defined subsurface features and only a few postholes. Primarily, the site consists of scatters of potsherds and flints across sand dunes. To some degree, the density of these scatters is correlated with the natural contours of the dunes, but it is uncertain how much post-occupation deflation has taken place and whether the artifacts themselves helped stabilize the areas where they were the densest. The high density of artifacts in some areas is quite striking, as is the high degree of fragmentation of the pottery. The overall impression is of an intense – yet short-lived – occupation, or perhaps a palimpsest of several occupations. There are literally hundreds of similar sites across the sandy areas of northwest Poland (Wiślański 1969: 73).

Another group of Funnel Beaker sand settlements is found along the Baltic coast of East Germany (Nilius 1973, 1975; Nilius and Warnke 1984) and inland in the lake belts of Mecklenburg (Schuldt 1974, Nagel 1980). These sites appear to be very similar in structure to the sand sites of the Polish lowlands. At Ralswiek, an

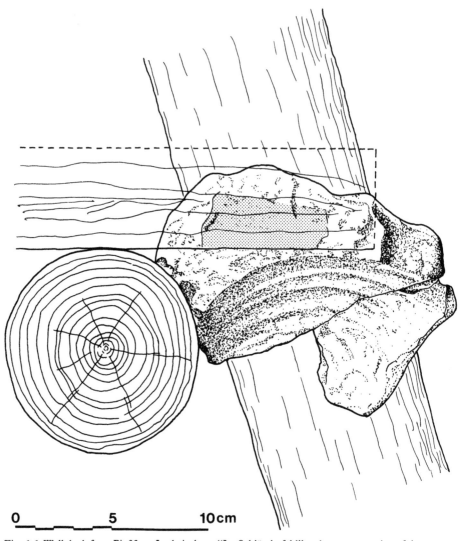

0   5   **10cm**

Fig. 6.6 Wall daub from Pit 32c at Ludwigsburg "Im Schlösslesfeld" and a reconstruction of the timbers responsible for the imprints (after Lüning and Zürn 1977: plate 120).

irregularly shaped depression 2.5 m in each direction contained hearths and suggested a habitation location. Gristow had similar dark discolorations which contained intrusive stones and a large amount of highly fragmented sherds, quite similar to the situation observed by the author at Nowy Młyn in Poland. One quite interesting site was the settlement at Basedow, on a sandy island, where a Neolithic settlement layer with burnt wall-daub was found over an area about 20 by 20 m. There is apparently evidence for a Mesolithic component at this site as well, although the stratification is not well defined.

At some Polish sites, such as Mrowino near Poznań (Tetzlaff 1978) and Brąchnówko near Toruń (Wawrzykowska 1981), rectangular concentrations of artifacts and burnt daub have been interpreted as reflecting the outlines of houses, although little in the way of direct structural evidence has been found. At both

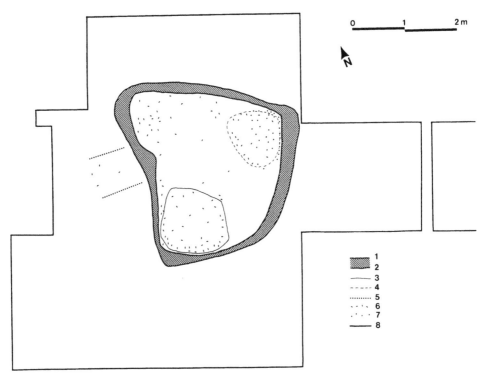

Fig. 6.7 Funnel Beaker features at Ralswiek (after Nilius and Warnke 1984: fig. 2.) Key: 1 – upper limit of structure; 2 – lower limit of structure; 3 – outline of pit; 4 – outline of hearth; 5 – possible entrance; 6 – sherds; 7 – burnt daub; 8 – limits of excavation.

sites, a single such structure (?) has been found. The house at Mrowino was 4 m by 5.5 m, while at Brąchnówko the structure is 4 m by 8 m. These two sites seem to be of roughly similar dimensions, although in both cases the size of the excavated area seems to exceed the actual extent of the Neolithic settlement in some directions yet does not seem to extend far enough in others. From the published plans, it is possible to estimate that they are about 300 m^2 in surface area. At Mosegården in Jutland, a living area and a dump area could be distinguished. To one side of a stone hearth several postholes indicated the presence of structures of indeterminate dimensions. Madsen (1982: 206) estimates that the site was occupied for at least two and a half years on the basis of the number of broken vessels.

One cannot fail to be struck by the similarities between the Funnel Beaker sand sites and those of the indigenous hunter-gatherers of the North European Plain. The far greater numbers of Funnel Beaker sites known is a result of several factors. The first is the greater archaeological visibility of the Neolithic sites due to their ceramic content. Not only are sherds more readily visible during archaeological survey in this area, but a few pots can produce a volume of archaeological material equivalent to a longer period of stone tool manufacture. Another contributing factor to the discovery of many Funnel Beaker sites seems to be that many were occupied for longer periods *on the average* than were the Mesolithic camps. Finally, it is not unreasonable to infer that the agricultural subsistence base of the

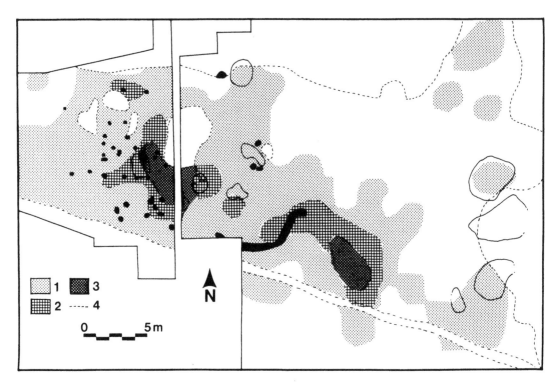

Fig. 6.8. Density map of pottery finds at Mosegården (after Madsen 1982: fig. 7.) Key: 1 – 0-100 g of pottery/m^2; 2 – 100-200 g of pottery/m^2; 3 – 200-400 g of pottery/m^2; 4 – limit of preserved deposits.

inhabitants of these sites permitted the maintenance of larger populations, hence the greater number of sites which have survived.

After about 2700 bc, a number of somewhat larger Funnel Beaker settlements appear, often in lacustrine and riverine habitats, particularly within a short distance inland from the Baltic and North Sea coasts. The character of some of these sites does not appear to be radically different from the smaller sand sites of the preceding centuries. Bistoft LA 11, for instance, has been interpreted as a seasonal exploitation settlement occupied during the summer and early autumn at which a limited amount of stockherding was carried out (L. Johansson 1981: 104). Szlachcin, despite the fact that good preservation conditions led to the recovery of a wooden platform, seems to have been a similar sort of specialized site in a marshy valley in northwest Poland. A similar type of economic specialization has been reported for two coastal Funnel Beaker sites in Denmark, Hesselø and Sølager (Skaarup 1973).

Other sites, such as Poganice (Jankowska 1980) and Hanstedgård (Eriksen and Madsen 1984), appear to represent permanently occupied settlements. These generally date towards the end of the Funnel Beaker sequence, approximately 2600/2500 bc. The Funnel Beaker settlement at Poganice is located on a terrace about 200 m from the bank of the Łupawa river. Settlement traces occur discontinuously over a 12 hectare area, within which four foci of occupation have been identified. Within these habitation areas, post structures have been found along with a density of refuse suggesting multi-phase occupations. Within several kilometers of Poganice are a number of clusters of earthen long barrows. Hanstedgård in eastern Jutland is situated on a low gravel and sand hill surrounded on three sides by water and on a fourth by a marsh. In a natural depression, 42 m long and 4–10 m wide, a deposit of settlement refuse was found, within which were a number of pits, postholes, and ard furrows. At the western end of the North European Plain, the Funnel Beaker site at Heede, on the Ems river, has yielded a number of postholes which appear to form the outlines of houses (Fröhlich 1985). The 17 houses at Heede measure approximately 11.5 by 5.5 m each. Four occupation phases have been identified, each with 3–5 houses.

In Schleswig-Holstein and Denmark, a few late Funnel Beaker sites with traces of enclosures have been found on promontories. Büdelsdorf (Hingst 1971), Toftum (Madsen 1978, 1982), and Sarup (S. Andersen 1980) are the most important of these sites, which are quite large but often without significant traces of habitation (although the interior of Büdelsdorf contained numerous hearths and a thick midden layer). Such sites have not been found on the outwash plains and meltwater valleys south of the Baltic moraine area.

There has been some discussion lately about the form of the structures found on Funnel Beaker sites, particularly in Denmark. Earlier claims for Danish "long-houses" on a parallel with the Primary Neolithic structures of the loess belt (e.g. at Barkaer and Troldebjerg) have recently been dismissed as representing traces of earthen long barrows or as fragments of palisades (Eriksen and Madsen 1984). The houses at Heede are among several claims for smaller rectangular post structures in Niedersachsen. At Flögeln-Eckholtjen, Kr. Cuxhaven, a 12.8 by 4.8 m house, with walls set in bedding trenches and a double row of center posts, has been reported (Zimmermann 1979), while another house at Wittenwater, Kr. Uelzen, measured 15.6 by 6 m (Voss 1965). Claims for similar structures in Denmark are all problematical (Eriksen and Madsen 1984: 78). Eriksen and Madsen have advanced the proposition that the least ambiguous evidence for Funnel Beaker houses in Denmark and Schleswig-Holstein between 3100 and 2500 bc is of small oval or D-shaped structures (Fig. 6.11). They argue that a prevailing desire to find more substantial structures has led some archaeologists to misinterpret ambiguous structural remains while in fact overlooking traces of smaller and flimsier structures. The hut at Hanstedgård appears to have been preserved due to its location in a natural depression that later filled with midden, protecting the small postholes from being obliterated.

If small oval or D-shaped structures were the prevailing Funnel Beaker house form in Denmark and perhaps elsewhere in the North European Plain, the parallels with the Mesolithic dwellings on the North European Plain should not be overlooked. Newell (1981) has evaluated the evidence for Mesolithic dwellings in north-central Europe to separate those that appear to be genuine structures from those that are features resulting from natural phenomena such as tree-falls. It is quite striking that a number of the best documented Mesolithic structures (e.g. those from Bergumermeer in the Netherlands) are oval or horseshoe-shaped. If Eriksen and Madsen are correct in their argument that, at least in Denmark,

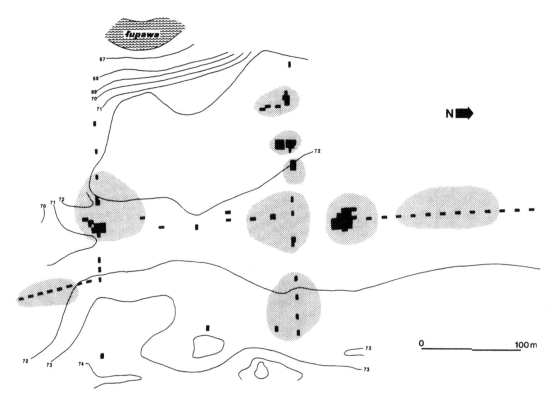

Fig. 6.9. Funnel Beaker settlement traces at Poganice (after Jankowska 1980). Shaded areas indicate extent of settlement traces; black rectangles indicate excavation units.

Funnel Beaker houses also took the form of small, roundish huts, this may reflect yet another instance of a Mesolithic tradition persisting past the appearance of domestic plants and animals in this area.

Special cases: Dümmersee, Late Ertebølle/Ellerbek, Rhine-Maas

Although the main approach used in this book has been one of simplification and generalization, there are several special cases of subsistence-settlement systems which do not fit easily into the various categories used here. These sites are on the North European Plain (as might be predicted due to the great environmental variability of the region) and are temporally at the very dawn of the establishment of agrarian communities in this area. They thus represent adaptations which slightly predate the Consequent Neolithic sites discussed above, falling between about 3600 and 3000 bc (4400–3800 BC). In each case, there are different dimensions to the anomalous character of the subsistence settlement system. At the Dümmersee, current information is confined to a single site – Hüde I am Dümmer – which was excavated in the early 1960s and has only recently been studied in greater detail. The best known of these anomalous subsistence-settlement systems in the European lowlands is the Ertebølle culture of Denmark and its Ellerbek variant in Schleswig-Holstein and Mecklenburg. Finally, in the Rhine-Maas delta, recent work has revealed a special type of estuarine adaptation.

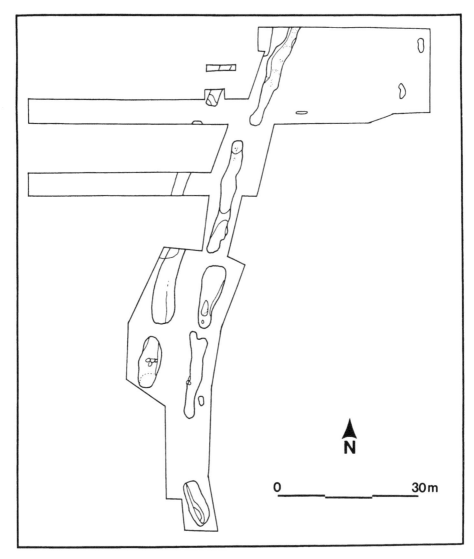

Fig. 6.10 Detail of ditch features at Toftum (after Madsen 1978: fig. 1).

Hüde I on the Dümmersee

The importance of the glacial lakes on the northwest German outwash plain for the transition from foraging to farming in this area has only recently been recognized. Very few early food-producing sites have been excavated, although numerous Mesolithic sites have been known from this area for many years. One lake basin, the Dümmer, appears to be of particular significance on the basis of the research which has been done there in the last two decades. The Dümmersee is the second largest lake in Niedersachsen, currently having a surface area of 15 km². It is both fed and drained by the Hunte river. In the early Holocene, the lake was clearly larger, and a perimeter of Mesolithic sites marks what must have been its shoreline during the Atlantic period (see Fig. 6.13; Fansa and Kampffmeyer 1985: 109). The

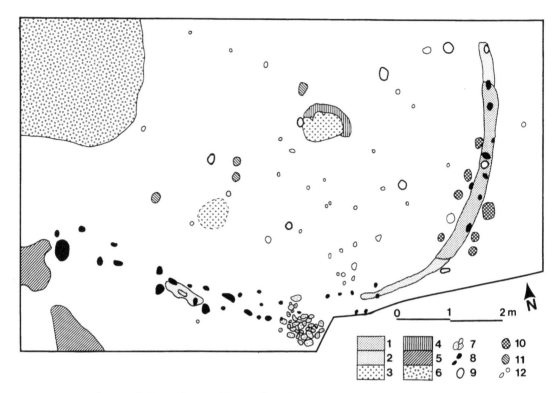

Fig. 6.11 D-Shaped house at Hanstedgård (after Eriksen and Madsen 1984: fig. 7). Key: 1 – foundation trench with grey-black fill; 2 – foundation trench with grey fill; 3 – red-brown sand (hearth); 4 – dark, grey-brown sand; 5 – pits; 6 – modern disturbance; 7 – entrance paving; 8 – stake holes in semicircular wall; 9 – postholes deeper than 30 cm; 10 – shallow postholes adjacent to foundation trench; 11 – postholes less than 30 cm deep; 12 – various stakeholes.

Neolithic sites lie considerably closer to the present lake margins. The first Neolithic settlement on the Dümmersee to be excavated was the so-called "Huntedorf", located near the spot where the Hunte flows into the lake (Reinerth 1939, Schirnig 1979). The "Huntedorf" is a site of the Funnel Beaker culture, datable probably to about 3000–2800 bc, and the excavations yielded traces of post structures and a fully agrarian economy.

Between 1961 and 1967, another Neolithic site was excavated on the Düm-mersee, also near the mouth of the Hunte. The Hüde I site, as it is known, was discovered during the drainage of moors along the lake and the lowering of the water table. 1,100 m^2 were excavated, and the preservation of organic material was exceptionally good. There were several occupation layers at Hüde I, although it was difficult to differentiate them. It appears that there are three main occupation phases: 4200–3700 bc, 3700–3200 bc, and 2950–2700 bc. The oldest phase is poorly represented, but yielded sherds of large vessels with pointed bases, very similar to those of the Ertebølle/Ellerbek culture of the west Baltic area. In all respects, however, the subsistence data recovered from the oldest occupation phase at Hüde I reflect a foraging economy with no empirical evidence of cultivation or stockherding.

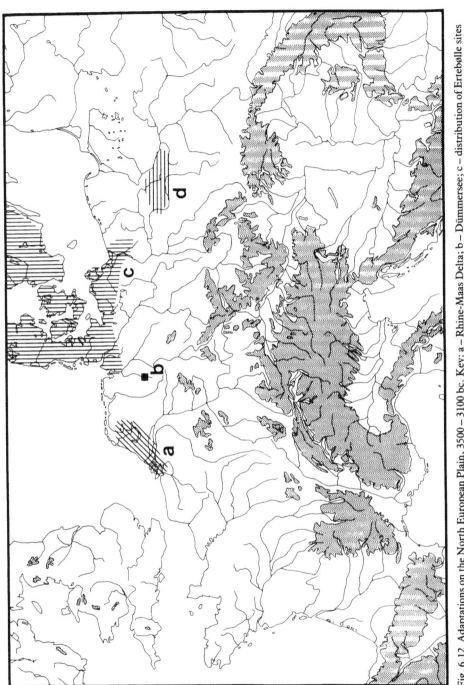

Fig. 6.12 Adaptations on the North European Plain, 3500 – 3100 bc. Key: a – Rhine-Maas Delta; b – Dümmersee; c – distribution of Ertebølle sites on the west Baltic littoral; d – distribution of settlements of the Brześć Kujawski Group.

The following settlement phase at Hüde I is marked by ceramics which, when decorated, show similarities to those of the Rössen culture of the loess belt. In general, however, the overall lack of decoration on essentially Rössen vessel forms led some to refer to this ware as "Dümmer-Keramik". Fansa and Kampffmeyer (1985: 109) report that analysis has shown that some vessels in this phase were made in the loess belt and were brought from there to the site, a distance of at least 80–100 kilometers. The final phase at Hüde I belongs to the Funnel Beaker culture, with ceramics ranging from early Funnel Beaker forms to the typical northwest German "Tiefstich" ware. Some structural remains appear to have been associated with this phase, which has a somewhat greater spatial extent that the previous phase (Fig. 6.16).

The faunal and botanical samples from the latest two settlement phases are difficult to separate completely, and the published discussions generally treat them as a single sample. From over 30,000 faunal specimens, 10,600 mammal, 1,001 fish, and 275 bird bones could be identified (Boessneck 1978; Hübner 1980; Saur 1980; Hüster 1983). At the moment, it is difficult to assess the relative importance of the various species present, since detailed quantification has not been available. On the basis of numbers of identified specimens, the major taxa represented are cattle (36.8%), pig (21.5%), and beaver (12.8%). The three same species are also shown to be of major importance on the basis of minimum numbers of individuals. A minimum of 250 individual mammals are represented in the Hüde I assemblage, with beaver accounting for 20%, cattle for 17.1%, and pig for 16.7%. Other mammalian taxa represented include wolf, fox, bear, otter, weasel, wild cat, wild horse, red deer, roe deer, sheep/goat, and dog. The majority of the pig bones are believed to come from wild individuals, and most of the cattle bones are thought to be those of aurochs, although in light of the debate over the degree of precision possible in the separation of wild and domestic forms of the same species, these assessments may be somewhat problematical. In any event, however, it seems clear that the representation of domestic taxa in the Neolithic faunal assemblage from Hüde I is markedly less than that of wild species.

Domesticated plants are known from both carbonized grain and imprints on ceramics, although an analysis has not been published. In addition, grinding stones have been found. Kampffmeyer emphasizes, however, that these data indicate only that grain was utilized by the inhabitants of Hüde I and provide no proof that it was grown in the immediate vicinity (Kampffmeyer 1983: 129).

Kampffmeyer (1983: 127) attaches particular importance to the large number of beaver and other fur-bearing mammal bones in the Hüde I assemblage, although it does not appear that the only function of the site was the exploitation of these species. Rather, the Hüde I site seems to have been devoted to the acquisition of a broad spectrum of wild resources whose ranges overlapped at the lake shore. The analysis of the age profiles indicates that the site was seasonally occupied in late summer and fall (Fansa and Kampffmeyer 1985: 110), and the model which has been proposed is of a pattern of autumn hunting to supplement an otherwise agrarian economy. Fansa and Kampffmeyer point out that the establishment of food production on the lowlands of northwestern Germany was a risky proposition, and it may have been necessary to treat the Dümmer basin as a reserve, especially in lean years.

The implication of this model is that other residential bases of the seasonal inhabitants of Hüde I are elsewhere. Kampffmeyer (1983: 129) suggests that the Dammer Berge, a hilly region on the western edge of the Dümmer basin, is a likely location, since ceramic analyses have shown this to be the source area for some of the clays in the pottery at Hüde I. Megalithic tombs are known from this area, coeval with the Funnel Beaker occupations at Hüde I and the "Huntedorf." In any event, the sites around the Dümmersee are perhaps the tip of an iceberg. The prehistoric settlement system in this area between about 4000 and 3000 bc may shed considerable light on the transition from foraging to farming on the lowlands of northwest Germany if it is fully investigated.

Late Ertebølle/Ellerbek
The unique situation of the Ertebølle/Ellerbek sites of Denmark and northern Germany has attracted a considerable amount of attention recently (Schwabedissen 1981; Jarman, Bailey, and Jarman 1982: 81-94; Rowley-Conwy 1984; Zvelebil and Rowley-Conwy 1984 among others). It is quite difficult to review briefly the range of both economic and settlement data from Ertebølle/Ellerbek sites. Interpretations of the data are affected by the fact that there has been a concentration on coastal sites at the expense of inland settlements. Moreover, there is a tendency for discussions to become sidetracked into debates over whether Ertebølle/Ellerbek is "mesolithic" or "neolithic" under the assumption that the two categories are mutually exclusive. The presence of pottery, long taken as a hallmark of an agrarian economy, in Ertebølle/Ellerbek contexts is frequently the source of much discussion.

Although Ertebølle/Ellerbek is most closely associated with the "kitchen midden" sites of the Danish littoral, it is important to realize that these are only one type of site of this culture. Of particular significance are the inland sites of northern Germany, which are usually situated around moors and lake basins, as well as coastal sites along the south Baltic margin which are not shell middens (Schwabedissen 1981). Schwabedissen argues that these continental Ertebølle/Ellerbek sites must be viewed separately from those of the Danish littoral when the establishment of an agrarian economy in this area is considered. Two localities are especially important in this discussion: the complex of sites around the Satrup Moor in Schleswig-Holstein and the site of Rosenhof on the Baltic coast.

Four major Ertebølle/Ellerbek sites are found on the margins of the Satrup Moor, all of which have yielded the characteristic pointed-base pottery and numerous wooden and antler artifacts. The radiocarbon dates for these sites all fall between 4000 and 3800 bc. At two sites, Südensee-Damm and Pöttmoor, an early Funnel Beaker component overlies the Ertebølle/Ellerbek component, separated by a sterile layer. Rosenhof lies to the southeast of the Satrup Moor on a small moraine along a former inlet of the Baltic. In addition to several hundred sherds, largely from pointed-base vessels, a large number of bone and antler artifacts were found. The antler T-axes especially are similar to those from sites of the Brześć Kujawski Group (cf. Grygiel 1986). Carbon-14 dates for Rosenhof lie between 4100 and 3500 bc.

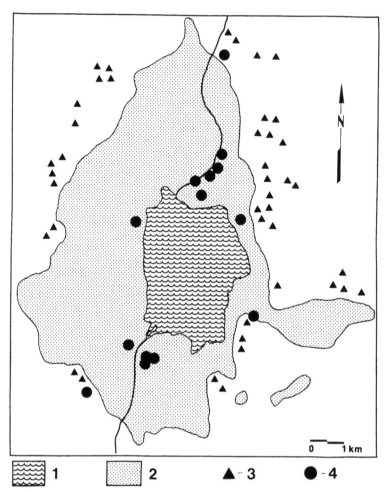

Fig. 6.13 Map of the Dümmer basin showing locations of Mesolithic and Neolithic sites (after Fansa and Kampffmeyer 1985: fig. 1). Key: 1 – current extent of Dümmersee; 2 – maximum extent of Dümmersee during the Atlantic period; 3 – Mesolithic sites; 4 – Neolithic sites.

At both the continental Ertebølle/Ellerbek sites and those on the Danish peninsula and islands, the evidence for the use of domestic plants and animals is equivocal at best. At the "classic" Danish sites, there is now believed to be no good evidence for domestic plants and animals (Zvelebil and Rowley-Conwy 1984: 109). At the continental sites, claims have been made for domestic animals (e.g. Nobis 1975), but the small sample sizes and lack of closed finds make these very problematical. At several of the sites at Satrup Moor, traces of cereal pollen have also been identified (Schütrumpf 1972), but there are problems with the accurate identification of cereal pollen (Andersen 1978), so this issue is in doubt as well. One pot from Rosenhof has an impression of a cereal grain, although it is uncertain whether this vessel was locally produced.

Schwabedissen (1981: 141) attaches great importance to the tenuous evidence of continental Ertebølle/Ellerbek food production, along with the evidence for

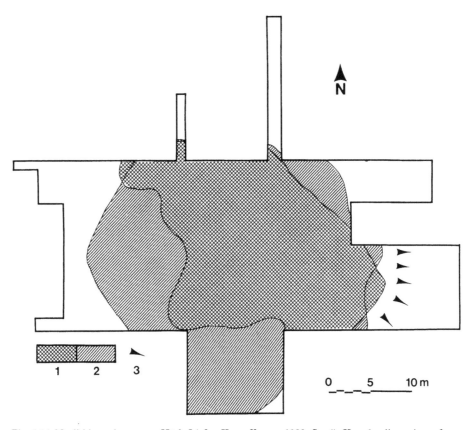

Fig. 6.14 Neolithic settlements at Hüde I (after Kampffmeyer 1983: fig. 6). Key: 1 – dimensions of earlier settlement component (Rössen-like ceramics); 2 – dimensions of later settlement component (Funnel Beaker ware); 3 – gentle slope to shore line.

contact with food-producing cultures further south in the form of pottery production and shoe-last celts (Schwabedissen 1966; see also Fischer 1982). There are several key research frontiers in the resolution of this issue. The first is the systematic recovery of cereal grains from the continental Ertebølle/Ellerbek sites through flotation or wet-sieving, or the demonstration that they are not present. The other is the investigation of early Neolithic and late Mesolithic settlement sites in the lake belts of Mecklenburg and Brandenburg, where research has hitherto concentrated on megalithic tombs. This area should be the crucial interaction zone, between the Primary Neolithic communities on the northern fringe of the loess near Braunschweig and Magdeburg and the late Mesolithic communities of the North European Plain.

The "classic" Ertebølle sites of the Danish peninsula and islands appear to represent a somewhat different matter, although the archaeological material is quite similar to the continental settlements (again, no more "package deal"). Here, a successful foraging adaptation successfully resisted the introduction of food-production until 3000 bc or even later, with virtually no evidence of domestic

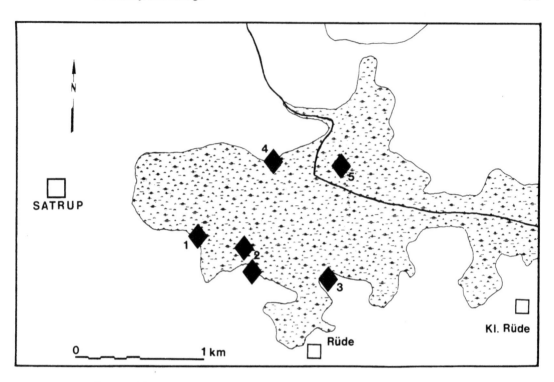

Fig. 6.15 Distribution of Ertebølle/Ellerbek settlements at Satrup Moor (after Schwabedissen 1981: fig. 2). Key: 1 – Förstermoor; 2 – Pöttmoor; 3 – Rüde 2; 4 – Bondebrück; 5 – Südenseedamm.

plants and animals prior to this date (save for some problematical specimens). Rowley-Conwy (1984; see also Zvelebil and Rowley-Conwy 1984) has explained this delay in the spread of farming into this area by the exceptional reliability and productivity of the coastal environment. He suggests that the eventual acceptance of food production by the foragers of the Danish littoral took place due to a decline in the productivity and reliability of the Ertebølle environment. Of particular importance was a decline in the availability of oysters, a relatively minor resource in the overall Ertebølle subsistence system but one which filled a crucial gap in the winter diet. The proposed cause of the oyster decline was a drop in sea level, leading to a decrease in salinity of the inshore waters, which took place about 3200–3100 bc. Cereals would have initially provided only a storable winter resource to offset the lack of shellfish, but soon expanded in importance to become a key element of the subsistence system.

The Rhine-Maas delta
The Rhine-Maas delta presents a special type of estuarine environment on the North European Plain, in which not only were there the usual lowland forest and riverine resources but also extensive marshes, tidal flats, and peat bogs. The most important sites of the Initial Delta Neolithic (Louwe Kooijmans 1987) are situated in the peat zone, often occurring on what were floating peat islands or along estuarine tidal creek systems. There are usually excellent conditions of preservation,

and a broad range of subsistence data is available from these sites. Of particular importance are two individual settlements, Hazendonk-1 and Bergschenhoek, and a complex of sites on a tidal creek at Swifterbant (Louwe Kooijmans 1976, 1980, 1987; Clason 1978; Price 1981b; van Zeist and Palfrenier-Vegter 1981; Bakels 1981; Wiel 1982; van der Woude 1984).

A detailed faunal analysis has not yet been published for Hazendonk-1, but Louwe Kooijmans (1987) reports that cattle, pig, and dog were present in the earliest phases. In the Swifterbant complex, the best data on subsistence are available from site S3 (Clason and Brinkhuizen 1978; van Zeist and Palfrenier-Vegter 1981). Here, a broad range of mammalian taxa, both wild and domestic, have been identified. Cattle and pigs are the major domestic species, while red deer, elk, aurochs, brown bear, otter, beaver, polecat, and wild horse comprise the wild component of the sample. In addition, there is a significant sample of avian remains, including cormorant, mute swan, crane, and white-tailed eagle. The sample of fish bones included both estuarine species but also anadromous taxa like sturgeon and salmon, the gray mullet which enters the tidal creeks only in the summer, and the large catfish. The catfish represented in the Swifterbant assemblage were quite large specimens, averaging between 100 and 120 cm in length (Brinkhuizen 1979: 260).

Bergschenhoek has yielded an extraordinary range of subsistence data on the exploitation of wild animals, particularly fish and waterfowl. In the fish bone sample, both large and small fish are represented, including eel, perch, carp, roach, bream, tench, and the large catfish. In addition to the faunal evidence, three large fish traps made from twigs of red dogwood were found at this site (Fig. 6.16). The waterfowl assemblage includes a variety of currently resident species such as mallard, tufted duck, and bittern, as well as winter visitors such as Bewick's swan, goosander, and widgeon. The mammalian assemblage is limited to aquatic mammals such as seal and otter.

The plant remains from the Initial Delta Neolithic sites are also of interest, for there is some question as to whether the estuarine and dune environment would support an agrarian economy. At Hazendonk-1, in the first phase, large amounts of carbonized grains as well as chaff and internodes were recovered (Bakels 1981). Bakels' current position is that although the carbonized material from this site is abundant, the surrounding ecosystem would have not have provided sufficient flat dry areas for fields and thus the grain was presumably brought to the site from the dry-land areas (personal communication 1985, 1986). Bergschenhoek, on the other hand, has yielded only wild fruits and nuts, including apples, hazelnuts, and blackthorn kernels.

Again, the richest data on plant exploitation in the Initial Delta Neolithic come from Swifterbant S3 (van Zeist and Palfrenier-Vegter 1981). Wild plants include apples, blackberries, hawthorn, rose hips, and hazelnuts. Naked barley is the predominant cultivated taxon in the assemblage, with close to 2,000 specimens, and is more abundant than emmer wheat by a ratio of approximately 25:1. In addition to grain, chaff and internodes were also found, which is taken to indicate local cultivation although the nearest field sites are at least a kilometer away (van

Fig. 6.16 One of three fish traps made from red dogwood twigs found at Bergschenhoek. The cut-off root systems of this scrub species suggest that the fish traps were made on the site. Photo copyright © Rijksmuseum voor Oudheidkunde, Leiden.

Zeist and Palfrenier-Vegter 1981: 143). This position is in contrast to that of Bakels concerning the similarly situated Hazendonk site. Louwe Kooijmans (1987) also believes that it is more likely that cereals were brought to the site on the ear.

The fact that relatively few Initial Delta Neolithic sites have been located and excavated makes it still impossible to study the distribution of sites on a regional level. The sites that are known all occur in the peat zone (see Chapter 2), where estuarine creek systems and freshwater reed-bordered lakes contributed to considerable ecological diversity. As a result, although it is not possible to study settlement patterns yet, the locations and configurations of these sites can shed some light on the nature of this adaptation.

The Hazendonk is a Late Glacial river dune, on which the original occupation surfaces have been eroded away. The top of the dune was so small, however, that the archaeological deposits extended down the sides under the later deposits surrounding the outcrop. In light of the subsistence data and the small size of the site, Louwe Kooijmans (1987) interprets Hazendonk-1 as a high and dry base camp for the exploitation of resources in the surrounding environment rather than a permanent settlement. Bergschenhoek, located in a system of freshwater lakes and reed swamps, is also not considered to be a permanent settlement. This site has yielded a complex microstratigraphy which has led to its interpretation as having been a floating raft of peat which became caught on a clay deposit, then reinforced and raised with bundles of reeds. The microstratigraphy shows alternating, presumably annual, depositions of clay and organic matter, which have led to the assessment that the peat raft was occupied over a span of about ten years. Like Hazendonk-1, Bergschenhoek is believed to be a subsidiary extraction camp for short-term fishing and fowling.

The Swifterbant sites, particularly S3, appear to reflect some longer-term occupations, situated on river dunes and creek levees. Swifterbant S3, about 800 m^2, has a habitation layer up to 75 cm thick. Within this habitation layer, 750 posts and stakes were found, which probably represent structural elements of small huts. Clay hearths which were periodically renewed also suggest a certain stability of occupation over time. Louwe Kooijmans estimates that 4–10 households or 20–50 individuals occupied S3 at any one time as a long-term residential base. The absence of winter indicators has led to the hypothesis that these were still not year-round occupations, however.

The similarities between the Rhine-Maas sites and those of both the Ertebølle/ Ellerbek culture and the local Late Mesolithic have been noted by a number of authors (Roever 1979; Price 1981b; Louwe Kooijmans 1987). The major difference is the concrete evidence for domestic plants, in the form of carbonized grain, at the Initial Delta Neolithic sites. As Louwe Kooijmans notes, however, the cereals could have been brought to these sites on the ear, so it is necessary to be cautious for the moment in calling these settlements fully agrarian. Nonetheless, the evidence for continuity from the local Mesolithic has led most to conclude that the Rhine-Maas Initial Delta Neolithic reflects the adoption of pottery, crop cultivation, and animal husbandry by indigenous foraging communities without, at first, major changes in other aspects of the settlement system.

Consequent Neolithic settlement

The loess belt

As was the case with the Primary Neolithic loess belt settlements, the seminal study of Consequent Neolithic settlement patterns on the loess was done in the early 1970s in southern Poland by Janusz Kruk (1973, 1980). Subsequent studies by Nicholas Starling in the Elbe-Saale region of East Germany have shown that although some of the patterns perceived by Kruk are replicated in other parts of the loess belt, there is some degree of variation among the different *Siedlungskammern* as well. Off the loess, in areas with dendritic drainage and well-defined valley-interfluve terrain, such as parts of northeastern France, similar settlement patterns are also found.

There are two major aspects to the shift in settlement patterns between the Primary and Consequent Neolithic observed by Kruk. The first is the penetration of the interfluves by human settlement, accompanied by a movement of settlement off the floodplains and floodplain margins favored by the Primary Neolithic

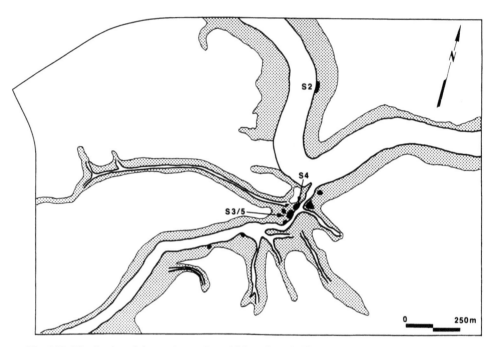

Fig. 6.17 Distribution of sites on levees along tidal creeks at Swifterbant (after Louwe Kooijmans 1980b: fig. 8c).

settlers. One must be careful in interpreting this change in settlement location, and it should not be taken to mean that the interfluves had been hitherto unexploited or that the floodplains stopped being used for cultivation and other activities. Rather, it should be taken at face value, reflecting a preference for settlement on the upper margins of the interfluve slopes as opposed to their lower margins and the floodplains.

The other aspect of the shift in settlement location observed by Kruk and others is the dispersal of settlement locations. No longer does one find the small clusters of Linear Pottery and Lengyel settlements located along a segment of the floodplain. Instead, the Funnel Beaker (and Baalberg and Michelsberg) sites are spread out along the interfluve edges, usually occupying the tops of most of the promontories and culminations in any microregion with a substantial amount of settlement. This observation does not mean that Consequent Neolithic sites are spread out over entire regions. Certain microregions still clearly have more sites than others. It is at the microregional scale, in areas of up to perhaps 10 kilometers across, that Consequent Neolithic sites have a more dispersed distribution.

The shift in patterns from the Primary to the Consequent Neolithic can be investigated statistically using measures of contagion and dispersion developed first in plant ecology. Hodder (Hodder and Orton 1976: 89–97) examined Kruk's maps and applied statistical measures to them, concluding that there was a significant difference between the Linear Pottery and Lengyel distributions on one hand and the Funnel Beaker distribution on the other. The pattern shift observed by Kruk, then, appears to be verifiable through both visual interpretation and statistical analyses, suggesting that it is not spurious but rather does reflect significant change in locational strategies.

Clearly, then, there was an expansion in the loess belt into areas not hitherto occupied by agricultural communities. This fact, however, should not be interpreted to indicate that there were markedly different associations in soil types between the two periods. In the loess belt, there continues to be a strong correlation between the patches of loess and Consequent Neolithic settlement, at least before 2500 bc. It is important to realize that within the loess belt, the development of Consequent Neolithic settlement patterns did not come with any movement off the loess, but rather into different landscapes and zones *within* areas covered by loess.

Ecologically, however, the interfluve margins are quite different from the energy-subsidized floodplains in their edaphic qualities. These areas would have been the first to suffer from nutrient loss in the soils due to leaching and downslope movement of minerals. More importantly, the removal of vegetation from this zone would have resulted in pronounced erosion, more so than in any other landscape zone in the loess belt. The interfluve margins would have been drier than the floodplains, but Kruk stresses, however, that if the interfluves themselves are considered as a single unit, then these margins are moister than the interior regions furthest from streams.

In the Elbe-Saale area of central Germany, Starling has noted that there are a number of Consequent Neolithic sites which are located on river terraces, just as in the Primary Neolithic, except that there is little continuity at individual settlement locations. The hilltop *Höhensiedlungen* described above are a new element in the pattern, and to the extent that these contain settlement remains, they represent a development parallel to the shift observed by Kruk in southern Poland. As in the southern Polish uplands, the Consequent Neolithic sites in the Elbe-Saale area display a tendency towards clustering on a regional level, but they are dispersed on a microregional level.

In the case of the Primary Neolithic settlements of the loess belt, there is considerable discussion as to whether they represent actual villages or rather accretions of individual homesteads. The Consequent Neolithic sites, even the ones where large concentrations of settlement debris have been found, fit the model of single or double household units even better than do the Primary Neolithic settlements, suggesting that the real difference between the two periods was not one of agricultural system but rather of the degree of agglomeration of the household units and the extent of their "obtrusiveness" in the archaeological record. At the Consequent Neolithic sites where actual house outlines (e.g. Niedzwiedz) or where features identified as the archaeological correlates of domestic structures (e.g. Tomice) have been found, the usual number of such house sites is of the order of one or two, with associated pits forming a "household cluster" in the immediate vicinity. At sites where multiple structures have been found (e.g. Wallendorf), they are usually sufficiently dispersed and irregularly oriented to conform with a model of individual households, not all of which were necessarily coeval.

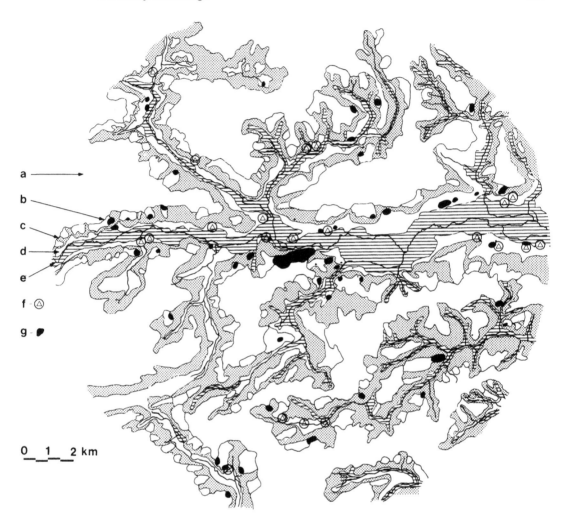

a ——————►
b
c
d
e
f ⊚
g ◗

0 1 2 km

Fig. 6.18 Comparison of Linear Pottery and Funnel Beaker settlement distributions in the Bronocice microregion (after Milisauskas and Kruk 1984, supplemental figure 1). Key: a – loess upland watersheds; b – upland margins; c – upland slopes; d – flood plain margins; e – alluvium; f – Linear Pottery settlements; g – Funnel Beaker settlements. Note that most Linear Pottery sites are on the flood plain margins, while Funnel Beaker sites are often on the upland margins.

Although the Primary Neolithic sites of the loess belt may have been similarly organized along household lines, the overall agglomeration of population took on the functional appearance of a village. This is clearly not the case in the Consequent Neolithic of the loess belt, where the small "generic" Funnel Beaker and Michelsberg sites represent very small-scale populations indeed, probably of the order of less than 20 individuals per site. Milisauskas and Kruk (1984) have proposed much higher population estimates for the Funnel Beaker sites in the Bronocice area, based on an extrapolation from the population estimates at the Linear Pottery site at Olszanica made using Naroll's method (Naroll 1962). In my opinion, these estimates are too high, for they are based on the floor space in what must have been multiple purpose structures, and then transposed for absolute areas of settlement. It is difficult to believe that there is such an absolute correlation between *site* area and population that it is possible to say that a 1.1 hectare site had 29 inhabitants while a 1.2 hectare site had 31. These small differences add up in the total picture, given the overall number of Funnel Beaker sites, and the resultant population estimates may be skewed significantly.

My argument, then, is that the overall population of particular microregions in the loess belt was not much different from that found during the Primary Neolithic (except in areas where there was an overall contraction of the settled area). The only real difference is that the method of the dispersal of settlements over the landscape was significantly changed. Apparent population growth when measured in terms of site numbers is offset by the fact that many of these sites are single-component sites occupied for a shorter period of time than many of the Primary Neolithic sites. Rather than having households clustered on floodplains as in the Primary Neolithic, there is now a greater tendency for households to pick and choose their settlement locations according to other criteria, many of which were probably not purely functional dictates of the subsistence system.

Neolithic settlement systems on the North European Plain
In discussing Neolithic settlement systems on the North European Plain, it is necessary to consider settlement patterns over time between ca. 3200 and 2500 bc, rather than to accept a static model of settlement development. Moreover, it is important to realize that there are significant regional variations even within the North European Plain area, but these are variations of degree rather than fundamental differences. Recently, there have been several attempts to develop models of Consequent Neolithic settlement systems in both Denmark (Madsen 1982), northern Germany (Johansson 1981), and northern Poland (Jankowska 1980). All are similar in their identification of several fundamental functional types of sites. To some degree it may be possible to extend these models to other parts of the North European Plain, although it is important to realize that against the variable backdrop of the ecology of this area, sociocultural developments in different areas probably proceeded at different rates.

Madsen's model is based on his study of a 1600 km^2 region of Jutland, morainic countryside very similar to that of Schleswig-Holstein and Pomerania, but with perhaps more marked topography than in the outwash plains and glacial meltwater valleys. The "early" and "middle"phases of his sequence fall within the temporal limits of this book. Madsen defines three fundamental types of habitation sites: exploitation ("catching") sites, residential sites, and central sites, which generally correspond to the site configurations identified on previous pages (pp. 00-0). Catching sites are generally small coastal or lacustrine sites, often located on former Mesolithic occupations. Residential sites are somewhat larger than the catching sites, and their dimensions grow over time. In Madsen's early phase these sites are of the order of 500–700 m^2, differentiated from coeval catching sites by their locations, while in the middle phase, they range up to 4,000 m^2, clearly larger than the coeval catching sites. The central sites appear in the middle phase and are located on promontories in the moraine belt or on hilltops. These are very large enclosures, between 10,000 and 50,000 m^2 in area, surrounded by ditch systems. In many respects, they are quite similar to the causewayed camps in Britain and to the Michelsberg and Funnel Beaker promontory sites in the loess belt. Toftum, which is within Madsen's study area, and Sarup, on South Fyn, are examples of central sites. Madsen's interpretation of these sites is that they are not residential bases but gathering places for the inhabitants of a broader hinterland.

Johansson's model for northern Germany identifies a similar three-tier typology of habitation sites. He considers Bistoft LA 11 to be a prime example of an exploitation site, since it was occupied during the summer only. Residential sites are larger, although few are known. Finally, central sites in Schleswig-Holstein are represented by Büdelsdorf, the only example of a site with ditch systems yet to come to light in this area. Johansson envisions a similar pattern of residence and seasonal exploitation to that proposed by Madsen, although his data are not as complete.

Jankowska's model, again very similar to those of Madsen and Johansson, is based on her work in the Łupawa valley in Pomerania. Poganice appears to be a good example of a residential base with dimensions similar to the residential bases of Madsen's middle phase in Jutland. Around Poganice are several sand dune sites, without faunal data, but which Jankowska considers to represent exploitation camps for hunting and collecting rather than field camps for agriculture, due to their location in infertile areas. She suggests that the central settlement of Poganice was either a permanent residential base or a location to which small groups frequently returned for prolonged stays.

It may be possible to identify elements of similar settlement systems elsewhere on the North European Plain. For instance, the settlements at Szczecin-Ustowo and Cedynia are also similar to residential bases like Poganice, and like the residential sites in Madsen's study, they are located near – but not directly on – streams and bodies of water. It is particularly striking, however, that the main evidence for the functional differentiation of Funnel Beaker sites comes from the morainic area to the north of the outwash plains and meltwater valleys. In the latter areas, there is some evidence for the emergence of a differentiation between exploitation sites and residential bases after ca. 2600 bc. At sites like Mrowino and Brachnówko in north-central Poland, concentrations of wall-daub and poorly defined house outlines suggest more permanent occupations than the small sand sites of the preceding centuries. Szlachcin, in a boggy valley near Środa Wielko-polska, has yielded a faunal sample which reflects a heavy reliance on the hunting of large wild herbivores, much in the same fashion as Bistoft LA 11. The majority of the Funnel Beaker sites in this zone, however, are the small sand settlements which do not produce copious amounts of subsistence data to permit them to be strongly differentiated. Nothing along the lines of the central fortified sites identified in Denmark and Schleswig-Holstein has been found in the outwash zone, although this may be due as much to the lack of similar morainic landforms as to any difference in the basic settlement systems. The overall pattern that

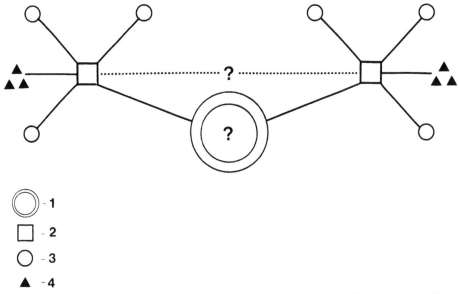

Fig. 6.19 A generalized model of Consequent Neolithic settlement in northern Germany proposed by L. Johansson (1981: fig. 3). Key: 1 – "fortified" settlements (e.g. Büdelsdorf); 2 – main settlements; 3 – satellite settlements (e.g. Bistoft); 4 – megalithic tombs.

emerges in the outwash-meltwater valley zone is of a fluid, poorly defined settlement system with little in the way of locational focus.

Consequent Neolithic subsistence systems

Since empirical data on Consequent Neolithic subsistence and especially the nature of the settlement systems are quite different in the various major ecological zones of central Europe, one can infer that there was probably regional variation in the nature of the subsistence systems as well. As in the Primary Neolithic, the nature of the settlement system has been presumed to reflect underlying economic factors, and particular importance has been attached to the nature of the changes in settlement distribution from Primary to Consequent Neolithic. That there were changes is difficult to dispute in light of the research of the last 20 years. The real issue lies in the interpretation of these changes as reflecting economic shifts, particularly in the agricultural regime.

Risk, dispersal, and intensification in the loess belt
The shift from a valley-bottom settlement distribution during the Primary Neolithic in the loess belt to an interfluve-margin distribution in parts of the loess belt in the late fourth millennium bc has led some archaeologists to infer a shift from the intensive "horticulture" of the Linear Pottery culture and its successors to an extensive agricultural regime based on swidden agriculture. This hypothesis was originally formulated by Janusz Kruk as an interpretation for the changes observed in settlement patterns on the loess uplands of southern Poland (Kruk 1973, 1980). The fundamental premise of this hypothesis is that the dispersal of settlement and the exploitation of the drier interfluve margins are the archaeologic-

al correlates of an extensive agricultural regime, using shifting slash-and-burn techniques. The assumption is made that the drier, higher parts of the valley slopes and watershed margins would have been better-suited to extensive techniques, and hence the occupation of these areas by dispersed farming settlements indicates that such a technique was, in fact, used.

Before this model enters the archaeological literature as "fact" in the same way that the notion of Primary Neolithic cyclical agriculture had in the 1960s, I would like to call attention to the fact that a shift in agricultural techniques to an extensive regime may not be automatically presumed to account for the change in settlement locations. In fact, it is possible to infer exactly the opposite. Jochim (1981: 155) has pointed out that "intensive farming ... may encourage population dispersal." The heavy and frequent work inputs of intensive horticulture may lead farmers to save effort in travel time to and from their plots by locating their residences nearby. Moreover, Jochim notes a connection between land scarcity and the need for farmers to protect their crops and fields, which would also encourage the dispersion of population.

There are no compelling reasons for equating the dispersal of settlement with extensive agricultural practices. Rather, it can be seen as a method of increasing the efficiency of energy capture by the subsistence system as a whole under the constraints of the linear patterns of optimal resource zones in the loess belt. The loess landscape was a relatively homogeneous environment, in which the soil was fertile but dry and the water sources were confined to streams. The valley bottoms probably would have remained the agricultural land of choice due to their mineral richness from flooding and slope wash. It is difficult to argue that a substantial portion of the agricultural activity shifted to the interfluves during the Consequent Neolithic. The richness of the valley bottoms and lower slopes would have been maintained through centuries of agricultural use through the continual refreshment of their nutrient content. Rather, local population growth within particular microregions may have resulted in greater demands on sections of the floodplains than during the Primary Neolithic, leading to a continuation of the linear expansion of agricultural lands away from the settlements. The costs of this expansion, particularly in travel time to and from fields and pastures, would have been a strong impetus for the decentralization of settlement.

It should also be remembered that agricultural products did not constitute the sole subsistence base of the Consequent Neolithic communities of the loess belt. In addition to grain and garden crops, it is probable that wild plants were also important, as was dairy production. Large nucleated settlements, after a certain point, are not the most efficient configuration for the exploitation of wild plant resources, for the environmental degradation that would result after even several years of exploitation would lead to increasing amounts of seed plants at the expense of the productive tubers and rhizomes. Rather, a much more effective settlement configuration for the exploitation of low-density wild plant resources is a dispersed pattern of small farmsteads, hamlets, and exploitation camps. The same holds true for the dairy sector of the economy, in which the need to provide sufficient grazing and forage for the herds would have been facilitated by the keeping of small groups of animals at separated sites rather than larger groups of stock at nucleated sites.

In fact, the shift from valley bottom settlements to the interfluve margins may be correlated with a greater reliance on animal resources in the economy of the Consequent Neolithic settlements, as a number of individuals have suggested began at this time (Sherratt 1983; Starling 1985). The valley bottoms, with their denser forests and alder carrs, had certain drawbacks for the keeping of large herds of livestock. Although water was more readily available in the valley floors, the stocking rates per unit of area were probably somewhat greater in the lighter forests of the drier interfluves. One possible explanation of the shift from the floodplain settlements to the interfluve margins was that this constituted a compromise, especially in terms of travel time, between the two major components of the subsistence economy, agriculture and stockherding.

Additional ecological perspectives can be brought to bear on the issue of settlement dispersal in the loess belt during the Consequent Neolithic. The loess landscape has a relatively small number of habitats when compared with the other major ecological zones of central Europe. Kruk (1973) identified them as the valley bottoms, the interfluve slopes, and the interfluve interiors. The large nucleated settlement clusters of the Primary Neolithic would have created anthropogenic ecosystems in particular microregions, but beyond the limits of these settlement clusters, the loess uplands would have had the same low degree of environmental diversity, and hence of productivity. The dispersal of settlement during the Consequent Neolithic would have had the effect of counteracting this broader environmental homogeneity by imposing an artificial patchiness on it. The dispersed settlement locations and field locations would have opened up more of the landscape on a broader scale than the old Primary Neolithic settlement clusters. The decentralization of Consequent Neolithic settlement would have had the effect of increasing the diversity of the environment in terms of the overall amount of resources which could be efficiently exploited in any particular microregion.

There are thus many reasons why it is not necessary to invoke a shift to extensive, slash-and-burn agriculture to explain the dispersal of Consequent Neolithic settlement in the loess belt. Rather, it can be seen as a method of increasing the efficiency of energy capture by the subsistence system as a whole within the constraints of the linear patterns of resource zones in the loess landscape. In fact, it is possible to argue with equal conviction that the shift in settlement patterns from Primary to Consequent Neolithic in the loess belt may actually indicate an *intensification* of the agricultural regime rather than a change to extensive agriculture.

The dispersal of settlement would have made more sense in the context of a strategy of intensification rather than one of extensification. The argument here returns to the question of environmental risks discussed previously in connection with the Primary Neolithic and the strategies for minimizing fluctuations in subsistence yields. The Primary Neolithic approach seems to have been one of risk-pooling and reliance on an interregional network of kinship ties. The environmental risks and fluctuations in crop yields which had been a factor during the Primary Neolithic did not disappear with time. The major difference from an adaptive perspective between the Primary and Consequent Neolithic in the loess belt was a growing familiarity with the variability in local habitats as well as a better agronomic sense of what worked and what did not. Nonetheless, the external factors such as crop blights and epizoötic diseases still were present, and there was a continued risk of subsistence shortfalls and outright crop failures. In addition, there was a new complication in the increased climatic variability which set in about 3400 bc (Schütrumpf and Schmidt 1977) and which seems to have led to the Piora cold phase several centuries later (Zoller 1977). The problem here was not the absolute effect of the changes in mean temperatures but rather the unpredictability of the climate from one year to the next which was introduced into the system. A factor which had been previously been relatively constant now began fluctuating.

I have described the loess habitat as relatively homogeneous, especially the interfluves between streams. Nonetheless, it is homogeneous only in relative terms, when compared to the other main habitats colonized by early farmers in central Europe, the North European Plain and the Alpine Foreland, where the greater variation in soils provides a dimension not found on the loess. There are, of course, variations in productivity between different areas within the loess belt and even locally, between floodplains and interfluves. In addition, there are highly localized differences in soil nutrients, precipitation, hydrology, temperature, and wind that would become apparent only after a group had become intimately familiar with a particular region.

Primary Neolithic fields had been concentrated on the floodplains and floodplain margins to take advantage of the "energy subsidy" that these areas offered. Nonetheless, there may have been areas of the interfluves which had a combination of the above factors which also made them attractive for cultivation. As these factors, which may not have been immediately obvious, were identified and mapped, a diversification in the types of field locations would be expected. Many of the non-pedological factors mentioned above would have been beyond the control of the Neolithic farmers. As a result, one can also see the diversification in field locations as part of a risk-minimization strategy, in which fields are located in a variety of zones in order to avoid the possibility of having the entire crop lost. In a situation of increasing environmental variability, this would have made even more sense, for certain factors would have selectively affected different configurations of hydrology and exposure.

Such a strategy of locational diversification does not result in an "extensification" of the agricultural system. On the contrary, it would require an intensification in the amount of labor, time, and energy expended in cultivation and travel to fields. There is no reason to assume that the duration of field use and the density of planting would have been changed. It should be remembered that Kruk's hypothesis of a shift from intensive floodplain horticulture to extensive interfluvial shifting cultivation was based on the idea that the interfluves would be more "suited" to slash-and-burn agriculture. This argument has gained such wide currency that to argue the opposite may not meet with a positive reception. Nonetheless, there are numerous reasons why the dispersal of settlement during the Consequent Neolithic is a reflection of an intensification in agricultural production.

Most importantly, the dispersal of settlement may be seen as an effort to minimize the investment of time in activity which is not directly productive, specifically travel time to and from fields and other locations of subsistence activity. If the fields were spread around a variety of zones within the loess landscape, it would seem to make sense to choose settlement locations which averaged out the travel time among them. The interfluve margins would have been quite suitable, for they form an intermediate location between the floodplains below and the potential areas for field locations in the interiors of the interfluves. A Neolithic household located here would have easy access to both areas. In addition, the location of settlements on higher terrain would have had other benefits. It would have given the inhabitants a better view of the surrounding countryside for spotting game, weather, and attackers, as well as providing a more defensible position. Moreover, the damp floodplains may have had high concentrations of insects and microfauna which would have contributed to disease transmission, decay of structures, and spoilage of stored crops.

It should also be remembered that field agriculture was not the only element in the Neolithic subsistence system in central Europe. Animal husbandry, and to a lesser degree hunting and collecting, also played a role in the subsistence economy. The concentration of Primary Neolithic settlement in tight agglomerations would have resulted in local depression of the availability of the browse that would have supported herds and in the amount of the subsidiary wild animal and plant resources. The interfluves would have been relatively poor in some of these subsidiary resources, particularly in wild fauna, but if certain species, particularly large wild herbivores like red deer, had become totally unavailable in parts of the floodplains, the exploitation of the populations inhabiting the interfluves might have been necessary. For stockherding, the interfluves may have been better suited in some instances than the floodplains, in that the drier and more open forests of the interfluves may have been better for grazing than the alder carrs and gallery forests of the lower zones.

When considered in the context of risk minimization strategies, it becomes unnecessary to invoke radical changes in the subsistence system to account for the changes in settlement patterns seen in the late fourth millennium bc in the loess belt. Instead of a shift to extensive slash-and-burn agriculture, the dispersal of settlement and the shift from floodplains to interfluves can be explained by a dispersal of field locations and a need to intensively exploit a wide variety of different biotic zones within the loess habitat.

Agriculture and indigenous foragers on the North European Plain
The establishment of agrarian communities on the North European Plain was quite different from the spread of farming settlements in the loess belt. Although the small indigenous foraging populations on the loess played a role in the spread of Primary Neolithic settlement, the extension of agriculture and stockherding onto the North European Plain occurred in areas where there were substantial

populations of hunter-gatherers. On the North European Plain, there is a clearer case for the derivation of the Consequent Neolithic communities from these local foraging populations (Schwabedissen 1981, among others.) It is very difficult to interpret the data from these sites as indicating the widespread colonization of these zones by the descendants of the Primary Neolithic communities of the loess belt and the subsequent displacement and replacement of local foraging popula- tions. There were cases of late Primary Neolithic outliers in these areas such as the Brześć Kujawski Group of the Polish Lowlands, but by 3000 bc, agriculture and stockherding had been adopted by indigenous foragers well beyond the immediate vicinity of these agrarian communities. The key issue is not so much from where the first farmers of the North European Plain came but rather *why* indigenous populations who apparently had a successful foraging adaptation began to exhibit a greater degree of sedentism and to explore the use of domesticated plants and animals.

Towards the end of the fifth millennium bc, the Mesolithic populations of the North European Plain appear to have undergone a considerable reduction in the size of their home ranges as well as a certain degree of population growth. One indicator of this is the development of possible Mesolithic "social territories" reflected in both artifact types and the distribution of raw materials (Gendel 1984; Vang Petersen 1984). Another indicator is an increase in the number of sites found in particular microregions. Across the North European Plain, in areas such as the Dümmer basin, the Satrup Moor, and the Plonia Valley, Mesolithic populations grew and became attached closely to certain habitats.

In the early fourth millennium bc, some of these regional adaptations approached sedentism, or at least "low mobility." Bocek (1985) has reviewed the conditions under which hunter-gatherer sedentism is likely to occur and notes that there is a strong correlation between non-mobile exploitation strategies and productive, predictable, and diverse ecosystems. All of these ecological variables are, of course, interrelated, and they are characteristic of many parts of the North European Plain. Although most sedentary hunter-gatherers are found in maritime habitats (e.g. coastal Peru or the Northwest Coast), Bocek notes that wetlands in lacustrine and riverine environments also commonly support low-mobility hunter- gatherer occupations. Examples of such adaptations are known from many parts of the world, and there are many habitats on the North European Plain that represent similar lacustrine, estuarine, and riverine environments with their attendant productivity and diversity. It is not unreasonable to infer that the wetlands in environments such as the Satrup Moor, the Dümmer basin, and the Rhine/Maas delta, among others, supported growing low-mobility hunter-gatherer populations by the mid-fourth millennium bc.

Coeval with the progressive decrease in the mobility of the indigenous hunter- gatherer populations of the North European Plain was the establishment nearby of Primary Neolithic agrarian communities and their congeners. On the North European Plain, Lengyel and Rössen sites are found in the same lacustrine and riverine zones which would have supported the non-mobile hunter-gatherer populations. For example, in the lake belt of the Polish Lowlands, sites of the

Brześć Kujawski Group represent a rare example of Primary Neolithic communities located outside of the loess belt. The large longhouse settlements, such as Brześć Kujawski and Krusza Zamkowa, are not much different from loess belt sites, but they are in a markedly different ecological zone. It is important to note, however, that they are not located in the very same type of habitat occupied by the indigenous foragers of this area. For the most part, sites of the Brześć Kujawski Group are found on glacial boulder clay, where fertile patches of Kuyavian "black earth" (a non-aeolian sediment) approximated the loess. In contrast, the Mesolithic and Consequent Neolithic sites of the Polish Lowlands are found on the sandy soils of the glacial meltwater channels and in the wetlands of the major river valleys. These two habitat types, however, are often adjacent or within a few kilometers of each other.

A different situation appears to have existed in the Dümmer basin. The Rössen component at Hüde I lacks the trapezoidal longhouses that characterize sites of this culture in the loess belt. The Rössen pottery at Hüde I also seems different from that made in the loess belt, although petrological analysis indicates that some vessels were made elsewhere. It is still uncertain whether the Rössen settlement at Hüde I represents a special-purpose site established by Primary Neolithic farmers in a productive habitat or the adaptation of Rössen ceramics by an indigenous sedentary foraging community.

In Chapter 5, the likelihood of interaction between indigenous foraging populations and Primary Neolithic farmers was discussed, and it appears probable that on the fringes of Primary Neolithic settlement in the loess belt various types of reciprocal relationships existed between farmers and foragers. In addition to the inferences possible from artifact types such as the so-called "Limburg pottery", Gregg's (1986) simulation of the nutritional requirements of Primary Neolithic communities suggests that there was a need for both agricultural and hunter-gatherer populations to exchange particular resources at certain times of the year. If this was the case, then it would appear that the outlying Primary Neolithic sites on the North European Plain would have entered into particularly close relationships with indigenous foragers. Communities like Brześć Kujawski and Krusza Zamkowa, separated by some distance from their congeners in the loess belt, would have been somewhat cut off from the mutual support network hypothesized in Chapter 5, and the economic relationships with neighboring foragers could have substituted for such a network.

It seems naive to assume that the hunter-gatheres involved in such relationships would not pick up a fundamental awareness of the agrarian economy. In fact, as Dennell (1985: 136) has noted, hunter-gatherers in such situations may be better informed about agriculture than farmers about foraging. By itself, the mere proximity of food production is no longer a reason to assume that they would have automatically adopted agriculture and stockherding, however. The disincentives to adopting food production for foragers are well known: they can usually eat better, stay healthier, and work less than their agricultural neighbors. Nonetheless, as Dennell (1985: 124) has noted, the agrarian lifestyle may have held some attractiveness for certain segments of the hunter-gatherer populations, particularly adolescents. It would have been precisely this constituency which would have been able to enter into integral relatioships with agrarian households by marrying into them and supplying them with additional labor. For an isolated Primary Neolithic community like Brześć Kujawski, the local foragers could have been a good source of mates, if the principle of household and community exogamy was strictly observed.

Hunter-gatherers will readily alter their subsistence strategies if they perceive that they will find it advantageous. In Chapter 3, I described the potential limitations on subsistence options posed by the increasing non-mobility and growing populations of the indigenous foragers of central Europe. One response to such limitations on the options normally afforded by mobility would have been the manipulation of the forest ecosystem to increase plant foods and game browse through deliberate burning. The artificial ecosystem maintained through burning, with plants at various stages in the vegetational succession, would have been structurally very similar to a tropical swidden. Such a pattern of environmental manipulation and intensified local resource procurement would have been a fertile situation for the integration of domestic plants and animals into the Mesolithic economy.

Many foraging groups around the world have been known to experiment with cultivation on a small scale. The Agta of the Philippines, often considered to be exclusively hunter-gatherers, are in fact "generalists" who experiment with whatever subsistence strategy feeds the most people at a particular time and location (Griffin 1985: 117). Hunter-gatherers in contact with agriculturalists rarely, if ever, retain their "pristine" subsistence systems, since domestic plants and animals are all too easily incorporated into the economy of a flexible group of foragers. The fundamental question is not how the hunter-gatherer populations of central Europe acquired the ability to farm and raise domestic livestock but rather *why* they chose to make these pursuits key economic strategies so that by the mid-third millennium bc, agriculture and stockherding were the key subsistence practices on the North European Plain.

The answer may lie in the climatic changes which occurred between 3500 and 3000 bc, coupled with the overall trend toward sedentism and population growth observed in the Mesolithic communities. A crucial limiting factor for Mesolithic communities in central Europe was a storable winter source of carbohydrates. Several were available – cattail rhizomes, hazel nuts, wild grass seeds – but none would have been reliable from year to year, particularly within circumscribed exploitation territories. The inherent unpredictability of these resources was overlaid with an additional source of variation with the onset of unsettled climatic conditions after about 3300 bc. Until this time, annual climatic variation, especially in rainfall, held within a narrow range, while the period after 3300 bc was characterized by considerably greater annual variation, including some very cold years (Zoller 1977; Schütrumpf and Schmidt 1977). Although the yields from domestic grain may not have been any more predictable, they would have provided an additional high-density storable resource which could have helped to support a foraging and farming group through the winter.

The incorporation of domestic plants into the intensively exploited habitats of the North European Plain may have had the ancillary effect of concentrating animal resources in more limited areas as well. In the faunal assemblages from some sites, such as Bistoft LA 11, the number of bones of red deer and wild pigs is quite striking. Red deer in particular would have flourished on the forest edges and in cultivated fields, and it is possible that an exploitation pattern on the model of the "garden hunting" proposed by Linares (1976) for the American tropics was practiced. In garden hunting, animals are hunted in cultivated fields and gardens as they are attracted to the growing crops. Some degree of crop loss to animal pests is considered acceptable, since the net effect is to concentrate the animals in the gardens and fields and thus reduce the expenditure in time and energy in hunting them. Moreover, the biomass of certain species increases when permitted access to cultivated crops. In garden hunting, still practiced by a number of Central and South American groups such as the Guaymi and Cuna, protein from wild animals becomes a by-product of farming. One way of testing the possibility that a similar strategy was followed by some Neolithic communities would be to examine the seasonal indicators such as tooth eruption and dental annuli in the pig and deer bones from sites like Bistoft LA 11 to see if the animals were in fact killed during the growing season.

Although the initial use of cultigens by the indigenous hunter-gatherers of the North European Plain may have been a tactical response to resource deficits, the well-known feedback cycle that commits a group to agriculture once it relies on domestic plants to meet dietary minima may have set in. Nonetheless, the use of domestic plants and animals may not have been integrated into the indigenous subsistence patterns of the North European Plain in a steady, unilinear fashion (although archaeologically the transition appears to have taken place fairly rapidly). The foragers-turned-farmers of these areas may have gone through cycles of population growth, intensified foraging, incipient farming, and back again, or fluctuating between primarily foraging and primarily farming. It is important to avoid viewing the transformation of an essentially fluid exploitation pattern as a pair of "snapshots" showing the beginning and end states only. The great degree of variability seen in the subsistence data from these sites perhaps reflects this fluidity over time in addition to spatial variation.

Animals and subsistence in the Consequent Neolithic

It was during the Consequent Neolithic that the complex of subsistence practices associated with animal husbandry which Sherratt calls the "Secondary Products Revolution" occurred. In its most general terms, the Secondary Products Revolution consists of a horizon marked by the initial appearance of several animal-related economic traits: dairy and wool production and cattle traction for the ard and cart. Whether this "revolution" represented a true economic transformation or whether it was simply the elaboration of a number of traits which had their roots deeper in antiquity is problematical (see Chapman 1982 for a critique). In Chapter 5 above, for instance, it was argued that dairying was practiced even during the Primary Neolithic. The use of animals for traction, however, represents a significant development in Neolithic life and may, in fact, be another reflection of some social developments suggested by other aspects of the archaeological record.

The dispersal of Consequent Neolithic "generic" settlements, in contrast to the denser groups of Primary Neolithic sites of the loess belt, has been interpreted here as reflecting the emergence of relatively independent households. In Chapter 5, I had proposed that a major consideration of any Neolithic community was the size of its available labor pool, particularly for land clearance and harvest, and that the size of the Primary Neolithic site groupings perhaps represented an effort to pool the labor force and its investment in the risk assumed by the community. Such large communities had other drawbacks, however, and the emergence of smaller hamlets and farmsteads in the Consequent Neolithic meant that individual households assumed a greater measure of the risk. To deal with this phenomenon, a variety of measures appear to have been taken, a number of which are discussed below. An immediate problem, however, would have been to extract the same or greater expenditure of energy from a reduced labor pool *per household*, and it is perhaps in this connection that the evidence for ploughing and wheeled vehicles becomes especially significant.

The labor-saving value of both inventions is quite apparent, in that they allow human energy expenditures in tillage and transport to be shifted onto the livestock. The labor required to manufacture the ards and wagons could be expended at times of the year when there was less to do in the realm of subsistence activities and more for the maintenance of structures and implements. It does not seem particularly reasonable to assume that the primary purpose of wheeled vehicles was for long-distance transport. Central European terrain, particularly the grades in the loess belt and the Alpine Foreland and the water barriers in the lowlands, would appear to preclude much long-distance use of carts before better tracks and roads were developed. Rather, it seems much more likely that Neolithic vehicles were used in a utility capacity within a short distance of settlements, transporting bulky items such as harvested crops, firewood, timber, animal carcasses, and the like, rather than exotic commodities like copper ingots between settlements. In such a utility role, their labor-saving value would have been maximized.

If it was possible to use animals for traction with wheeled vehicles, certainly other uses would have been known as well. One possible use of animal traction, which could even pre-date the use of wheeled vehicles, would have been in forest clearance by dragging away felled trees. These could then be cut up more gradually on the side, rather than as a prerequisite for clearance of the intended field. It has been argued in this volume and elsewhere that slash-and-burn was probably not used in Neolithic European agriculture, and thus the ashes from the felled trees were not needed to maintain field fertility. Again, the use of animal traction in this capacity would have promoted the existence of the household as a discrete productive unit by reducing the need to depend on neighboring households for activities requiring pooled labor.

Finally, ploughing would have been of significant benefit in maintaining soil fertility through aeration and incorporation of new organic material. In the loess belt, it would have freed Consequent Neolithic households from their dependence

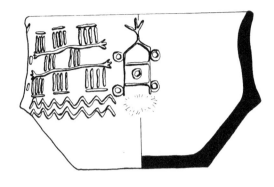

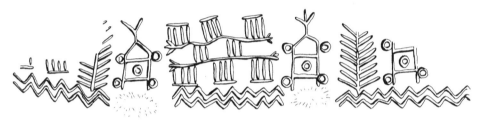

Fig. 6.20 Decoration on vessel from Bronocice believed to depict a wheeled vehicle (after Milisauskas and Kruk 1982: plate 8).

on energy-subsidized floodplain habitats, enabling the occupation of the inter-fluves described by Kruk (1973) and others. In the lowlands, it would have been ideally suited to the lighter, sandier soils favored by the nascent agrarian communities. In any event, it would seem that ploughing would have been incompatible with any sort of extensive agricultural regime, and its use can be taken to reflect continued intensive agriculture. As was noted above, this argument contradicts one of the fundamental tenets of recent Neolithic settlement studies, which argue for an "extensification" of agriculture during this period. Ploughing would promote the concentration of farming on a much more limited parcel of land and increase in effectiveness if regeneration were suppressed, even perhaps through annual cropping.

7

The consequences of food production

Just as subsistence practices and settlement patterns differed between the North European Plain and the loess belt, so the social correlates of these varied as well. The mythical Neolithic "package deal" dissolved still further. In large part, this variation is due to the role that the indigenous foragers played in the new agrarian economy, which in turn derived from the ecological conditions which determined the distribution of the hunter-gatherer populations. In the discussion below, then, it will be necessary to be explicit about the locale of the change in question: was it a general phenomenon or was it peculiar either to the loess belt or to the North European Plain.

In the discussion of Consequent Neolithic developments in the loess belt, a key assumption is that – as did the Primary Neolithic longhouses – the small "generic" settlements represent the archaeological remains of independent households. This assumption is extraordinarily difficult to prove except by recourse to the ethnographic generalization that the fundamental unit of production in small-scale agrarian societies is the household and that the discrete Consequent Neolithic settlements of the loess belt suggest independent productive units. For the North European Plain, this assumption is more problematical, since the ephemeral and extensive nature of many of the sites makes it difficult to isolate individual habitation units. The overall impression, particularly from the larger habitation sites, is that the occupation is by groups somewhat larger than a nuclear household but not at the level of the agglomeration of several such units. One hypothesis would be that they represent some sort of extended household that possibly would have been not far removed from a foraging band in its structure.

The model of Primary Neolithic social interaction proposed in Chapter 5 was one of very broad interregional ties as part of a mechanism for offsetting subsistence shortfalls. The emergence of dispersed household settlement during the Consequent Neolithic and an apparent decrease in broad geographical mobility options does not necessarily mean that these households were wholly autonomous or that these interregional ties atrophied completely. Rather, the transformation appears to have been much more subtle, leading to a degree of regional integration within individual *Siedlungskammern* that set the stage for the emergence of true regional polities during the Late Neolithic and Early Bronze Age.

The Social Consequences of Food Production
The establishment of what appears to be a relatively stable pattern of agrarian settlements in the area initially occupied by the Primary Neolithic communities

now makes it possible to return to a consideration of social organization. In European prehistory, there is a general tendency to see the development of Neolithic social organization in evolutionary terms, from lesser to greater degrees of complexity. A case was made above for the essentially egalitarian nature of Primary Neolithic society, noting that there were various factors in the process of the agrarian colonization of central Europe that may have suppressed trends towards any degree of ranking or hierarchy and which encouraged the maintenance of multilateral kinship links with other households. In the evolutionary model favored by European prehistorians, then, the successful establishment of an agrarian economy in central Europe should be followed quite rapidly by the establishment of unilineal kinship systems. But was this actually the case?

Kinship and social behavior
The focus on unilineal kinship systems in archaeology reflects the attention such systems have received in anthropology in general. Beyond the household, anthropologists have tended to focus their study on kinship systems in which activities, affiliations, and obligations are determined by unilineal descent. In particular, agrarian societies with such kinship systems have received a great deal of attention. As a result, a dichotomy between multilineal foraging bands and unilineal agrarian communities has, often implicitly, found its way into models of prehistoric social development. In some cases, the issue is one of terminology. For instance, Renfrew (1976) has characterized Neolithic society as "segmentary", by which he means simply that they do not have the centralized, hierarchical structure of the state. This is quite reasonable, except that the use of the term "segmentary" has entered anthropological literature in the context of the *segmentary lineage,* a particular form of unilineal social structure (Sahlins 1961). The concept of segmentary lineage systems is considered problematical by some social anthropologists, however. In fact, recent reanalysis suggests that the Nuer, a paradigmatic segmentary society in the literature of social anthropology, did not have any lineages, segmentary or otherwise (Verdon 1982). The inference that Neolithic societies in central Europe had this form of social organization is unfortunate, for there seems to be no reason to believe that the ecological conditions or population densities of Neolithic central Europe would have favored the emergence of such lineages.

Although some anthropologists would propose that a "lineage principle" operates in almost every society, it is important to realize that it is quite possible to have kinship and descent systems which are non-unilineal or "non-lineal" (Gulliver 1971). These are found today in many parts of the world, on virtually every continent and frequently among small-scale agrarian societies similar to those under consideration here. In particular, these non-lineal kinship systems are often characterized by low population densities, while the "classic" lineage systems, especially in Africa, are characterized by quite high densities. The relevance of this is that since lineages are exogamous corporate groups, they require quite substantial population densities over reasonably large areas in order to remain viable. Without being able to make specific estimates of the thresholds required, it appears that such densities were simply not present in central Europe before 2000 bc.

Goodenough, in fact, has argued that the crucial distinction is not so much between unilineal and non-unilineal societies as it is between those which have ancestor-based groups where common descent aggregates kinsmen into a corporation and those which have personal kin groups where groups of individuals have common relatives but not necessarily common ancestors (Goodenough 1961: 1343). Such personal, "ego-oriented" kin groups are commonly called "kindreds", although Gulliver (1971) has proposed a different way of conceptualizing these groups (see below). These groups are laterally organized, with relatively little linkage across many generations. The ancestor-based groups, on the other hand, may be either unilineal or non-unilineal, but always have considerable time-depth in their reckoning of kinship ties. Thus the question of whether or not Neolithic societies in temperate Europe developed segmentary lineages is somewhat irrelevant. Rather, the question is whether it made more sense to have kinship groups which were either lineal or lateral in the context of the ecological and social conditions which can be argued to have prevailed between 3500 and 2500 bc. The relatively low population densities on a regional level and the continued need for flexibility in social relationships would appear to argue strongly in favor of a model of non-lineal descent rather than a strict lineage system. Supporting such a model, though, necessitates a refocusing of attention away from the regional or territorial social grouping as a key element in Consequent Neolithic society to the individual residential units, the households.

Households and social organization
In the loess belt, the "generic" Consequent Neolithic settlements can be argued to represent household-size social units similar in structure to those contained in Primary Neolithic longhouses. The differences between the highly visible Primary Neolithic household remains and the more ephemeral Consequent Neolithic occupations can be accounted for in several ways. First, the high rate of population growth along the Neolithic frontier and in its wake probably meant that mean household size in the Primary Neolithic was somewhat larger, with a commensurate difference in the amount of refuse generated. Secondly, the average duration of a Primary Neolithic settlement seems to have been considerably longer than that of Consequent Neolithic settlement sites. Many Primary Neolithic sites seem to have been occupied for several hundred years, often over 10 or more generations, while many Consequent Neolithic sites seem to have occupation spans of under a hundred years, approximately five or fewer generations.

The result is that in the loess belt, there are many more Consequent Neolithic sites that appear to be *of shorter duration*, than there are Primary Neolithic sites. Arguments for substantial population increase during the Consequent Neolithic (e.g. Milisauskas and Kruk 1984), based on increased numbers of sites and their total areas, may be difficult to support. Instead, one might expect that the suppression of unrestrained population growth in the wake of what had been a frontier situation would be found in the Consequent Neolithic, as the demographic patterns discussed in Chapter 5 above (pp. 93-100) would suggest. If this is the case, then population levels during the Consequent Neolithic in the loess belt would have stayed approximately the same as found in later Primary Neolithic times, or even have declined somewhat.

One possible explanation for the decrease in occupation spans of Consequent Neolithic sites would be to link it with declining agricultural yields and increasing shifting of settlement to fresh soils. This explanation would be consistent with the Kruk hypothesis of an extensification of loess belt agriculture at this time, reflected in the dispersal of settlement along the interfluve margins. Yet above, I argued that this dispersal of settlement may actually reflect just the opposite phenomenon, one of the *intensification* of agriculture. If this argument is to be consistent, another way must be found to account for the reduction in settlement duration during the Consequent Neolithic.

The answer may lie in the viability of households through time and the differences in household viability between the Primary and Consequent Neolithic. By a household's "viability", I mean its ability to provide adequate labor and offspring to support itself as a discrete social unit. The question is not one of year-to-year, or season-to-season, survival, as it might have been during the Primary Neolithic, but rather one of the viability of the household unit across generations. The factors which may have conditioned the differences between the Primary and Consequent Neolithic would have included the demographic composition of individual households and the nature of exogamous social relationships on a regional scale.

A number of anthropologists have emphasized that domestic groups cannot be viewed as static but rather display changes over time, as old members age and die and new members are born and reach maturity (see, for instance, the essays in Goody (ed.) 1962). As a result, it is possible to view Neolithic settlements not as reflecting unchanging domestic groups but rather as the venues for changing patterns of social relationships among their members over time. Once such dynamic time-behavior is recognized, then it is possible to explore a new realm of explanations for features of the archaeological record instead of relying on external factors operating on unchanging social groups.

Of particular importance is the fact that households are established in some regular pattern, usually related to the betrothal or marriage of the founding husband and wife. They then pass through a series of developmental phases (Fortes 1962: 4–5). The first phase lasts from the marriage of the nuclear pair until the completion of their procreation. The second is one of dispersion or fission, during which the children form their own households. Finally, there is a phase of replacement, during which the founding pair dies (either physically or "socially") and their household is replaced by one formed by their heirs among their children. This process of succession is made possible through an orderly system of apportionment of the productive and reproductive resources of a household during the phase of dispersion.

The fission of domestic groups is normally translated into spatial separation, and the extent of this separation appears to have been amplified during the Consequent Neolithic. In the Primary Neolithic, new households appear to have been established within several hundred meters of the original homestead (until fissioning of the community on a broader scale took place), while new Consequent Neolithic households seem to have been located somewhat further afield. The reasons for this increased spatial separation are unclear, although it is possible that it is linked to a developing sense of household autonomy and the authority of the heads of individual households (an idea that is developed further below).

The orderly succession in households from one generation to the next also depends on the existence of suitable heirs able and willing to take over the physical household of their parents. If Primary Neolithic households had more offspring than Consequent Neolithic ones (an undocumentable assertion but within the realm of possibility), then the likelihood that such an heir would exist within a particular household would have been larger, on the average. A smaller pool of potential heirs would increase the potential for all of them to be unable or unwilling to take over the parental homestead, leading to its eventual abandonment. Offspring of one gender (depending on the exogamous marriage rules) would go off to join other families, while other potential heirs might die prematurely, become estranged, or otherwise be unwilling to take over. The Primary Neolithic houses themselves, solidly constructed with a high investment of labor, would have provided some incentive for heirs to continue to occupy their ancestral homestead as long as possible. Consequent Neolithic settlements, however, may not have been so attractive after several generations, and abandonment may have been a reasonable option. The ultimate result of such changed patterns of household establishment and decreased household size was that while agglomerated Primary Neolithic communities could last for several hundred years, with households succeeding each other within a spatially concentrated area, the dispersed Consequent Neolithic households had the odds stacked against their remaining viable social units in one location for more than five or so generations.

The identification of the Consequent Neolithic sites of the loess belt as dispersed households indicates that the real implication of the shift in settlement patterns observed between the Primary and Consequent Neolithic may be one of household autonomy rather than of a shift in the agricultural system. Although the Primary Neolithic sites were composed of individual households, there still appears to have been a considerable degree of joint decision-making involving groups of households perhaps linked very closely by kinship and other interests. With the firm establishment of agriculture in central Europe by appearance of the Consequent Neolithic in the loess belt, whatever decision-making occurred seems to have taken place primarily on the level of the individual household, especially concerning settlement location and, by inference, about the allocation of various resources.

Clearly, however, these individual households could not exist in a vacuum, since there must have been a formal structure of kinship and marriage rules. One effect of the dispersal of households was that the pool of available mates would have been considerably enlarged. There are two ways that this was brought about. The first is that the dispersal of settlement meant that inter-household contact was less structured, although by no means less important. Rather than one Primary Neolithic settlement cluster relying for support on a limited number of other settlement clusters, some or all of which were presumably linked by very direct kinship ties, the Consequent Neolithic household could deal with a range of other dispersed settlements, within and outside its home microregion. There was thus more opportunity for contact with households which presumably contained suitable mates, rather than with households which were already kin and hence unacceptable sources for further mates. The somewhat greater certainty of the subsistence system also meant that the need to call on the support of other households may have been less frequent, thus putting inter-household interaction on a more social basis rather than out of dire necessity.

The other benefit of the settlement dispersal would have been that the size of the operative exogamous unit would have been decreased, opening up new possibilities in terms of mate selection. The tight kinship links hypothesized to have existed within the clusters of Primary Neolithic settlements meant that it would have been almost always necessary to look outside for acceptable mates. The Consequent Neolithic households, on the other hand, probably would have been more loosely linked to most of the other households in the same microregion, while directly linked to a limited number. The result would have been that previous linkages which would inhibit the further intermarriage would be with smaller-scale exogamous units. As generations passed, these linkages would have either been forgotten or diluted to the point where further intermarriage between two households would be acceptable. In other words, the marriages would be between individual households rather than groups of households. The net effect of this would have been that the sort of "intermarriage gridlock" suggested for the Primary Neolithic settlement clusters would have been ameliorated by the greater number of potential sources of mates on a local level.

Although this discussion of household dynamics has been highly speculative, the key proposition is that the Consequent Neolithic of the loess belt saw the further expression of the household as the fundamental unit of Neolithic organizational structure. The increasing familiarity with particular regions and the desire for greater social autonomy may have been the root causes for the dispersal of settlement so often interpreted as a reflection of changing subsistence patterns. Of course, this proposition is a hypothesis which will require testing, but so is the theory of agricultural extensification which others have proposed to account for settlement dispersal and shorter occupation spans. In fact, a social basis rather than an economic basis for this shift would better account for the fact that different *Siedlungskammern* display different configurations of settlement distribution.

Kin-sets, action-sets, and networks
On ecological grounds, then, a case can be made for the maintenance of flexible systems of social relationships, based largely at the household level. A lineal system of social organization, with its linkages across generations, would have greatly limited the social options of young members of individual households, given the ecological circumstances of the loess belt. Instead, a flexible system of personal kin groups, which could be defined and re-defined by individuals, would have made much more sense. Thus households, and their heads, are the critical elements of Neolithic society, rather than corporate lineages. The question now becomes one of

how to conceptualize Consequent Neolithic social interaction once agrarian households and communities are attached to particular microregions over a number of generations and once the factors which hindered the development of social differentiation were reduced in importance.

Gulliver (1971: 16–27) has developed some useful conceptual tools in analyzing non-lineal kinship, which in turn may be useful in thinking about Consequent Neolithic society. The first of these is the "kin-set", which is the group of individuals with whom a person has cognatic and affinal links and with which he maintains an active relationship. The kin-set is usually smaller that the total number of an individual's kin, but it generally has no fixed boundaries. These are the people against whom a person can exercise claims, with whom he cooperates, and to whom he acknowledges obligations. Gulliver (1971: 18) emphasizes that the kin-set is a social category, not a social group.

From time to time, an individual may need to seek the support of members of his kin-set, although it is unlikely that he will call on all of them at any one time. Gulliver terms the ad hoc subsets of the kin-set called upon by a person to take collective action on his behalf the "action-set" (1971: 18). The action-set is a temporary constituency, recruited for a particular purpose, then disbanded. Its composition depends on a number of factors, including the nature of the collective action, the special talents of certain individuals in the kin-set, pressures of time and competing interests, residential proximity, and the personal relations between kin. Rarely do action-sets recruited by the same indivdual have identical compositions, and those recruited by different individuals are based on different kin-sets. Most importantly, an action-set is not a corporate group which has some permanence but rather an ephemeral collection of individuals mobilized by one or a few members for collective action.

If an individual consistently mobilizes the same body of supporters and is recognized as a successful leader, there is the possibility of the emergence of a political faction. In societies with strict unilineal forms of organization, participation in political activity is often limited to those from the proper lineages. The implication of the model of action-sets in non-unilineal societies is that individuals in them can rise to political prominence regardless of descent. This theme will be taken up further later in this chapter.

The kin-set of any one individual, however, overlaps and interlocks with those of many others. This is important, for the degree to which an individual can mobilize others for concerted action does not stop with the limits of his own kin-set. In other words, the action-set can go beyond the limits of the kin-set, forging new relationships outside those normally recognized on the basis of kinship (although with time, such relationships can be formalized through fictive kin links). Gulliver terms the broader web of non-lineal kinship connections within a society a "network." Although theoretically unbounded and infinite, a real network contains some fault lines, determined by geography, common interests, and other limits on interaction.

It may be possible, then, to view Consequent Neolithic social organization in the loess belt as a network of personal kin-sets, theoretically unbounded but effectively separated by the spacing between microregions within individual *Siedlungskammern* and the relatively uninhabited zones between *Siedlungskammern*. There seems to be no compelling reason to argue that lineages were an immediate and inevitable result of the establishment of stable agrarian communities in the loess belt. Instead, a focus on lateral ties between individuals and households would have made much more sense from a social and an economic point of view. This is not to argue that the Consequent Neolithic communities of the loess belt were absolutely egalitarian. Significantly, some degree of ranking is not incompatible with non-lineal descent, but the ranking is one along lines of age, gender, and influence rather than a hereditary position. This theme will be taken up again later in this chapter.

Foragers turned farmers on the North European Plain
The situation on the North European Plain during this period seems to have been rather different. The actual impression from sites such as Poganice is one of social groups larger than simple households taking up a settled agrarian lifestyle. The lack of discrete structures in settlements like Mosegården and Nowy Młyn suggests that the fundamental unit of socioeconomic organization was rather broader than the nuclear household, although there are then sites such as "Im Hassel" with a number of house outlines. Perhaps it may be more accurate to refer to it as a "descent group" consisting, perhaps, of several related families. Such descent groups could be expected to be outgrowths of the organizational structure of the indigenous foraging peoples of these areas, since the new agrarian communities were arguably composed largely of individuals descended from forager stock.

I noted in Chapter 3 that the general demographic trend during the Late Mesolithic of the North European Plain was towards larger and more concentrated populations. Nonetheless, there was a limit to the degree of this concentration, since their use of many different types of resources, both wild and domestic, necessitated home ranges that covered a wider area than the catchments of sites during this period in the loess belt. Moreover, there was a need for a certain degree of flexibility in residence locations, since the exploitation of these different resources was seasonal and probably, to some degree, opportunistic. As a result, the Consequent Neolithic social system of this area may have represented a compromise between the remnants of Mesolithic band structure and the new constraints and labor requirements posed by the agrarian element in the economy.

In contrast to the situation presented by the loess belt, this compromise may have provided the conditions for the emergence of lineal forms of social organization and descent in these areas. There would have been two crucial elements contributing to this. The first is the relatively larger size of the emergent agrarian social grouping derived from the band structure of the foraging society. If small households, founded when an individual reached social maturity, were not the fundamental social units, then each band-like unit may have had multiple representatives of several different generations. The trans-generational links that this situation may have fostered would have enhanced the opportunities for the emergence of ancestral patterns of kinship reckoning rather than ego-centered lateral networks. Second, the model of Consequent Neolithic resource exploitation

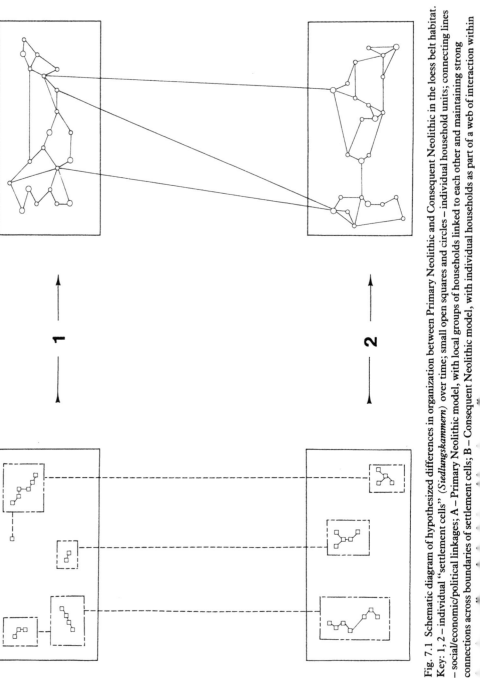

Fig. 7.1 Schematic diagram of hypothesized differences in organization between Primary Neolithic and Consequent Neolithic in the loess belt habitat. Key: 1, 2 – individual "settlement cells" (*Siedlungskammern*) over time; small open squares and circles – individual household units; connecting lines – social/economic/political linkages; A – Primary Neolithic model, with local groups of households linked to each other and maintaining strong connections across boundaries of settlement cells; B – Consequent Neolithic model, with individual households as part of a web of interaction within

on the North European Plain presented in Chapter 6 had a strongly territorial focus, rather than fixed settlements occupied by individual households as in the loess belt. In such a territorial system, it may be necessary to establish the rights of a group to a tract of land in ways other than the obvious location of a settlement. Thus, although overall population density was low, a group could establish its claim to a territory through its identification with ancestors who also controlled that territory. Once immoveable resources such as crops were involved, this territorial demarcation was doubly important. The hypothesis, then, is that in areas in which foragers adopted an agrarian economy, there were ecological considerations which promoted the development of lineal (but not necessarily unilineal!) systems of reckoning kinship.

On the North European Plain, this ancestor-based sense of corporate identification was expressed particularly vividly: the newly agricultural communities of this area began to build large burial monuments. Across the lowlands of northern central Europe, the adoption of agriculture by indigenous foragers is followed within a century or two by the appearance of monumental burial architecture. The basic form of the earliest such tombs in northern Poland and Germany is the unchambered long barrow, often with the mound outlined by a kerb of boulders. The plan of these structures can be either rectangular, as in the *Hünebedden* (from the Old German *Hüne* = "giant", thus "giant beds") of northern Germany, or trapezoidal, as in the case of the so-called "Kuyavian" long barrows of northern Poland. The Kuyavian tombs are directly associated with foci of Funnel Beaker settlement and are not found in areas of Primary Neolithic settlement in the lowland zone. Similarly, the *Hünebedden* are associated with the *Tiefstich* Funnel Beaker ware in the western province of this culture.

The most interesting aspect of these tombs, particularly in the Polish lowlands, is that they are often clustered in groups of up to ten. Of course, the surviving distribution is greatly affected by the extent to which these monuments have been leveled by later agricultural activity. Nonetheless, their distribution is different from that of the megalithic tombs along the Atlantic fringe of Europe, where each grave may be separated from the next coeval monument by several kilometers or more.

Although the tombs themselves are large, the actual burials are fairly simple, without elaborate ritual. A possible inference from this is that the tombs served a more global purpose in the Funnel Beaker social order than simply commemorating the deceased individual. Rather, it may be possible to view them as having a significance for the living members of the community which extended beyond their mortuary aspect.

It is in this connection that the increased tendency towards territorial grouping first observed during the late Mesolithic can be raised again. The shift from gathered plants and hunted game to domestic plants and animals necessitated one fundamental change in the foraging way of life. Whereas before there was a focus on spatially ubiquitous resources, the domestic plants would have been fixed in space prior to their harvest. While the Funnel Beaker agriculturalists eschewed the nucleated settlements of the Primary Neolithic farmers for smaller and more

Fig. 7.2 Reconstructed Kuyavian earthen long barrow at Sarnowo, site 1. Photo: Museum of Archaeology and Ethnography, Łódź, Poland.

ephemeral occupations, there would have been an even greater need to identify a "home range". The catchments exploited by the inhabitants of sites like Brześć Kujawski were defined by the central residential base and the radius exploited by its inhabitants. Funnel Beaker territories, on the other hand, would have been characterized by a number of small, discrete settlement locations, none having the permanency or visibility of residential bases like Brześć Kujawski. The establishment of clusters of earthen long barrows could have alleviated this problem, in that they clearly provided a central focus for the home range of a community of foragers-turned-farmers.

The notion of burial monuments as territorial markers of incipient agriculturalists was first brought forward by Colin Renfrew over a decade ago (C. Renfrew 1973, elaborated in Renfrew 1976). Renfrew's proposal dealt with newly agrarian groups seeking to preserve their territorial integrity in the face of encroaching farming populations. In his view, it is possible that megalithic tombs were erected to stake the claim over time of communities to particular territories as their ranges were reduced by the exogenous agricultural populations. The suggestion made here, however, is somewhat different in that the Funnel Beaker barrow builders had already adopted agriculture and domestic animals and were not in competition with exogenous agriculturalists for land or resources. Rather, the issue was one of local group territoriality, which could be seen developing through the regionalization of tool types during the late Mesolithic. The Funnel Beaker settlement system by itself did not establish the claim of a local group to a particular tract. So long as game was mobile and foraging resources ubiquitous this was not a problem. Once, however, fixed-location resources – cultivated plants – entered the picture, the

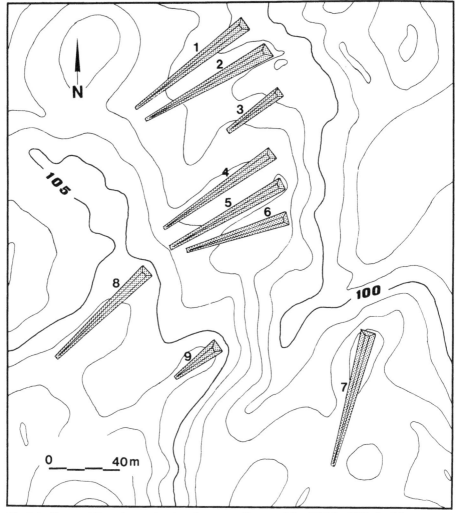

Fig. 7.3 Cluster of Kuyavian earthen long barrows at Sarnowo (after Midgley 1985: fig. 24).

situation took on a new complexion. The establishment of large, visible mortuary monuments would have been a way of mitigating this problem by defining a fixed focus to a home range in which the actual settlements were small and short-lived.

V. Gordon Childe was the first to remark on the similarity between the trapezoidal plans of the Kuyavian earthen long barrows and the longhouses at Brześć Kujawski and other sites (Childe 1949: 135). If these two types of remains were coeval, it would simply be a nice example of mortuary architecture imitating domestic architecture. There is, of course, a temporal separation between the Brześć Kujawski Group settlements at 3500–3200 bc and the Kuyavian tombs at 3100–2800 bc. Perhaps, however, these similarities are *not* coincidental. If the Kuyavian tombs played the same role in the territorial perception of the Funnel Beaker foragers-turned-farmers as the nucleated settlements did for the Primary Neolithic agriculturalists, then it is not unreasonable to expect some formal similarities between the two sorts of remains. For the farmers at sites like Brześć Kujawski, the fixed central settlement defined the focus of the home range. For the Funnel Beaker farmers elsewhere on the North European Plain, the groups of earthen long barrows may have defined the focus of a looser settlement system, yet one with a similar geographical extent.

If one accepts the notion that the development of lineal descent systems serves a similar function, then the rationale for the building of these monumental tombs is immediately apparent. These were, quite simply, the settlements of the ancestors, which legitimized the occupation of the surrounding territory using a subsistence-settlement system which did not lend itself to the establishment of long-term residential bases.

The Social Context of Exchange
The considerable evidence at Consequent Neolithic sites for the use of raw materials which were obtained from distant sources again brings up the issue of trade and exchange. In the earlier discussion of the Primary Neolithic, I argued that what archaeologists often perceive as commodity-exchange systems may only reflect household-level exchanges in the context of mutual assistance, bridewealth, and the like, and that formal trading networks did not really exist as such. It might be possible to make a similar case for the Consequent Neolithic, except for the existence of evidence which points towards the concerted exploitation of particular resources, especially flint, by the inhabitants of settlements near their sources. From this, it is possible to infer that there was a certain level of economic motivation behind the extraction and distribution of these resources beyond the level of household necessity. Moreover, there is evidence for the broader distribution of other non-subsistence resources, such as copper, well beyond their source areas and in a pattern which does not present a regular fall-off. These data also imply the existence of exchange networks which extended beyond the household economy.

At the outset, it is important to differentiate between two broad categories of materials, essential goods such as flint and subsistence products and "exotic" commodities such as copper and amber. Flint, of course, is of variable quality and unevenly distributed in central Europe, and many parts of the loess belt are some distance from the sources of the better flint. On the North European Plain, the main source of flint outside of Denmark and northern East Germany was the erratic flint pebbles which lay strewn across the landscape. The erratic flint is of very poor quality and unsuited to tasks which require a sharp, straight working edge (such as antler working). Copper during this period was not used for utilitarian products but rather was manufactured primarily into ornaments (Ottaway 1973). In fact, copper "awls" and other artifacts which have been identified as tools are more likely to represent scrap from ornament manufacture rather than finished products (certainly the case at Brześć Kujawski, for instance).

Some have suggested that the trade in "exotic" raw materials during this period was a mechanism for the regulation of a more vital trade in staple commodities, specifically subsistence resources and raw material for tools (e.g. Sherratt 1976).

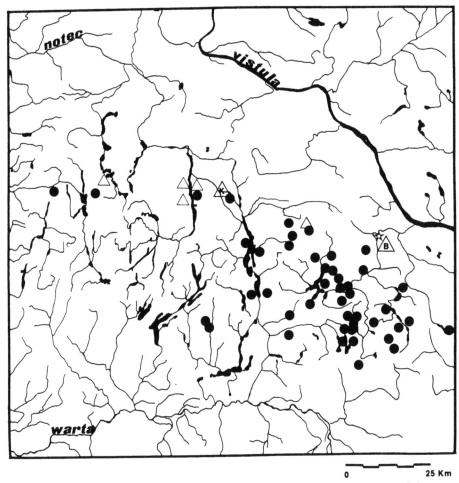

Fig. 7.4 Relationship between distribution of Funnel Beaker earthen long barrows and late Primary Neolithic settlements of the Brześć Kujawski Group in the eastern part of the Kuyavia region of Poland (distribution of barrows after Midgley 1985: fig. 5). Key: triangles – Brześć Kujawski Group settlements (B – Brześć Kujawski; K – Krusza Zamkowa); circles – Funnel Beaker barrows; star – Funnel Beaker settlement site at Nowy Młyn near Brześć Kujawski.

The continuous demand for imported copper, amber, and similar materials would have supported a parallel exchange in essential commodities. In question, however, are the dimensions of this demand and whether it was really large or continuous. For instance, the extent to which copper reached a given site or area often fluctuated markedly. At Brześć Kujawski very late in the Primary Neolithic, for instance, copper was plentiful only during the apex of the settlement about 3400–3300 bc. During this period it was frequently removed from circulation through inclusion in grave inventories. After 3300 bc, copper became progressively scarcer at Brześć Kujawski and does not appear in graves, suggesting either that the supply was cut off or that some form of "social storage" was practiced rather than the disposal of wealth. Elsewhere in central Europe during this period the distribution and consumption of copper seems to be similarly sporadic.

It seems difficult to support the argument that the circulation of "exotic" commodities during this period acted as a "flywheel" for trade in essential goods. Instead, it appears that the exchange of "exotic" items must be placed in a social context rather than strictly related to subsistence-level economic decisions. This is not to argue that trade in subsistence commodities did not take place. On the contrary, the conditions of subsistence risk which prevailed during the Primary Neolithic also very probably continued to exist in the Consequent Neolithic, although it is also likely that the better knowledge of central European ecosystems would have reduced the uncertainty of the situation somewhat. It is, of course, virtually impossible to document the existence of trade in food products, but it is perhaps sounder to hypothesize its existence on ecological grounds rather than to infer that it existed as a transparent aspect of the exchange in "exotic" materials. The increase in the distribution of flint and stone, however, is quite apparent in the archaeological record of many areas, and more importantly, there are changes in the nature of the extraction and initial working of the flint. Of particular importance is that for the first time, there are settlements which seem to have been primarily concerned with the extraction and preparation of flint for distribution well beyond their own catchments.

Trusted networks and trading partnerships
The usual impression that one receives about exchange in Neolithic Europe (although it is never made so explicit in the literature) is of individuals and communities bartering and trading with almost everyone around them. Such a picture of essentially opportunistic entreprenurial behavior is not at all in keeping with what is known about how exchange is actually conducted in simple societies. Instead, trading links exist among individuals, households, and corporate groups in ways which are defined and reinforced by kinship, inheritance, custom, and trust. It is not possible to say which of the above was the primary determinant of the nature of trade relationships during the Consequent Neolithic, but the end result would have been the establishment of a network of trade partnerships rather than the sort of blanket first-come, first-served situation often implicit in discussions of this topic. Burns (1977: 32) has defined a "trusted network" as any set of individuals in whom a trader seeking to open exchange relations can have relatively more confidence than he can in others. A network generates trust among its members when the interpersonal relationships in it yield reliable information and permit the manipulation of sanctions reinforcing desired behavior. The stronger the bonds of trust among trading partners, the greater the probability that disputes among members of the network will be fairly settled. The question of dispute settlement in trading is crucial, for not only does exchange provide the circumstances for disputes to arise, but it also supports a mechanism for the resolution and avoidance of conflicts as well. Trusted networks vary considerably in their size, the ease with which they are initiated, and costs of their maintenance. Nonetheless, their existence means that the exchange relationships pursued by any single individual, household, or group are not random or identical in all circumstances. Moreover, traders are more likely to search for new partners within the

trusted network than outside of it. In short, people are more likely to trade with others whom they trust than with individuals or groups whose behavior would tend to increase the risk or uncertainty in the exchange relationship.

A trusted network is a parallel of the kinship network discussed above, for it is centered on individuals rather than corporate groups. In fact, many of the nodes in the trusted network of an individual may also be nodes in his kinship network as well. In circumstances where the relationship between two trading partners is particularly strong, this may be then formalized in kinship terms as well. Hughes (1977: 210) suggests that the linkages in an individual's trusted trading network may serve various ends. Some may be established primarily to acquire subsistence resources, others to obtain luxuries, while others may further political and social ends. It may thus be spurious to assign a single motivation or goal to exchange in Consequent Neolithic central Europe. There were perhaps a variety of reasons why certain classes of materials and artifacts were exchanged, ranging from the purely utilitarian, such as salt, to the exotic, like copper. It is important, however, to keep in mind the social context of this exchange as an activity essentially between individuals as heads of households, either singly or in groups.

Hughes' study of New Guinea trade patterns has shown that the strongest trading linkages between non-related individuals for material benefit were *between* major physiographic, ecological, and cultural divisions (Hughes 1977: 210). In other words, differences in resources made it possible for trade to develop, and only areally specialized products were traded. Within regions of similar resources, exchange took the form of ceremonial exchanges, which were generally among relatives for sociopolitical benefit. In the ceremonial exchanges, the goods exchanged were often the same and not the product of specialized resources or labor. It may be possible to see the movement of materials in Consequent Neolithic central Europe in a similar light, with the actual trading links being between different *Siedlungskammern* or even between major habitat zones (such as the loess belt and the North European Plain). Then, within *Siedlungskammern* or within microregions contained therein, the exchange that took place may have been more ceremonial in nature, conducted for sociopolitical reasons rather than for strictly economic gain.

Consequent Neolithic flint distribution

The Consequent Neolithic in the loess belt was marked by the first concerted extraction and preparation of flint by communities which set up operations near to the flint sources. In the Primary Neolithic, alien flint was found at the settlements of the end users, but it is unclear how it came from the sources, often several hundred kilometers distant. Workshop areas near to flint sources were sometimes found (e.g. Sąspów in southern Poland), but these did not project the impression of complete functioning residential bases.

In the Consequent Neolithic, however, settlements are found which appear to have had direct connections with flint sources and also to have been functioning residential bases. Two of these are known from the area of the Holy Cross Mountains in south-central Poland (Balcer 1975). Ćmielów is located 9 kilometers

from the flint source at Krzemionki and 22 kilometers from the source at
Świeciechów, while Zawichost is 15 kilometers from Świeciechów. Both of these
appear to have been "production settlements" at which the high quality
Świeciechów and banded Krzemionki flint was worked into blade blanks for
further distribution. A thousand kilometers to the west, at Spiennes in Belgium,
Michelsberg communities appear to have played a similar role, and it may be
possible to identify others in central Europe. Such "production settlements" in the
loess zone are relatively rare, however, for most of the inorganic raw materials
exploited by Consequent Neolithic communities were in areas away from the loess
deposits. It should also be remembered that the initial working of flint is a
particularly "obtrusive" process in the archaeological record, whereas axe production, for instance, would result in grinding residues which would not appear
archaeologically. Nonetheless, the existence of settlements like Zawichost and
Ćmielów attests to the existence of at least an "atmosphere" which permitted the
development of production for exchange rather than for internal household
consumption.

Salt as an essential commodity

One subsistence resource whose exchange it may be possible to infer is salt, and
during the late fourth millennium and early third millennium bc there are the first
indications of the production of salt on a large scale in certain areas. Salt is a
fundamental human physiological requirement, and the lack of it forces the body
to secrete water in order to maintain the proper concentration of salt in the blood.
Human populations subsisting primarily on a meat diet do not require extra salt,
for the mineral salts in animals and fish can be readily absorbed by the body.
Agricultural peoples, however, require additional salt, estimated at approximately
6 grams/day in temperate climates (Dauphinee 1960: 413). There are three
potential sources of salt that can be exploited by inland populations. These are the
mining of rock salt, the burning of plants with a high salt content and the leaching
of salt from their ashes, and the evaporation of brine from salines. It appears that
large-scale salt mining in central Europe did not begin until quite late in antiquity,
since it required great inputs of labor and technology and was worthwhile only if
extensive exchange networks existed to distribute the product. The burning of
salt-bearing plants would leave little or no evidence archaeologically, so it is
difficult to assess its importance for the Neolithic inhabitants of central Europe. It
seems, however, that the evaporation of brine from salines was probably the
principal method of salt extraction during this period, for these sources are widely
distributed in central Europe and the process is uncomplicated and requires low
inputs of time, energy, and technology.

The best evidence for Neolithic salt production at salines comes from the area
around Kraków in southern Poland. Here, at Barycz, Jodlowski (1976: 90) has
identified salt pans dating to a late stage of the Lengyel Culture, including several
holding-basins, small ditches, and hearths. Godlowska (1985: 128) has indicated
that this evidence for salt production continues into the Funnel Beaker occupation
of this area. The ditches conducted the brine from the saline into the basins and

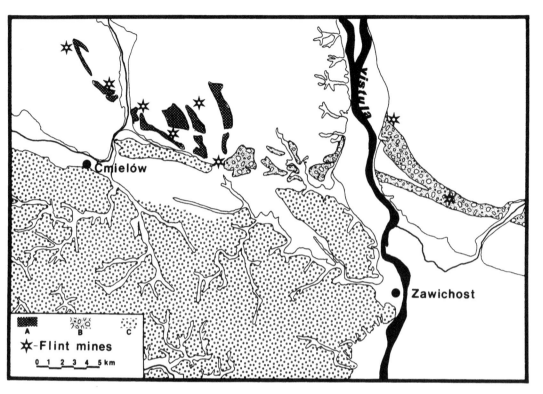

Fig. 7.5 Map of mining area in eastern Holy Cross mountains and the location of settlements at Ćmielów and Zawichost (after Balcer 1975: fig. 40). Key: A – Astartian deposits ("chocolate" flint); B – Turonian deposits (Świeciechów flint); C – loess.

were plastered with a thin layer of clay. The sediment in the basins was subjected to chemical analysis and it was found that it contained a markedly higher percentage of NaCl and Na$_2$O than the surrounding subsoil. A similar ditch system was identified at the site of Kraków-Pleszów IIk, but it is less certain that it was associated with salt production. The identification of the Lengyel salt basins and trenches at the Barycz saline was rather fortuitous, and it is likely that similar features could be found at Neolithic sites near other salines as well. In the same way that many Linear Pottery houses were missed before 1935, many Neolithic salt-production features have probably been overlooked by archaeologists.

Another piece of evidence pointing toward an elaboration of salt-production at this time is the appearance of what may be vessels used in salt-making at some Neolithic sites. Again, the best evidence comes from Barycz. Vessels were found here that have a conical shape and interior residues high in NaCl content. Similar cups are known from other Late Lengyel and Funnel Beaker sites in the Kraków area. Elsewhere in central Europe, the evidence for such vessels is slim. The suggestion has been made, however, that the Michelsberg "tulip beakers" are connected with salt production, and Lichardus has called attention to the occurrence near salines in the Saale valley and Harz Mountains (Lichardus 1976:

fig. 56). It should also be noted that the ceramic evidence of salt production should not be confined to tall, thin vessels. The shallow bowls which are common in the ceramic inventories across this area could easily have functioned as salt pans, much as similar vessels did in prehistoric North America (Brown 1980: 20–37).

Whatever the technique used for salt extraction, it may be significant that there is a correlation between clusters of Neolithic settlement, especially in the late fourth/early third millennia bc, and areas where salines are common. The most striking examples of these are the concentrations in the Kraków area of southeastern Poland and the Saale valley near Halle in East Germany. It is in these two areas that the overall density of settlement during this period appears to have its greatest increase, whereas elsewhere it generally declines. There is also a concentration of Lengyel and Funnel Beaker settlement near Inowrocław in the Polish Lowlands (whose German name is Hohensalza), where a number of salines can be found.

The significance of salt in the Neolithic diet would suggest that it must have been an item of exchange alongside stone and metals. Moreover, it was the only dietary item apparent in the archaeological record that was necessary for the survival of those communities which did not have access to their own sources, whereas local items could usually substitute for the other traded materials. The identification of salines would also have provided some motivation for communities to remain nearby, both to have access to the salt for their own consumption and to be able to produce a valued commodity for exchange. The demand for salt, in contrast to that for materials like copper, probably would have been relatively constant over time. Salt, then, may form a category of traded commodity during this period different from the sporadic exchange in subsistence resources and exotic materials.

The exchange of exotic materials
Among the exotic raw materials used during the Consequent Neolithic in central Europe are copper (Ottaway 1973; Sherratt 1976; Wiślański 1979) and amber (Wiślański 1979; Mazurowski 1983). Copper made its first appearance in this area among the various Lengyel groups which occur right at the Primary-Consequent Neolithic transition in Poland – Brześć Kujawski, Jordanów, Wyciąze-Złotniki, and Lublin-Volhynian White Painted Ware. In the settlements and cemeteries of these groups, copper ornaments generally occur as ornaments in graves. Several characteristic ornament forms are found (Ottaway 1973), including "spectacle spirals", beads, and disks. These artifacts are not cast, but rather the smelted copper was cold-hammered into sheets and wire, then bent into shape. Fifteen years ago, Ottaway counted close to 500 such ornaments known from Late Lengyel contexts (Ottaway 1973: 312). By now, the number is substantially more as the result of recent finds at Brześć Kujawski and Krusza Zamkowa. Perhaps the most striking aspect of the distribution of copper in Late Lengyel contexts is the amount of it found on the North European Plain, over 500 km from the presumed source of the copper in Slovakia. Certain sites and regions are very rich in Late Lengyel copper finds, while others have produced very few ornaments. Much of the copper was ultimately removed from circulation through its use as grave goods. A few

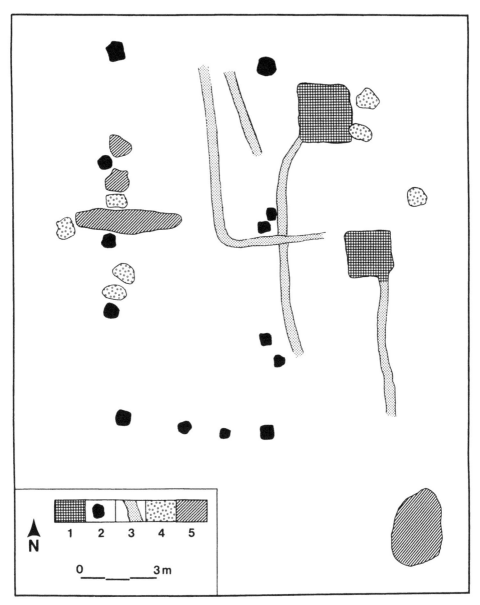

Fig. 7.6 Late Lengyel salt production features at Barycz (after Jodłowski 1977: fig. 2). Key: 1 – salt pans; 2 – postholes; 3 – ditches; 4 – pits; 5 – boiling-hearths.

sites, like Brześć Kujawski and Złota, appear to have evidence for local metalworking, including the smelting of ores (Kulczycka-Leciejewiczowa 1979: 145; Grygiel 1986).

This florescence of extensive copper use and procurement was not evenly distributed over north-central Europe, and in many areas it was relatively short-lived. The amount of copper which is found in Funnel Beaker contexts in the loess belt is substantially less than that at the Late Lengyel sites. For instance, in the Elbe-Saale area in SE Germany, isolated copper beads and pieces have been found at a few Consequent Neolithic sites. (The beads of rolled copper sheet from Preusslitz are often described in isolation (e.g. Behrens 1973: 75; Schlicht 1979: 173) and most of the finds from this area discussed by Ottaway (1973) are from later Neolithic periods.) A small piece of copper was found at the late Rössen settlement at Schernau in Bavaria, like Brześć Kujawski right at the very end of the Primary Neolithic sequence (Lüning 1981: 141-2), but at later Michelsberg sites in the German loess belt, very little copper has been found (although it should be noted that to the south in the Alpine Foreland copper artifacts have been found at Cortaillod and Pfyn sites that are coeval with the Consequent Neolithic of the loess belt). Of particular significance is the paucity of copper artifacts in graves, suggesting that even its limited abundance was not enough for it to be removed from circulation through its inclusion in burials. One possibility is that this represents a form of "social storage" in which valuables were not removed from circulation but were needed more in the living economic system. Another may be that it reflects changing patterns of interaction which accompanied the other changes associated with the transition from the Primary to the Consequent Neolithic in the loess belt.

It is important to note that about the same time there is a decline in the number of other exotic materials, such as the *Spondylus* shell ornaments that were utilized by Primary Neolithic groups in central Europe and obsidian. It appears that there was an *across-the-board decline* during the Consequent Neolithic in the amount of exotic materials which were widespread during the Primary Neolithic in the loess belt. Elsewhere in Europe, the opposite seems to have occurred about this time, and thus this decline has been overlooked when the European Neolithic is considered to be a "package deal". Yet, this decline may actually have *more* significance for social and political developments than if the level of *Spondylus* and copper movement had continued unabated.

The frequency of Consequent Neolithic copper finds is far greater on the North European Plain, although again, they are not uniformly distributed. There is a focus of copper finds in the western group of the Funnel Beaker culture, particularly west of the Weser. As of 1979, 47 copper specimens had been found in 21 megalithic tombs (Schlicht 1979). These are often beads of rolled copper sheet, presumably imported from the southeast. East of the Weser, however, the distribution falls off. In Denmark, there is an additional concentration of copper finds, from both burial and hoard contexts (Ottaway 1973; Randsborg 1980). The Polish earthen long barrows have yielded virtually no copper artifacts, surprising perhaps in view of the probable derivation of these tombs from house forms of the Brześć Kujawski Group (Midgley 1985; Bogucki 1987). In general, however, the pattern of copper use on the North European Plain between 3200 and 2500 bc is far more extensive than that in the loess belt during this period.

Other exotic materials found in Consequent Neolithic contexts on the North European Plain include gold and jet. A single gold armring has been reported from Himmelpforten in Niedersachsen, and Schlicht (1979: 169) has proposed an Irish origin on the basis of the sourcing of continental Bronze Age gold finds. Jet ornaments are known from several north German megaliths along the Ems and are also suggested to have come from sources in the British Isles (Schlicht 1979: 177).

In this connection, it is also worth mentioning amber, which is frequently believed to have been a widely used exotic commodity in the northern part of central Europe during this period, particularly along the Baltic coast. It seems clear that in Denmark, amber is quite frequently encountered in burial contexts in a variety of forms and often in quite great quantities (Midgley 1985: 197). This is not unexpected, considering the availability of amber along the Baltic littoral. Inland, the best data on the spatial and chronological distribution of amber during the Neolithic come from Poland, where Mazurowski (1983) has compiled an inventory of amber finds. Mazurowski points out that it is erroneous to assume that amber comes from only a limited source area on the Baltic coast but that rather it can occur naturally in deposits far inland. From a total sample of close to 1,500 amber finds, only 26 – less than one percent – come from contexts dating before 2500 bc. There appears instead to have been a marked florescence of amber use associated with late Neolithic groups after about 2200 bc, well beyond the scope of this book. Mazurowski points out (1983: 188) that the raw material for the few amber artifacts found in Funnel Beaker contexts could easily have come from random local finds, perhaps in the course of activities such as the construction of earthen long barrows. Amber, then, may not be so exotic a material after all.

Changing patterns of interaction

The *decline* in the amount of exotic commodity exchange observed between the Primary and the Consequent Neolithic in the loess belt could be interpreted in two contrasting ways. One possibility would be to suggest that it represents increased social isolation of the Consequent Neolithic farmsteads as a result of the breakdown of the broader support networks inferred to have existed during the Primary Neolithic. Such an explanation would seem to be an entirely plausible way of accounting for the relative scarcity of copper and *Spondylus* shell ornaments after about 3300 bc. Yet, there is something intuitively unsatisfactory about leaving the matter at this, for it may be a symptom of the changes at only one level of interaction.

Braun and Plog (1982) have studied changes in patterns of exchange in prehistoric North America and note a very similar decline in the exchange of valuables in the midcontinental United States after about AD 200. The traditional explanation for this has been something akin to the one presented in the paragraph above – that it marks an end to a complex system of interregional interaction and hence more social isolation of individual communities. This florescence of interregional interaction, known as Hopewell, is viewed as something which could have ultimately led to the emergence of supralocal polities but did not. Braun and Plog propose an alternative explanation which treats this development as a positive social phenomenon. They take the position, as has been taken here, that regional and interregional cooperation and interaction is an adaptive mechanism to deal with local environmental unpredictability. In their view, valuables exchange requires some social distance between the trading partners and may reflect short-term negotiated connections for the most part. Decreasing valuables exchange may, Braun and Plog propose, indicate decreasing social distance between the interacting parties and the development of more long-term, stable connections. They conclude that decreased valuables exchange could represent *increasing*, not decreasing, regional integration.

The model presented by Braun and Plog is intriguing for it seems equally plausible as an explanation for decreased valuables exchange in the loess belt during the Consequent Neolithic. The decline in copper, *Spondylus*, and obsidian exchange may have been accompanied by a rise in the archaeologically transparent exchange of subsistence commodities. As was noted in the New Guinea case cited above, trade *within* regions often involves such mundane items. In central Europe, the increased use of animals in household production would have been a step in the direction of generating exchange commodities not readily apparent in the archaeological record. In fact, a crucial element in this may have been breeding strategies which promoted herd growth, for it would have been necessary at times to put surplus stock to a use more rewarding than just their meat. The exchange of salt and flint, again mundane commodities where exchange seems to have continued through the Consequent Neolithic, has been discussed above.

It may be possible, then, to interpret the evidence from temperate Europe, particularly the loess belt, in the same way that Braun and Plog have interpreted the changing patterns of exchange in the midwest United States. Although the decline in the exchange of valuables such as copper, *Spondylus*, and obsidian may represent a cessation of the long-distance connections of the preceding millennium, it may also reflect an increasing density of short-range, but long-term, connections of a more regional character, perhaps on the scale of *Siedlungskammern*. Rather than reflecting an atrophying of most supralocal interaction as the data may suggest at first glance, the Consequent Neolithic evidence may indicate the emergence of stable integrated regional exchange networks which in the long run had greater sociopolitical import than the Primary Neolithic kin-based or ad hoc connections. A major role in such increased regional cooperation would have been the interlocking trusted networks described above. It would not be unreasonable to believe that the elaboration of such trusted networks would have been of major interest to individual households. This would have been particularly true for those whose kin-sets were somehow abbreviated or for whom geographical mobility was not at all an acceptable option for dealing with environmental unpredictability. These trusted networks in turn would have overlapped with the kin-sets and action-sets mobilized by other household heads for local collaborative activities. On a regional scale, then, Consequent Neolithic society may have exhibited a high level of integration, although interregional links may have declined in importance. The question addressed later in the chapter is how this socioeconomic integration may have been translated into sociopolitical integration.

On the other hand, the greater use of copper in parts of the North European Plain suggests different socioeconomic patterns. In particular, the concentration of copper artifacts found in the Funnel Beaker culture west of the Weser in Niedersachsen as well as the copper finds in Denmark suggests spatially well-defined regions where the population acquired artifacts of this material. These materials were obtained from some distance, presumably from sources in southeast or south-central Europe, across the intervening loess belt. The situation in Denmark and Niedersachsen contrasts with the lack of copper finds in the earthen long barrows of north-central Poland, and it is worth noting that there may be a correlation between the distribution of copper in Neolithic contexts on the North European Plain and areas where increased territorial integration appears to have occurred toward the end of the Mesolithic. The possible significance of this will be developed further below.

Warfare and the management of risk

Using social and economic networks to buffer shortfalls and uncertainty works only if the shortages are more localized than the network and where a household or community is in a position to reciprocate. Although this may often have been the case, there were certainly instances of larger-scale environmental events which caused problems on a regional or even wider scale. The Consequent Neolithic period in central Europe is the time when possible evidence of warfare begins to surface. Milisauskas and Kruk (1984: 27), for instance, propose that the numerous finds of "battle axes" and the fortified settlement at Bronocice (discussed above) may reflect a degree of warfare not previously found in Neolithic society. Earlier, Milisauskas had suggested that there was an increase in warfare between communities as land with good soils became scarcer (Milisauskas 1978: 177), yet his subsequent studies in the Bronocice area indicated that there were large tracts of fertile land available. The theme of Neolithic competition for land is not a new one in European prehistory. Thirty-five years ago, Grahame Clark described the "uneasy" situation which started at this time, when "instead of peaceful peasants ...one finds warriors", reaching its climax with the pastoral tribes of late Neolithic times (Clark 1952: 97–8). Other authors tend to skirt the question of warfare and competition, categorizing certain artifacts as "weapons" but avoiding the implications of such an identification (e.g. Behrens 1973: 214).

It seems, however, that conflict and its resolution are significant issues and that it may be possible again to draw on anthropological perspectives on warfare to develop some hypotheses about the nature of Neolithic conflicts.

In social and cultural anthropology, warfare is a topic which has received a considerable amount of attention (Fried, Harris, and Murphy 1967; Vayda 1976; Ferguson (ed.) 1984, among many). The literature of ecological anthropology in particular has considerable discussion of warfare and conflict, as it is a seemingly maladaptive institution which plays an adaptive role in many small-scale societies. The most frequent approach to warfare in the ecological literature is to view it as a response to some sort of resource imbalance. The definition of such an imbalance can be broadly defined. In various cases, shortages of food, protein, mates, and land have been cited as underlying factors. The exclusive use of such a framework, however, may not always be warranted and may lead to overly simple "prime mover" explanations. A case in point is the Amazonian protein-deficiency debate, where there has been a search for very specific limiting factors which provoke warfare in a society with a relatively low population density (Harris 1974; Chagnon 1977; Beckerman 1979; Harris 1984).

A particularly helpful approach to warfare in its ecological context is that presented by Jochim (1981: 194–201). Jochim examines warfare both as a response to ecological problems and as a strategy for the management of intergroup relationships. In both these areas, warfare can be viewed as very similar to the role of exchange, although the contexts of the two institutions can be quite different. Trade is a response to short-term shortages, while warfare is an alternative response to prolonged deficits. Moreover, trade requires portable resources for redistribution, whereas the redistribution of fixed resources, such as land, requires the movement or displacement of people through war or emigration. If the deficits of resources are either localized or are occurring at the same time over broad regions, emigration ceases to be an option for the redistribution of consumers. Warfare, then, should occur if there are shortages involving fixed resources such as land or if adjacent communities experience either different degrees of environmental risk over time or experience resource shortfalls at the same time.

The implication of this is that the differences in risk may be found along environmental boundaries while simultaneous shortfalls are more likely to occur within environmental zones. As a result, groups occupying adjacent environmental zones may be likely to engage in warfare due to differential risk, while groups within the same zone (perhaps in adjacent valleys, for instance) would engage in warfare when both parties were exposed to the same shortfalls. In both cases, emigration as an alternative response would be unacceptable, since neighboring groups may be unwilling to accept refugees or they may be suffering from the same sort of shortages.

If warfare is viewed as a way of redistributing people in relation to fixed resources, then it would seem to follow that it would be more common in groups which are largely sedentary and have fixed home ranges. If land in particular is the key fixed resource in question, then shortages of land would most likely increase with population density. The question, especially in the case of Neolithic Europe, would be the scale of the critical population density, since it is apparent that even a millennium after the original penetration of central Europe by agriculturalists there were large tracts of sparsely inhabited territory. Perhaps a more accurate hypothesis would be that the *perception* of decreasing social and economic options which comes with increased local population densities is the critical factor, rather than an absolute population threshold over which warfare is invoked as an adjustment mechanism.

The issue of the perception of economic options brings up the question of warfare as a manifestation of aggressive competition for resources (Jochim 1981: 198). Generalizing from the ecological literature, Jochim proposes that the more similar the economies of two groups in the same habitat, the greater the amount of competition which may be expected. This proposition has a considerable amount of empirical support. In contrast, groups exploiting different resources in the same habitat tend to have peaceful relationships, marked by mutualism rather than competition. Such a relationship has already been proposed for the interaction

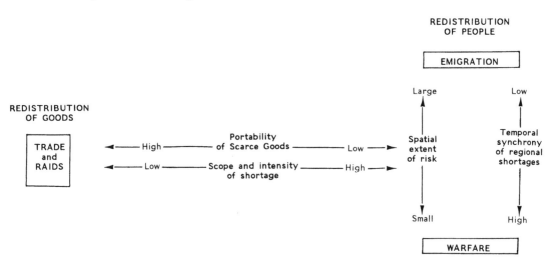

Fig. 7.7 Options for redistributing imbalances of populations and resources, including warfare (after Jochim 1981: fig. 7.1).

between foragers and farmers in Neolithic Europe, but it is possible that such relationships were also found between agricultural groups exploiting different habitats and resources.

Another approach to warfare in an ecological context is that it can also serve as a management strategy in order to regulate conflicts (Jochim 1981: 213). Within any human group or set of groups there are inevitably conflicts about motivations, goals, and strategies. Some potential conflicts have already been discussed above in connection with environmental risk. Warfare, then, can represent a method of dealing with these conflicts. To some degree, this is the other side of the resource coin, for many of the conflicts can be reduced to matters of resource allocation. In treating warfare as a management, rather than a maintenance, mechanism, however, it is possible to view its role in ecological adaptation as extending beyond the functional view of it as a procedure for the reallocation of resources.

Common strategies in warfare
Morren (1984) has proposed that there are three common strategies in warfare, which can be correlated with environmental characteristics and human responses to them. Although he associated them with several broad ecological zones in New Guinea, it may be possible to generalize from his model to reflect on the European Neolithic case. Morren perceives these strategies as a continuum of escalation, rather than being mutually exclusive.

The first strategy is to deny the opponent the use of unoccupied territory, including the interdiction of movement and the exploitation of the territory's resources. The goal of such strategy is to maintain buffer zones between communities. In such a strategy, the tactics are limited, involving short engagements and terrorism. Another goal of warfare is to plunder the transportable resources of the opponent, the "pursuit of trade by other means." Essentially, this is the sort of raiding which corresponds to the small-scale redistribution of resources by means of warfare. In economic terms, such warfare involves the exploitation of another group's resources without direct input of capital or labor (Morren 1984: 171). A final strategy of warfare involves the displacement of people and the occupation of their territory. This aim is the more radical approach to the adjustment of people and resources discussed above. The tactics involved in this sort of warfare are different from those used in the previous two types. Here, large engagements, with defined objectives and opponents, are the norm.

Some models of Consequent Neolithic warfare
In his study of New Guinea warfare, Morren was able to correlate different types of strategy and tactics with different ecological situations. Within the limits of analogy, it may be possible to draw on his work and our discussion of the social dimensions of Consequent Neolithic adaptations above and formulate some hypotheses about patterns of warfare in central Europe during this period. In attempting to apprehend the forms of warfare that might be expected in the different ecological zones of central Europe, it is important to recall the salient characteristics of the major habitat types, especially the loess belt and the North European Plain. If the premise that warfare is a mechanism for redistributing population in relation to resources is accepted, then it is also necessary to reflect on the distribution of Consequent Neolithic population within the major habitat zones.

Although the Consequent Neolithic in the loess belt saw a trend towards the dispersal of settlement and the exploitation of the interfluves, the focus of settlement was still on the tertiary streams and minor rivers. The basins of these streams were still the most productive areas, and as a result the attractive resources of the loess belt, in terms of preferred settlement locations, were concentrated in a linear fashion and separated by tracts of relatively unattractive landscape. As a result, it would appear that buffer zones between groups were already largely a function of the natural distribution of resources. Within this network of linear optimal resource zones, the Consequent Neolithic population was clustered into smaller microregions. The degree of clustering is not as great as in the Primary Neolithic, where the settlements are strung closely together along the floodplains. Nonetheless, on a regional scale the settlement is still not completely random, and hence displays some degree of aggregation. More importantly, the settlements now appear to represent individual household units which have a greater degree of autonomy than the Primary Neolithic hamlets. As a result, the possibility of local and regional disputes arising from conflicting goals and motivations would appear to be even greater than in the Primary Neolithic. Above, I noted that although the subsistence system was probably more finely tuned than in the Primary Neolithic, there would still appear to have been considerable opportunity for crop failure and the attendant stress and anxiety. More importantly, the apparent increase in the amount of annual variability during the late fourth millennium bc would have resulted in potential shortfalls spread over entire regions, in contrast to the more localized shortfalls hypothesized to have occurred during the Primary Neolithic.

The lowlands of the North European Plain presented a different set of ecological conditions and hence the potential existed for different causes and effects of warfare during this period. The lowlands lack the concentrated resource zones of the loess belt. Here, the optimal resources occur in small patches rather than in strips. Although on a broad macroregional scale there are unproductive areas which would have served as buffer zones, the penetration of Consequent Neolithic populations into a variety of habitats resulted in a greater potential for interdigitation of regional groups than in the loess belt. Nonetheless, there is some degree of variability in the distribution of Consequent Neolithic populations in this area, and this distribution is not entirely explainable by ecological factors. In some areas, potentially productive zones appear to have been sparsely inhabited, while other regions have dense concentrations of Consequent Neolithic population. In short, the distribution of Consequent Neolithic population in the lowland zone is as patchy as the ecosystem. The distribution of these patches, however, is not entirely contiguous.

The other significant aspect of lowland Consequent Neolithic populations is the degree to which they reflect a continuation of the territorial patterns which appear to have emerged in the late Mesolithic. The small sites reflect ephemeral occupations, and the larger sites in lacustrine and riverine settings, while indications of longer-term foci of settlement, are by no means as permanent as the residential bases of the Primary Neolithic. The pattern that emerges, as discussed above, is one of the effective group being small groups of households, perhaps of the order of 25–35 people, or single extended households exploiting somewhat flexible territories and practicing agriculture alongside gathering and collecting. Presumably these groups would have been affected by the same increased level of environmental variability as the populations in the loess belt. The option of increasing the size of the territory would have been greater for the inhabitants of the lowlands. The net result would have been a type of readjustment of the relationship between population and resources unavailable to the inhabitants of the loess belt. The problem would have been how to keep this option open when neighboring territorial groups were experiencing similar sorts of challenges.

The loess belt and the lowland zones, then, presented different configurations of fixed resources and population distributions. In the uplands, the optimal fixed resources, the linear stream valleys, are separated by less attractive interfluves. Within these resource zones, the population, in the form of dispersed household units living in reasonably long-term habitations, was focused on particular microregions. In the lowlands, the fixed resources, in the form of fertile soils and naturally abundant habitats, were more uniformly distributed in the patchy ecosystem of the North European Plain. Here, Consequent Neolithic populations appear to have been somewhat larger groups, perhaps extended households or groups of households, following the pattern established during the Mesolithic in this area. The exploitation patterns of these groups were more territorial in nature, and habitations tended to be rather impermanent.

The different habitats presented different sorts of problems for the relationships between people and their resources. The first category could be termed "environmental", in the sense that the fundamental challenges are posed by the habitats themselves. In the upland zone, shortages and shortfalls were probably often broadly distributed within individual *Siedlungskammern*, with adjacent drainages experiencing problems at roughly the same time. As a result, population movement within the *Siedlungskammer* would not be an option to alleviate local problems, nor would cashing in on exchange relationships within the region. In contrast, in the lowlands, the inherent patchiness of the ecosystem and the overall abundance of alternative resources would have resulted in greater possibilities for local groups to weather shortfalls in resources provided they had access to a sufficient catchment and could enlarge their range in order to compensate for these events. The trick would have been for them to maintain buffer zones separating them from neighboring groups in order to be able to ameliorate the effects of shortages in one critical resource such as their crops.

The other category of problems with the distribution of populations could be called "social" issues. Again, there are grounds for hypothesizing that there were differences between the situation in the loess belt and those in the lowland zone. Earlier, I characterized Consequent Neolithic communities the upland zone as being prone to a variety of social problems which had earlier been suppressed by the settlement fissioning and movement during the Primary Neolithic. In particular, it can be hypothesized that there was a certain degree of difficulty in locally obtaining suitable mates, assuming household and descent group exogamy. The basis for this hypothesis is that the overall regional population densities were still relatively low yet on a microregional scale the "intensity" of social relationships and linkages would have been high. The options of individuals reaching adulthood and seeking to establish households of their own would have been constrained under such circumstances. The result would be high degree of anxiety and frustration on one hand and more opportunities for the violation of rules involving exogamy, avoidance, and other institutions on the other. In the lowlands, the territorial groups would also presumably have been exogamous, but the issue would not have been the relative density of social interrelationships but rather the opposite. Although it is probable that various formal systems for inter-group marriages and exchange of mates existed, there may have been circumstances in which these would have not worked for a particular group. The recruitment of new members by birth or marriage alone may not have been enough in some cases to ensure the survival of the group as a social unit.

The result of these differing sets of environmental and social problems is that it may be possible to hypothesize that the institution of warfare had a somewhat different cast in the loess belt than in the lowlands. In the loess belt, it is possible that the greatest tensions existed on the local level, within particular microregions or between adjacent microregions. At stake would have been both material and social resources. Some of these conflicts can be presumed to have grown out of the paradox of local success: as households budded off and microregional populations grew, the exposure to failure, both material and social, would have increased at the same time. Material failure could exist on a variety of levels, from the most basic kinds of subsistence shortfalls through a lack of success in acquiring raw materials, both mundane and exotic. Competition within particular microregions could have been as prevalent as conflict with near neighbors. As a result, Consequent Neolithic warfare in the loess belt can be seen as perhaps an extreme condition of the management of the risks to which a Neolithic household and community would have been exposed.

Within particular microregions, the need to manage conflict along with the risk would perhaps have been the most pressing. The limitations on social options, which would have probably affected young males the most, could have resulted in heightened social tension and an increased opportunity for violations, both real and imagined, of social rules. As a result, it is possible to propose a model of Consequent Neolithic warfare in the loess belt that does not have territorial goals but rather one which involves a certain amount of raiding between microregions at one level and some degree of intragroup conflict, perhaps violent, on the other.

The lowlands of the North European Plain presented a different set of issues. Here, populations were not as sedentary and wedded to grain crops as were the inhabitants of the loess belt. For the lowland groups, the question was the maintenance of the exploitation territories which enabled them to have a sufficiently diverse resource base. Warfare in this situation would have presumably had a territorial dimension, to deny adjacent groups the use of space which may well remain unoccupied. Morren (1984: 170–1) has proposed that in such instances, warfare is symbolic, using token violence and terror in order to deliver a message. Another possible goal of warfare in the lowlands may have been the recruitment of new members for local groups. While in the uplands the presumed occasional local deficits of mates would have led more to limitations of social options of individuals, in the lowlands it may well have been a matter of group survival requiring the reproductive capacity of additional women.

It may therefore be possible to consider Neolithic warfare in a new light, not in terms of territorial expansion but in terms of conflict resolution, maintenance of buffer zones, and small-scale raiding. There are certainly good ecological grounds for thinking along these lines. It seems doubtful that the sorts of organized campaigns associated with chiefdoms and states actually occurred in Neolithic Europe, nor can one portray early European farmers as warring barbarians. Rather, warfare should probably be considered to be another option, albeit an extreme one, for the management of the risks and tensions inherent in Neolithic existence. The presumption of the existence of warfare (as opposed to feuding, revenge, and other violent activities), however, assumes the existence of some supra-household forms of political organization, and this issue is addressed in the next section below.

Suprahousehold political structures in the Consequent Neolithic

In Chapter 5, I argued that the sociopolitical organization of Primary Neolithic communities was essentially egalitarian and that management and decision-making lay almost exclusively with individual households. The question for the Consequent Neolithic, then, is whether this pattern of relatively autonomous household-based political systems continues unchanged or whether it is transformed into something more complex, as some have suggested (e.g. Milisauskas and Kruk 1984). If this transformation indeed took place, whatever changes occurred were probably rather modest. Unfortunately, the nature of the transition from egalitarian household-based political systems to simple supra-household systems is very poorly understood and has received relatively little attention (Lightfoot and Feinman 1982: 63). The actual organizational changes might have been so subtle that their archaeological correlates may not be perceived, due to their being within the normal range of variation for the previous egalitarian situation. Then, of course, there is the problem of defining the archaeological correlates of the emergence of supra-household political organization themselves.

Before considering the emergence of supra-household political organization in the Consequent Neolithic, it is perhaps worth noting a few fundamental elements on which this sort of organization is predicated. In small-scale societies, without hereditary elites, political authority can be thought of as an effect of a hierarchy of achievement within certain age classes. Even in societies which do not formalize age differences, the establishment of an independent household is a sign that a man has reached social maturity. In most societies, male adult status, headship of a household, and an independent role in public affairs are closely associated (La Fontaine 1978: 16). In light of the ongoing theme of household structure and organization, this is particularly germane. LaFontaine has noted (1978: 16) that "in any society in which the control and management of resources is located in households, and political influence depends on the manipulation of resources, management of such a household is the basis of a man's political capital." Political power and authority, then, begin at home. Successful management of one's own household is a prerequisite for success in political activity in supra-household contexts. LaFontaine points out that the "long-term survival of a household depends on the alliances and exchanges outside of it, so like any political leader, a household head is concerned with external relations." His success in developing these external relations, particularly among constituencies which are not obligated to him through kinship ties, is the first step in acquiring authority within the larger community

Presumably the most basic form of social differentiation is along the lines of sex and age. Households cannot exist in isolation, and there is a need for some sort of structure to regulate relations among domestic groups. The net effect of social differentiation by sex and age is to create a social order beyond the household. Domestic authority then takes its place at the bottom of a hierarchy of authority to which most, or all, men aspire. Once an individual is identified within the community as successful in the management of the exchange and alliance relationships necessary for household survival, then it is relatively easy for that individual to move into making decisions which affect other households as well.

One probable effect of the environment of risk management described above was to elaborate this social order beyond the household. Heads of households were probably continually balancing the immediate interests of the residential unit against the greater security that could be expected from exchange and alliance relationships with other households and groups. The differing degrees of success of heads of households in managing these relationships would have provided the conditions for the emergence of supra-household political organization, since the economic and social success would have been quite visible achievements to other individuals. Being the head of a household, then, is a necessary precondition for aspirations beyond the household. The degree to which these aspirations can be realized depends on a man's achievement in social and economic endeavors. In any given society, household heads can be assumed to have the same degree of domestic authority. What differentiates them beyond the household is their age and the effects of longevity: experience, knowledge, skill, respect, accumulated wealth, productive alliances, decision-making ability, and the like.

It was argued in Chapter 5 that Primary Neolithic society did not exhibit a particularly high degree of social differentiation beyond the household. In particular, the pattern of settlement fissioning and colonization of new microregions would have suppressed many of the tendencies in this direction. To argue this is not to propose that individuals did not develop greater prestige and authority as the result of age during the Primary Neolithic, for clearly the effects of longevity described above could be expected. Rather, the Primary Neolithic political environment must be viewed in contrast with that of a millennium or so later in the context of the opportunity for *differential achievement* beyond the household.

During the Primary Neolithic, successful household management can be viewed as having been a yes-or-no proposition. Either your household perpetuated itself as an independent residential group or it did not. If the model presented in Chapter 5 is reasonably plausible, household survival was predicated on spatial flexibility and the richness of the network of kinship ties on which it could draw in lean times. Management of risk was a matter of pooling that risk with other households rather than actively devising methods of increasing security through alliances, exchange, and – when necessary – warfare. Conflicts could be resolved through settlement relocation and fissioning. Under such conditions, opportunities for demonstrating achievement through successful household management would have existed, but the amount of authority beyond the residential group to which successful heads of households could aspire would have been limited.

The model of social and economic developments during the Consequent Neolithic presented earlier in this chapter would have provided the conditions under which political authority beyond the household could emerge, especially in the loess belt. First, individual households and kin groups would have been anchored to particular microregions to a far greater degree than in the Primary Neolithic. The option of out-migration to resolve conflicts and imbalances of resources and population would not have been available to the degree to which it was a millennium earlier. Second, the establishment of alliances, participation in exchange relationships, and organization of raiding parties would have provided opportunities for individuals to distinguish themselves that had been hitherto scarce. In short, within particular age classes, more opportunities for men to compete to achieve the degree of authority to which their age entitled them probably existed during the Consequent Neolithic than had done previously.

An additional factor which could have acted as an "accelerant" on the emergence

of supra-household political authority would have been the environmental variability which has been discussed as a factor in other developments during this period.
This increased annual variability would have put successful risk management by
individual households at a premium, because it would have introduced an element
of uncertainty into the annual regime. Rather than accept passive measures of risk
minimization as are hypothesized to have been practiced during the Primary
Neolithic, there was now a greater incentive to actively seek to minimize risk in
order to buffer the effects of uncertainty. The result would have been a climate in
which competition for authority through successful management first at the
household level and then beyond would have been able to flourish.

It is important to realize that when dealing with the Consequent Neolithic of
central Europe and the emergence of supra-household political organization, a
simple concept of "hierarchy" does not seem adequate. One does not find a regular
hierarchy of settlement sizes or a marked differentiation of elites in burial rituals.
Instead, there is a clear emphasis on communal activities, perhaps communal
ritual, as reflected in the *Höhensiedlungen* (Starling 1985, 1987: fig. 10). The
suggestion is *not* that these *Höhensiedlungen* were the seats of powerful individuals
who controlled other households. Rather, the mobilization of dispersed households
for collective action implies the existence of the community leaders mentioned
above, even if the prevailing ethos was egalitarian and even if the authority of these
individuals beyond their own households was ephemeral. The broad diversity in
burial types also implies some sort of social differentiation, although Consequent
Neolithic burials do not normally contain indicators of wealth and status. It would
seem that in this context, wealth, status, and power may not have been as directly
correlated as has often been thought.

It may be necessary to take a much more modest view of Consequent Neolithic
political organization, particularly in the loess belt. At the moment, it appears that
one cannot argue for the same degree of hierarchization during the Consequent
Neolithic that characterizes later periods such as the Bronze Age, but rather that
there were much less coherent, less integrated polities. Some have argued (e.g.
Kristiansen 1982) for the emergence of "chiefdoms" during the Consequent
Neolithic on the basis of perceived settlement hierarchies and diversity in burial
practices. Others (e.g. Voss 1982; Starling 1985) have argued that this is not the
case and that Consequent Neolithic groups remained essentially egalitarian. The
crucial issue is the concept of the "chiefdom" with its political centralization, as
defined by Service (1962: 114) based on Polynesian examples. It may be that the
focus on the "chiefdom" as an ideal type is the real problem in evaluating
Consequent Neolithic sociopolitical organization, and it may even be a hindrance
in determining the real nature of political relationships beyond the household
during this period.

Feinman and Neitzel (1984) have pointed out the problems with an overly
typological approach to pre-state sedentary societies, especially in the realms of
social differentiation and political leadership. The tremendous diversity which
Feinman and Neitzel document in pre-state societies in the Americas was
presumably also the case in prehistoric Europe. They found that there is not clear

dichotomy between egalitarian and stratified societies, but rather a continuous range of variation. It appears that the Consequent Neolithic communities of central Europe had only just begun to move along this continuum towards some degree of stratification. The development of regional exchange systems, involving mostly mundane goods, would have resulted in the sort of integrated local networks of kin and trusted partners which would have provided ideal conditions for the emergence of small-scale polities. There may have been a relatively long period characterized by community leaders with ephemeral power – individuals whose success in household management made them stand out at the community level but who could not sustain their authority beyond their households for an extended period.

Interestingly, the areas where social complexity beyond this level may have developed sooner than in other parts of central Europe may have been those where the Neolithic sequence began the latest, such as Denmark and other parts of the North European Plain where the Neolithic communities appear to have been derived from indigenous foraging populations. In Chapter 3, the proposition was advanced that the Late Mesolithic communities of the North European Plain had developed some degree of organizational complexity. Despite the appearance of agriculture and domestic livestock about 3000 bc, it appears that there is considerable continuity between the Late Mesolithic and the Neolithic of the lowlands of north-central Europe. The most visible difference between the two periods was the appearance in the latter of burial monuments like earthen long barrows, accompanied by evidence in some areas for the acquisition of "exotic" resources. One social correlate of this transition may have been the emergence of aggrandizing systems of resource allocation, a process that may have begun already in the Late Mesolithic.

The concept of aggrandizing systems of resource allocation was put forth by Richard Gould (1975), who contrasted them with systems that emphasize sharing and reciprocity. In an aggrandizing system, individuals or households accumulate and store surpluses as security against shortages. These accumulations may be unequal and lead to concentrations of wealth. Gould (1975: 168) has proposed a general hypothesis that in hunter-gatherer societies "'aggrandizing behavior' increases in respect to the total economy in direct proportion to the opportunity for optimal harvesting with minimal risk by individual family or household groups." By contrast, sharing of subsistence resources should be more adaptive in ecosystems with a greater element of risk. Although Gould developed this hypothesis in connection with maritime hunter-gatherers of the Pacific Northwest, it could be investigated as well in the case of the newly agrarian foragers of the North European Plain, particularly those that emerged in rich ecosystems.

Denmark is the case that springs immediately to mind, with evidence of conspicuous wealth appearing shortly after the establishment of agrarian communities (e.g. Randsborg 1975; S.J. Shennan 1982), but it is also worth considering the case of the Funnel Beaker groups in Niedersachsen, where grave goods in megalithic tombs reflect the long-distance acquisition of copper, gold, and jet. In both these areas, a certain degree of territorial integration appears to have emerged at the end of the Mesolithic (Vang Petersen 1984 in the case of Denmark and Arora 1973 for Niedersachsen). It may be that in these areas there was already a sufficient degree of security in the subsistence economy, even before the introduction of domestic plants and animals, to result in the local organizational complexity that permitted the type of aggrandizing behavior which led these groups to acquire these exotic commodities and to deposit large quantities of resources such as amber in burials. Elsewhere on the North European Plain the construction of megalithic tombs and earthen long barrows also reflects a degree of organizational complexity on a local scale that does not seem to have occurred in the loess belt.

Conclusion

The argument has been presented that the social developments in the loess belt and on the North European Plain proceeded along two different trajectories. The next question, too broad to be considered here, is what lay beyond, after 2500 bc. A hypothesis that requires further investigation is that the later emergence of social and political complexity in the loess belt was based on regionally integrated polities, while on the North European Plain the process took place on a much more local level, involving small groups of households and extended families. The latter situation is the more "volatile" of the two, in which the potential for considerable variation from community to community could exist. The examination of this idea, however, will require the comparative study of developments in the late Neolithic and early Bronze Age across a wide area.

There is still much to be done in the study of Consequent Neolithic political organization. The focus of investigation must be on the subtle shift from household-based political systems to simple supra-household systems, leaving aside the gross dichotomy between egalitarian societies and chiefdoms. The indicators of this shift may be difficult to perceive in many areas and may not appear in mortuary remains at all. Rather, such things as differences in house construction and size, variation in wealth among households, and larger storage facilities in particular households may be much more informative. These may not be easy to isolate and identify, but it is in such household-level analyses that major insights into the problem of the emergence of supra-household political organization in Neolithic Europe will be found.

8

The social archaeology of Neolithic central Europe

The social implications of agrarian colonization

By 5,000 years ago, agrarian societies were successfully established in most parts of central Europe. This process took close to 2,000 years and involved many generations of farmers and foragers. It was not as orderly or simple as a superficial examination of the archaeological record would suggest, nor did it follow the same course in every corner of central Europe. This book has been an attempt to understand this process and to propose a set of models for conceptualizing the transformation of the early pioneer farming settlements into settled agrarian communities.

I do not expect the reader to agree with everything proposed in this book. In fact, the first reaction may be, "Well, that's an interesting model but the evidence does not yet support it." But if the reader has at least considered what has been written here, that may be significant in its own right. Perhaps the underlying goal of this book was to write something about the European Neolithic that tried to go beyond subsistence yet which did not search for hierarchies where none may have existed. As this is being written in 1986, it appears that this is still the prevailing binary position of European prehistory: either one deals with subsistence or one deals with hierarchy. Although much space is devoted to the former, this book tries to use subsistence as a tool to discover underlying social conditions.

The models used in this book have drawn on anthropological data from societies studied in the last hundred years. It has meant some leaps of faith and perhaps some arguments which are less than airtight. Yet perhaps it has yielded some fresh insights that can now be tested and refined. For several decades there has been a general doctrine of pessimism in European prehistory about the degree to which social and political structure can be inferred archaeologically. Still, if one wants to penetrate beyond subsistence and palaeoeconomy, it is necessary to develop some hypotheses which can then be either disproven or maintained as valid when they are tested in the field.

European ecological diversity

Frequently, attempts to develop coherent models of European Neolithic sociocultural development lose sight of the tremendous environmental diversity of the continent. Even on a sub-continental scale, such as that considered in this book, there is considerable variation in habitats that were encountered by the first agrarian communities. Nonetheless, the recognition of this environmental diversity helps greatly in making sense of the various configurations of Neolithic adaptations to central Europe.

Perhaps the most crucial distinction to be drawn is between what has been referred to here as the "loess belt" and the lowlands of the North European Plain. Although the southern border of the loess belt is somewhat indistinct, the northern edge is quite sharply demarcated, and the difference in soils between the loess and the outwash further north was a significant determinant of Primary Neolithic settlement. This is particularly true in northwest Germany and the Netherlands. Of course, the loess belt is not a solid band of loess across central Europe, but the marked differences found in terrain elements such as drainage between this area and the regions to the north and south of it cannot be overemphasized. In fact, it may be that drainage rather than just soil types may have been a crucial factor, since the edaphic characteristics of particular locations would make them the "energy-subsidized" habitats favored by the Primary Neolithic farmers.

An underestimated element in the ecological picture of Neolithic temperate Europe is the varying role of indigenous foraging populations in the ultimate establishment of agrarian communities. In the loess belt, these native hunter-gatherer groups were sparsely represented, and as a result, the Primary Neolithic communities were relatively unconstrained in their choice of settlement locations. Nonetheless, it is clear that there were probably circumstances in which the Primary Neolithic communities entered into symbiotic relationships with neighboring foragers (see Chapter 6 above and Gregg 1986). The role of indigenous foragers becomes of major significance on the North European Plain, which supported much larger hunter-gatherer populations than the loess belt.

Households and decisions

Most attempts to investigate social issues in the European Neolithic have considered the fundamental unit of Neolithic society to be a local community, a village or a collection of dispersed households, which functioned as a corporate entity in decision-making. Renfrew (1976) for instance, has borrowed the concept of a "segmentary society" from social anthropologists to conceptualize the effective fundamental social unit. This way of thinking actually has its roots in nineteenth-century views of "progress", in which the household was viewed as having evolved from primitive larger kin groups. Moreover, "the household was judged to be a transitory group that precipitated in each society from the action of culturally specific systems of kinship, marriage customs, and rules of residence" (Netting, Wilk, and Arnould 1984: xiv). The prevailing assumption was that pre-modern society was organized into large corporate kin groups and that individual residential groups were of relatively little significance.

About thirty years ago, this view began to change in social anthropology, with a number of scholars arguing that individual residential groups should be a major focus of study (e.g. Goodenough 1956; Goody (ed.) 1962). In particular, a consensus emerged that the understanding of the social structure of society did not involve fitting it into a broad ethnological category but rather meant the study of the rules and options which affected the decision-making individuals. Over the course of these three decades, the household has come to be viewed as the crucial social unit of virtually all societies, particularly of small-scale agrarian groups. Kunstadter (1984: 300) notes that the household appears to be "an important social unit in all (or almost all) societies, with widely proliferating implications for many important aspects of behavior, including reproductive and other demographic behavior."

In Neolithic central Europe, unlike in other times and places around the world, it may be actually possible to isolate households archaeologically (e.g. Grygiel 1986). Admittedly, this involves a leap of faith that the archaeological configurations which can be called "household clusters" actually correlate with living households. Nonetheless, the imagination is not especially taxed to consider the Primary Neolithic longhouses and the small isolated "generic" Consequent Neolithic settlements as representations of the archaeological remains of discrete residential groups. In light of ethnographic data from similar small-scale agrarian societies, then, it is quite likely that the nexus of decision-making in Neolithic central Europe lay in the household and not in some larger corporate group. The implication of this is that the reasons for any changes, both local and regional, lay in the motivations, goals, and aspirations of individual households and their heads.

Major themes I – Primary Neolithic
Aside from the empirical data summarized in this book, a number of major themes have been stressed. Most of these themes are not entirely novel, but in some respects the emphasis laid on them is. These themes could be considered to be some key areas for hypothesis testing in European prehistory, for although the interpretations of the empirical data may vary, it seems reasonably certain that within the framework of these themes it may be possible to pose new questions about the introduction of food production to Europe and its consequences.

Uncertainty of subsistence
The first theme which deserves emphasis is the overall uncertainty of Neolithic subsistence. A notion which appears to be particularly questionable is the idea that Neolithic farmers, particularly those of the Primary Neolithic, had such an understanding of their crops and the European ecosystem that harvests were constant from year to year. Even up into recent times, it was difficult to predict how much a European harvest was going to yield, and until the development of national systems for offsetting crop shortfalls, famine was a real possibility in central Europe. Moreover, the potential for predation on Neolithic crops and herds as well as for blights and epizoötic diseases has to be recognized. During the initial period of the establishment of food production in central Europe, focused primarily on the loess belt, these concerns must have played a prominent role in conditioning the behavior of the agrarian communities. Most importantly, the loess belt is not especially rich in alternative resources, and hence Primary Neolithic communities would have had to rely largely on the output of their crops and herds.

The decisions of these early agricultural communities were made in an environment of uncertainty. The issue was not one of risk, in which the effects of a possible shortfall could be gauged and fall-back positions could be established. Instead, it would have been impossible to predict how much of a crop yield there would be until it was too late to replant or to mobilize a broad range of alternatives. Such a decision-making environment would have inevitably necessitated the development of a number of coping mechanisms for dealing with the possibility of hunger or near-starvation. Furthermore, it is likely that there were often times where alternative sources of food were not able to satisfy the dietary minima of some Neolithic communities. It is likely that these fundamental issues of subsistence had a crucial impact on social relationships. This would have been especially true during the Primary Neolithic, but the uncertainty of the subsistence base probably would have diminished only slightly during the Consequent Neolithic.

Potential for stress

The general environment of uncertainty in making fundamental household decisions for survival provided the conditions for a certain degree of stress in the Neolithic community. A failure to meet dietary minima, of course, would result in physical stress on the inhabitants of the settlement, which can provoke a range of psychological reactions. Of greater significance, however, would have been the social stress caused by differing perceptions of environmental conditions and their consequences, as well as by variation in the goals and aspirations of different households. All of these sources of stress would have had an impact on the social relationships in the Neolithic community, and presumably mechanisms would have developed to deal with this stress. One such mechanism would have been the fissioning of settlements when differences between households or factions could not otherwise be resolved. In fact, it seems no longer necessary to invoke spurious models of Neolithic shifting agriculture to account for the spread of agrarian communities across central Europe. Rather, the prerogatives of individual households to seek the best circumstances for their economic growth and development would probably have led to a rapid dispersal of food-producing communities throughout this area.

Labor mobilization

The necessity for individual households to clear and plant virgin forest, not to mention build substantial houses and carry out all other domestic activities would have meant that each would have to mobilize sufficient labor to meet these needs. This would have been especially true in the case of the clearance of virgin forest in the energy-subsidized habitats favored by Primary Neolithic farmers. Thus, the availability of labor, and its scarcity, would have had considerable relevance for the organization of Neolithic behavior, particularly during the Primary Neolithic. One immediate possibility would have been that settlement fissioning may have been a last resort, and there would have been a number of tradeoffs to be weighed before this actually took place. New settlements would have had a quite difficult time, especially at the time of the initial clearance of land. It is quite possible that among the primary determinants of Neolithic settlement location were ephemeral clearings in the forest caused by tree falls and beaver activity.

The need to maximize labor resources would have been an impetus for a relaxation of controls on popuation growth. This may account for the demographic "wave" that usually accompanies such colonization situations and which seems to be reflected in the archaeological record of central Europe around the middle of the Primary Neolithic. Yet, such population growth would have had an impact on a local scale, as individuals grew to social maturity and established households of their own. There would soon have been the conditions for the sort of stress described above, with the resultant cycle of settlement fissioning.

The conditions of labor availability which probably presented themselves to Neolithic households can be argued to have invited the development of relationships with indigenous foraging groups, when such opportunities presented themselves. Instead of hunter-gatherers being driven before the Neolithic frontier, as the prevailing view suggests, it seems more likely that the new farming communities would have been better advised to accommodate the indigenous peoples and to incorporate their labor into their subsistence cycle. Although the indigenous populations of the loess belt were sparse, there seems to have been some degree of interaction, especially on the northwest fringe of Primary Neolithic settlement.

The suppression of complexity
This environment of labor scarcity, settlement fissioning, and uncertainty over subsistence would have been a powerful counter to the development of social differentiation and political factions. Aggrandizive behavior would have been particularly suppressed, largely on ecological grounds, since the concentration of resources in the hands of any one household or group of households would have been difficult to maintain. The need to maintain as broad a network as possible of kin ties which could be counted upon in times of subsistence shortfalls would have hindered the emergence of lineal kinship structures, meaning that relationships among households would have been largely among equals.

This did not mean that certain individuals did not emerge as leaders or with some degree of heightened status. What it does mean is that this status was ephemeral. The pattern of settlement fissioning meant that the constituencies over which an individual in a leadership role had authority could dissipate quickly. Moreover, if new individuals and households moved into a community, they would not necessarily have recognized the authority of an individual who may have achieved some status. As a result, it would seem that any accumulation of status and rank by a household and its head would have been suppressed, and social differentiation would have been a product of sex and age alone.

Major themes II – Consequent Neolithic
The Consequent Neolithic of the loess belt, contrary to many current models, did not really represent a major transformation in agrarian society from the Primary Neolithic. Rather, it could be argued to represent an elaboration of a number of trends which can be observed developing through the preceding millennium. There were relatively few changes in crops and domestic livestock (except that pigs

generally usurp the percentage of the faunal assemblages previously held by sheep and goat, which was not an unreasonable development). The evolutionary model held by most European prehistorians would assume increased social complexity in the Consequent Neolithic. Just how much evidence there is for such complexity is questionable. If anything, more variation is visible archaeologically, but it is uncertain how this translates into complexity that was radically different from that observed during the preceding thousand years following the penetration of temperate Europe by farmers and stockherders. Instead, it seems also possible to take this variability to reflect a situation where local communities were coping with limited options and a degree of subsistence risk.

In fact, perhaps the most fundamental change between the Primary and Consequent Neolithic was the trading of an environment of uncertainty for one of risk in decision making. The potential and drawbacks of the loess environment were well understood by now. Rather than attempt to pool their collective risk in maintaining large settlements in energy-subsidized habitats as the Primary Neolithic communities did, the Consequent Neolithic households were able to take steps to manage their exposure to risk, particularly by engaging in alliances, exchange, and warfare.

Limitations on options
The better cognitive mapping of the loess belt was accompanied by some limitations on the options enjoyed by Primary Neolithic communities to deal with stress. In particular, the option of out-migration in order to deal with stresses, particularly social, would not have been available. Most of the preferred habitats in the *Siedlungskammern* of central Europe were already occupied. Moreover, as a microregion became increasingly familiar to its inhabitants, the uncertainty of moving to a new region would have been a powerful disincentive to household relocation. During the Primary Neolithic, one microregion was as poorly known as another, so this factor would not have worked against the pattern of settlement fissioning.

The limitations on options would have been felt not only in the realm of logistics and decision-making. As particular microregions filled up, social options would have been limited as well. The large Primary Neolithic residential bases were presumably exogamous, if they consisted of related households. The degree of flux in Primary Neolithic settlement and the presumed maintenance of broad lateral support networks meant that there would have been a certain degree of flexibility of action for individuals reaching social maturity in finding mates and establishing independent households. With the tethering of Consequent Neolithic populations to particular microregions, it meant that before long the entire microregion would have become effectively exogamous, for virtually everyone would have been related to everyone else. Moreover, the local foraging populations would have been already absorbed into the Neolithic communities, so that option would not have been available. All this meant that individuals reaching social maturity would have had a more difficult time finding suitable mates and establishing households. Demographically, this may have inhibited population growth still more by delaying marriages.

Foragers turned farmers
On the North European Plain, very little Primary Neolithic settlement had taken place, save for the lowlands of north-central Poland where Linear Pottery and Lengyel sites are found. A millennium after the establishment of agrarian communities in the loess belt, food production finally made its appearance in these areas. Although there are some cultural similarities between the Consequent Neolithic of the loess belt and the regions to the north, the settlement and economic data from these areas are quite different. Of particular importance is that in many respect the settlements have a distribution not much different from that of the indigenous foraging communities of these areas, and the faunal remains in particular show a continued reliance on wild taxa for a major part of the diet. The conclusion that must be drawn from this is that in contrast to the situation in the loess belt where there were no substantial populations of indigenous hunter-gatherers, the introduction of food production to the North European Plain was the result of the adoption of agricultural techniques by foraging peoples. This idea is not particularly earth-shattering, for it has been argued for a long time that the Funnel Beaker culture of the North European Plain indicates continuity with late Mesolithic traditions. The issue is why the apparently successful foraging adaptation required the addition of domesticated plants and animals to the subsistence economy.

It is difficult even to develop hypotheses to explain this change. It is clear that in the case of the North European Plain, communities which may represent pioneering agrarian adaptations may be of crucial importance. Sites like Hüde I and those of the Brześć Kujawski Group are significant not because they were successful in their own right but because they provided the nucleus around which indigenous foraging populations could coalesce and form symbiotic relationships. Then, as the central European climate became more variable after 3500 bc, as tree ring data appear to indicate, the additional carbohydrate source of domestic grain and the protein source of domestic animals became more important in maintaining the growing local hunter-gatherer populations. Some areas such as the west Baltic coast were buffered against this variability at first by the maritime resources, but soon they too adopted agriculture.

The management of risk
The replacement of uncertainty by risk in the decision-making process of the Neolithic farmers of central Europe, particularly in the loess belt, meant the emergence of a new range of social and economic relationships. The risk could not be completely mitigated, but it could be managed in order to relieve individual households of as much of it as possible. The key actors in this strategy would have been the heads of households, and as in most societies, status would accrue to the household heads who were most successful in managing their external relationships.

The breakup of the large nucleated Primary Neolithic settlements into small independent farmsteads would have had a number of implications for interhousehold relationships. No longer would there have been a considerable degree of aggregate genealogical "memory" in each settlement in the form of a several co-resident generations and possibly co-resident individuals more distantly related than siblings. Rather, the discrete households would have had a relatively short "memory" if they were constantly going through developmental cycles. Moreover, the well-defined links among microregions within particular *Siedlungskammern* which could be argued for the Primary Neolithic pattern, may have been less pronounced a millennium later. There was a need for individual households to replace these linkages with an overlay of different relationships and mechanisms for altering the distribution of population and resources.

I have argued that the Primary Neolithic communities of central Europe maintained a broad network of kinship bonds both within particular microregions and beyond. The establishment of this network would have been facilitated by the frequent fissioning of settlements and the high rate of demographic increase in the wake of the frontier. Once a stable pattern of settlement was established, however, and the demographic growth had leveled off, the dispersed Consequent Neolithic farmsteads needed to establish an alternative set of relationships which could be mobilized for collective behavior. The long generational "memory" held in long-lived Primary Neolithic settlements would have been able to maintain the kinship links over generations and at a level beyond immediate siblings. The discrete Consequent Neolithic households, established when an individual reached social maturity, would have had a relatively short "memory" of kinship links dependent on ancestors, and as a result it would have been necessary to establish and maintain a variety of relationships with other households.

This is where the kin-sets, action-sets, and trading partnerships described in Chapter 7 come into play. It would have been necessary for the heads of each household to maintain a "portfolio" of such relationships of varying degrees of intensity which could be mobilized for collective activity or relied upon for mutual assistance. These relationships would not have been fixed, and different linkages might have been invoked for different purposes. Nonetheless, on the basis of ethnographic evidence, it is not unreasonable to assume that a household could maintain at least some of these relationships across generations. In the type of decision-making environment proposed here, the strength of the external relationships of any one household would have mitigated some of the risk involved in making economic decisions. A household might pursue a daring agricultural regime which could potentially pay great dividends if its "safety net" in the event of failure was reasonably secure.

The maintenance of this network of relationships required a considerable degree of exchange, to a much greater degree than was seen in the Primary Neolithic. Although there is a temptation to see Consequent Neolithic exchange as a "package deal" which served essentially one purpose, it may perhaps be more useful to divide it into a few categories which cross-cut each other. First, there is the distinction which must be made between "exotic" and utilitarian items. Into the former category fall copper and amber, while the latter includes salt and in some cases special flint types. Second, there is a distinction between trade for material gain and ceremonial exchanges for social gain. In certain ethnographic cases, trade for material gain is most pronounced across ecological borders and involves the exchange of dissimilar commodities, while trade for social gain usually occurs among households and factions within the same general area and often involves the exchange of similar items. So, the distribution of copper, salt, and flint in Consequent Neolithic Europe, which often spans ecological areas, may have been motivated largely by material gain, while the social exchange which served to cement alliances may be largely transparent archaeologically or have involved the secondary distribution of materials acquired through trading channels.

The evidence for warfare in the Consequent Neolithic suggests that at times a more radical approach was needed to adjust the relationships between people and resources. I have argued that the sorts of warfare which took place in the loess belt and on the North European Plain were different. In the loess belt, the question appears to have been one of portable resource acquisition and factional disputes, and in cases studied by modern ethnographers, raiding is the general tactic employed. On the North European Plain, where local population densities appear to have been less but where communities seem to have had a pattern of territorial resource use, the purpose behind warfare may have been to maintain these territories and the buffer zones between them. Such cases ethnographically are characterized by an ad hoc approach to warfare, with hit-and-run tactics being sufficient to accomplish the desired effect.

Supra-household political organization

The repeated recruitment of action sets for communal activity by certain individuals could well have resulted in the emergence of political factions. Although there is little evidence from Consequent Neolithic sites of the loess belt to suggest that social differentiation was based on anything other than sex and age, particular household heads could have risen to positions of political prominence in such an environment. For the time being, such political prominence would have been difficult to sustain across generations, for it presumably would have been based largely on skill in decision-making and management of a household by a single individual who would eventually reach old age and die. Nonetheless, in societies where social differentiation is based on age and sex, political authority is something to which all heads of households can aspire. The emergence of rudimentary forms of supra-household political organization during the Consequent Neolithic would have laid the groundwork for more complicated forms of sociopolitical organization at the end of the Neolithic and in the Bronze Age.

Anthropological archaeology and Neolithic Europe

I would like to close this book with some optimistic thoughts about the prospects for addressing social and political questions in the European Neolithic. It is only upon examining the literature from other continents that one realizes that the archaeological data base in most areas of temperate Europe from the Neolithic onward is among the best in the world. There are few regions where there is not at least a chronological sequence on which to build, and over the last two decades a host of comparative studies has resulted in a firm knowledge of the regional variation in artifact types. Numerous radiocarbon dates are available, which have led to well-supported chronological sequences for most regions. In most places, a high standard of excavation prevails, and the exposure of broad areas of settlement sites is standard procedure. Sieving for small-scale finds, particularly organic residues, is becoming accepted as a worthwhile pursuit, and the analysis of faunal and floral remains is viewed as an integral part of archaeological research. Despite economic problems, archaeological research in Europe has certainly been better supported than in many other parts of the world, frequently by corporate donors. Among the few hindrances are the preservation conditions found in some types of soils, such as loess, but these are actually no worse than those found in the tropics or in the sandy soils of the northeastern United States.

In recent years, many European archaeologists have moved away from what had been a prevailing doctrine of pessimism about the ability of archaeology to shed light on questions of prehistoric social organization. In the course of doing so, however, an agenda has developed that focuses on questions of emergent social complexity and hierarchy. Much of this derives from the impact that evolutionary typologies of social organization (e.g. Service 1962) have had on archaeology. There are two dangers in such an agenda, however. The first is that archaeologists who are employing anthropological models may lose sight of the fact that typological approaches are not the only valid constructs of social organization. In fact, there are numerous anthropologists who do not embrace them, perhaps now more than those who do. A second problem is that archaeologists may lose sight of the fact that simple, non-hierarchical societies are interesting in their own right. There is no need to find traces of hierarchies or marked social stratification in Neolithic Europe to somehow justify it as a topic worthy of a place on the agenda. Anthropologists find simple, egalitarian societies interesting not because they are "not complex" but because they present social configurations that are intriguing of themselves. So, too, should Neolithic Europe.

These are exciting times in the study of the European Neolithic. The last two decades have seen the collection of tremendous amounts of data. It seems that the pace of fieldwork has slowed a bit, and it is time to relate these data to theory. This book represents one attempt in that direction, and there will undoubtedly be more such efforts. It will be important not to ignore the data base but to exploit its richness. At the same time, it is vital to exploit the richness of the anthropological literature, relying not on a limited number of key sources or approaches. Finally, there is the question of scale, both of data and of models. Detailed and exhaustive typological studies (of pottery decoration, for instance) are useful up to a point, but in many respects they produce few insights about social relationships. On the other hand, "coarser", larger-scale data, such as site sizes and settlement distributions, may actually be more useful. At the same time, complex models often demand data at a quantity and scale not available to archaeologists, and hence they must often be simplified. The real insights will come at the point where the data base and theoretical models can be successfully linked. It does not seem overly optimistic to suggest that this is possible in the study of the earliest farmers and stockherders of north-central Europe.

BIBLIOGRAPHY

Albrethsen, S.E., and E. Brinch Petersen 1976. Excavation of a mesolithic cemetery at Vedbaek, Denmark. *Acta Archaeologica* 47: 1–28.

Aldrich, H.E. 1979. *Organizations and Environments*. Englewood Cliffs: Prentice-Hall.

Ammerman, A.J., and L.L. Cavalli-Sforza 1971. Measuring the rate of spread of early farming in Europe. *Man* (N.S.) 6: 674–88.

1973. A population model for the diffusion of early farming in Europe. In *The Explanation of Culture Change*, Renfrew, C. (ed.), pp. 343–57. London: Duckworth.

1984. *The Neolithic Transition and the Genetics of Populations in Europe*. Princeton: Princeton University Press.

Andersen, N. 1981. Sarup. Befaestede neolitiske anlaeg og deres baggerund. *KUML* 1980: 63–103.

Andersen, S.T. 1978. Identification of wild grass and cereal pollen. *Danmarks Geologiske Undersøgelse*. Arbog 1978: 69–92.

Arora, S. 1973. Mittelsteinzeitliche Formengruppen zwischen Rhein und Weser. In *The Mesolithic in Europe*, Kozłowski, S.K. (ed.), pp. 9–22. Warsaw: University of Warsaw Press.

Bakels, C.C. 1978. *Four Linearbandkeramik Settlements and their Environment: a Palaeoecological Study of Sittard, Stein, Elsloo, and Hienheim*. Leiden: Institute of Prehistory (Analecta Praehistorica Leidensia 11).

1979. Linearbandkeramische Früchte und Samen aus den Niederlanden. *Archaeo-Physika (Festschrift Maria Hopf)* 8: 1–10.

1981. Neolithic plant remains from the Hazendonk, Province of Zuid-Holland, The Netherlands. *Zeitschrift für Archäologie* 15: 141–8.

1982. Zum wirtschaftlichen Nutzungsraum einer bandkeramischen Siedlung. In *Siedlungen der Kultur mit Linearkeramik in Europa*, Pavuk, J. (ed.), pp. 9–17. Nitra: Archaeological Institute, Slovakian Academy of Sciences.

1983/4. Pflanzenreste aus Niederbayern: Beobachtungen in rezenten Ausgrabungen. *Jahresschrift der bayerischen Bodendenkmalpflege* 24/25: 157-66.

1984. Carbonized seeds from northern France. *Analecta Praehistorica Leidensia* 17: 1–27.

1986. Akkerbouw in het moeras? *Rotterdam Papers* 5: 1-6.

Bakels, C.C., and C.E.S. Arps 1979. Adzes from Linear Pottery sites: their raw material and their provenance. In *Stone Axe Studies*, Clough, T.H. McK., and Cummins, W.A. (eds.), pp. 57–64. London: Council for British Archaeology (Research Report 23).

Bakels, C.C., and R. Rousselle 1985. Restes botaniques et agriculture du néolithique ancien en Belgique et aux Pays-Bas. *Helenium* 25: 37–57.

Bakker, J.A., J.C. Vogel, and T. Wiślański 1969. TRB and other C14 dates from Poland. *Helenium* 9: 3–27, 209–38.

Balcer, B. 1975. *Krzemień Świeciechowski w Kulturze Pucharów Lejkowatych. Eksploatacja, Obróbka, i Rozprzestrzenienie*. Wrocław: Ossolineum.

Barker, G. 1976. Morphological change and neolithic economies: an example from central Italy. *Journal of Archaeological Science* 3: 71–82.

1981. *Landscape and Society: Prehistoric Central Italy.* London and New York: Academic Press.

1985. *Prehistoric Farming in Europe.* Cambridge: Cambridge University Press.

Barlett, P. (ed.) 1980. *Agricultural Decision Making: Anthropological Contributions to Rural Development.* New York: Academic Press.

Bayerlein, P.M. 1985. *Die Gruppe Oberlauterbach in Niederbayern.* Kallmünz/Opf.: Michael Lassleben (Materialhefte zur bayerischen Vorgeschichte 53).

Beaudry, M., J. Long, H. Miller, F. Neiman, and G.W. Stone 1983. A vessel typology for early Chesapeake ceramics: the Potomac typological system. *Historical Archaeology* 17(1): 18–39.

Beckerman, S. 1979. The abundance of protein in Amazonia: a reply to Gross. *American Anthropologist* 81: 533–60.

Behrens, H. 1973. *Jungsteinzeit im Mittelelbe-Saale-Gebiet.* Berlin: VEB Deutscher Verlag der Wissenschaften.

1981. Radiokarbon-Daten für das Neolithikum des Mittel-Elbe-Saale-Gebietes. *Jahresschrift für mitteldeutsche Vorgeschichte 63: 189–193.*

Behrens, H., and E. Schröter 1980. *Siedlungen und Gräber der Trichterbecherkultur und Schnurkeramik.* Berlin: Landesmuseum für Vorgeschichte in Halle (Veröffentlichungen 34).

Bender, B. 1985. Emergent tribal formations in the American Midcontinent. *American Antiquity* 50: 52–62.

Beyer, A.J. 1972. *Das Erdwerk der Michelsberger Kultur auf dem Hetzenberg bei Heilbronn-Neckargartach, Teil II: Die Tierknochenfunde.* Stuttgart: Müller and Graaf (Forschungen und Berichte zur Vor- und Frühgeschichte in Baden-Württemburg 3/II).

Binford, L.R. 1980. Willow smoke and dogs' tails: hunter-gatherer settlement systems and archaeological site formation. *American Antiquity* 45: 4–20.

1983. Long term land use patterns: some implications for archaeology. In *Lulu Linear Punctated: Essays in Honor of George Irving Quimby*, Dunnell, R.C., and Grayson, D.K. (eds.), pp. 27–53. Ann Arbor: Museum of Anthropology, University of Michigan (Anthropological Papers 72).

Bloch, M 1963. The social influence of salt. *Scientific American* 209(1): 88–98.

Bocek, B. 1985. Toward a theory of hunter-gatherer non-mobility strategies. Paper read at Annual Meeting of the American Anthropological Association, Washington, DC, December 1985.

Boessneck, J. 1977. Die Tierknochen aus der Siedlung der Rössener Kultur von Schoningen, Kreis Helmstedt, Eichendorfstrasse und die Probleme ihrer Ausdeutung. *Neue Ausgrabungen und Forschungen in Niedersachsen* 11: 153–8.

1978. Die Vogelknochen aus der Moorsiedlung Hüde I am Dümmer, Kreis Grafschaft Diepholz. *Neue Ausgrabungen und Forschungen in Niedersachsen* 12: 155–69.

Bogucki, P. 1979. Tactical and strategic settlements in the early Neolithic of lowland Poland. *Journal of Anthropological Research* 35(2): 238–46.

1982. *Early Neolithic Subsistence and Settlement in the Polish Lowlands.* Oxford: British Archaeological Reports (International Series 150).

1984. Linear Pottery ceramic sieves and their economic implications. *Oxford Journal of Archaeology* 3(1): 15–30.

1987. The establishment of agrarian communities on the North European Plain. *Current Anthropology* 28(1): 1–24.

in press. The Neolithic and Early Bronze Age chronology of Poland. In *Chronologies in Old World Archaeology* (third edition), Ehrich, R.W. (ed.). Chicago: University of Chicago Press.

Bogucki, P., and R. Grygiel 1981. The household cluster at Brześć Kujawski 3: small-site methodology in the Polish Lowlands. *World Archaeology* 13: 59–72.

1983. Early farmers of the North European Plain. *Scientific American* 248(4): 104–12.

Boureux, M., and A. Coudart 1978. Implantations des premiers paysans sédentaires dans la vallée de l'Aisne. *Bulletin de la Société Préhistorique Française* 75(5): 341–60.

Braun, D., and S. Plog 1982. Evolution of 'tribal' social networks: theory and prehistoric North American evidence. *American Antiquity* 47: 504–25.

Brinkhuizen, D.C. 1979. On the finds of European catfish (Siluris glanis L.) in the Netherlands. In *Archaeozoology*, Kubasiewicz, M. (ed.), Vol. 1, pp. 256–61. Szczecin: Agricultural Academy in Szczecin.

Britan, G., and B. Denich 1976. Environment and choice in rapid social change. *American Ethnologist* 3: 55–73.

Bronitsky, G. (ed.) 1983. *Ecological Models in Economic Prehistory*. Tempe: Arizona State University Anthropological Research Paper 29.

Brothwell, D., and P. Brothwell 1969. *Food in Antiquity*. London: Thames and Hudson.

Brown, I.W. 1980. *Salt and the Eastern North American Indian. An Archaeological Study*. Cambridge (Mass.): Peabody Museum (Lower Mississippi Survey Bulletin 6).

Bukowska-Gedigowa, J. 1980. *Osady Neolityczne w Pietrowicach Wielkich pod Raciborzem*. Wrocław: Ossolineum.

Burchard, B. 1973. Z badań neolitycznej budowli trapezowatej w Niedzwiedziu, pow. Miechów (stan. 1). *Sprawozdania Archeologiczne* 25: 39–48.

1981. Kultura pucharów lejkowatych w Małopolsce zachodniej. *Kultura Pucharów Lejkowatych w Polsce*, Wiślański, T. (ed.), pp. 221–38. Poznań: Polish Academy of Sciences.

Burns, J.J. 1977. The Management of Risk: Social Factors in the Development of Exchange Relations among the Rubber Traders of North Sumatra. New Haven: Unpublished doctoral dissertation, Yale University.

Buttler, W., and W. Haberey 1936. *Die bandkeramische Ansiedlung bei Köln-Lindenthal*. Berlin: Walter de Gruyter (Römisch-Germanische Forschungen 11).

Butzer, K. 1971. *Environment and Archaeology* (2nd edition). Chicago: Aldine.

1983. *Archaeology as Human Ecology*. Cambridge: Cambridge University Press.

Cahen, D., C. Constantin, P.J.R. Modderman, and P.-L. van Berg 1981. Éléments non-rubanés du néolithique ancien entre les vallées du Rhin Inférieur et de la Seine. *Helenium* 21: 136–139.

Caldwell, J.C. 1977. The economic rationality of high fertility. *Population Studies* 31: 5–27.

Carlstein, T. 1982. *Time Resources, Society, and Ecology*. London: George Allen and Unwin.

Casteel, R. 1978. Faunal assemblages and the Weigenmethode or weight method. *Journal of Field Archaeology* 5: 71–7.

Chagnon, N. 1977. *Yąnomamö: the Fierce People* (2nd edition). New York: Holt, Rinehart, and Winston.

Champion, T., C. Gamble, S. Shennan, and A. Whittle 1984. *Prehistoric Europe*. Orlando: Academic Press.

Chaplin, R.E. 1975. The ecology and behavior of deer in relation to their impact on the environment of prehistoric Britain. In *The Effect of Man on the Landscape: the Highland Zone*, Evans, J.G., Limbrey, S., Cleere, H. (eds.), pp. 40–2. London: Council for British Archaeology Research Report 11.

Chapman, J.C. 1982. 'The Secondary Products Revolution' and the limitations of the Neolithic. *Bulletin of the Institute of Archaeology* (London) 19: 107–22.

Childe, V.G. 1929. *The Danube in Prehistory*. London: Oxford University Press.

1949. The origins of Neolithic culture in northern Europe. *Antiquity* 32: 129–35.

1957. *The Dawn of European Civilisation* (6th edition). London: Routledge and Kegan Paul.

Chmielewska, M. 1954. Grób kultury tardenuaskiej w Janisławicach, pow. Skierniewice. *Wiadomości Archeologiczne* 20: 23–48.

Clark, J.G.D. 1952. *Prehistoric Europe. The Economic Basis.* London: Methuen.
  1953. The economic approach to prehistory. *Proceedings of the British Academy* 39: 215–38.
  1974. Prehistoric Europe: the economic basis. In *Archaeological Researches in Retrospect*, Willey, G.R. (ed.), pp. 33–57. Cambridge (Massachusetts): Winthrop.
  1975. *The Earlier Stone Age Settlement of Scandinavia.* Cambridge: Cambridge University Press.
Clark, P.J., and F.C. Evans 1954. Distance to nearest neighbor as a measure of spatial relationships in populations. *Ecology* 35: 445–53.
Clarke, D.L. 1976. Mesolithic Europe: the economic basis. In *Problems in Economic and Social Archaeology*, Sieveking, G., Longworth, I., and Wilson, K. (eds.), pp. 449–81. London: Duckworth.
Clason, A.T. 1967. The animal bones found at the Bandkeramik settlement of Bylany. *Archeologické Rozhledy* 19: 90–6.
  1972. Some remarks on the use and presentation of archaeozoological data. *Helenium* 12: 139–53.
  1978. Worked bone, antler, and teeth. A preliminary report. Swifterbant contribution 9. *Helenium* 18: 83–6.
Clason, A.T., and D.C. Brinkhuizen 1979. Vogeln en vissen, een glimp van de Nederlandse vogel- en viswereld uit het verleden. *Westerheem* 28: 9–23.
Clay, R.B. 1976. Tactics, strategy, and operations: the Mississippian system responds to its environment. *Midcontinental Journal of Archaeology* 1: 137–62.
Constandse-Westermann, T.S., and R.R. Newell with C. Meiklejohn 1984. Human biological background of population dynamics in the Western European Mesolithic. *Proceedings of the Koninklijke Nederlandse Akademie van Wetenschappen* (series B) 87: 139–223.
Constantin, C., A. Coudart, and M. Boureux 1981. Céramique du Limbourg: Vallée de l'Aisne. *Helenium* 21: 161–75.
Constantin, C., and L. Demarez 1981. Céramique du Limbourg: Aubechies (Hainaut). *Helenium* 21: 209–26.
Cyrek, M., and K. Cyrek 1980. La sépulture mésolithique de Janisławice. *Inventaria Archaeologica (Pologne)* 44: 273.
Czarnecki, M. 1981. The Mesolithic in the Szczecin Lowland. In *Mesolithikum in Europa*, Gramsch, B. (ed.), pp. 345–54. Potsdam: Museum für Ur- und Frühgeschichte, Veröffentlichungen 14/15.
Czerniak, L. 1980. *Rozwój Społeczeństw Kultury Później Ceramiki Wstęgowej na Kujawach.* Poznań: Adam Mickiewicz University (Archaeological Series 16).
Czerniak, L., and J. Piontek 1980. The socioeconomic system of European neolithic populations. *Current Anthropology* 21: 97–100.
Dauphinee, J.A. 1960. Sodium chloride in physiology, nutrition, and medicine. In *Sodium Chloride*, Kaufmann, D.W. (ed.), pp. 382–453. New York: Reinhold Publishing Company (American Chemical Society Monograph Series).
Degerbøl, M., and B. Fredskild 1970. *The Urus* (Bos primigenius Bojanus) *and Neolithic Domesticated Cattle* (Bos primigenius domesticus Linne) *in Denmark.* Copenhagen: Det Kongelige Danske Videnskabernes Selskab (Biologiske Skrifter 17/1).
Degerbøl, M., and H. Krog 1951. *Den europaeiske sumpskildpadde* (Emys orbicularis L.) *i Danmark.* Danmarks Geologiske Undersøgelse 2(78).
Dennell, R. 1983. *European Economic Prehistory: a New Approach.* London: Academic Press.
  1985. The hunter-gatherer/agricultural frontier in prehistoric Europe. In *The Archaeology of Frontiers and Boundaries*, Green, S.W., and Perlman, S.M. (eds.), pp. 113–39. Orlando: Academic Press.

Desse, J. 1976. La faune du site archéologique de Cuiry-lès-Chaudardes (Aisne). *Les Fouilles Protohistoriques dans la Vallée de l'Aisne*, vol. 4, pp. 187–96. Paris: University of Paris.

Dickinson, R. 1953. *Germany: a General and Regional Geography*. New York: Dutton.

Dieck, A. 1977. Giftpfeile aus der Zeit der Linienbandkeramik im Diepholzer Moor. *Nachrichten aus Niedersachsens Urgeschichte* 46: 149–54.

Dirks, R. 1980. Social responses to severe food shortage and famine. *Current Anthropology* 21: 21–44.

Dohrn-Ihmig, M. 1979. Bandkeramik an Mittel- und Niederrhein. *Beiträge zur Urgeschichte des Rheinlandes* III (Rheinische Ausgrabungen 19), pp. 191–362. Cologne: Rheinland-Verlag.

    1983. Ein Rössener Siedlungsplatz bei Jülich-Welldorf, Kreis Düren. *Archäologie in den Rheinischen Lössbörden*, pp. 287–97. Cologne: Rheinland-Verlag.

Dyson-Hudson, R., and N. Dyson-Hudson 1970. The food production system of a semi-nomadic society: the Karimojong, Uganda. In *African Food-Production Systems*, McLoughlin, P. (ed.), pp. 91–123. Baltimore: Johns Hopkins University Press.

Dzieduszycka-Machnikowa, A., and J. Lech 1976. *Neolityczne Zespoly Pracowniane z Kopalni Krzemienia w Sąspowie*. Wrocław: Ossolineum (Polskie Badania Archeologiczne 19).

Easterlin, R.A. 1976. Factors in the decline of farm family fertility in the United States. *Journal of Economic History* 36: 45–75.

Ellen, R. 1982. *Environment, Subsistence, and System. The Ecology of Small-scale Social Formations*. Cambridge: Cambridge University Press.

Emery, F.E., and E.L. Trist 1965. The causal texture of organizational environments. *Human Relations* 18: 21–32.

Eriksen, P., and T. Madsen 1984. Hanstedgård. A settlement site from the Funnel Beaker culture. *Journal of Danish Archaeology* 3: 63–82.

Fagan, B.M. 1983. *People of the Earth. An Introduction to World Prehistory*. Boston: Little, Brown.

Falinska, K. 1973. Flowering rhythms in forest communities in the Białowieża National Park in relations to seasonal changes. *Ekologia Polska* 21: 827–67.

Fansa, M., and H. Thieme 1985. Eine Siedlung und Befestigungsanlage der Bandkeramik auf dem "Nachtwiesen-Berg" bei Esbeck, Stadt Schöningen, Landkreis Helmstedt. In *Ausgrabungen in Niedersachsen, Archäologische Denkmalpflege 1979–1984*, Wilhelmi, K. (ed.), pp. 87–96. Stuttgart: Konrad Theiss.

Fansa, M., and U. Kampffmeyer 1985. Vom Jäger und Sammler zum Ackerbauern. In *Ausgrabungen in Niedersachsen, Archäologische Denkmalpflege 1979–1984*, Wilhelmi, K. (ed.), pp. 108–11. Stuttgart: Konrad Theiss.

Farruggia, J.P., C. Constantin, L. Demarez 1982. Fouilles dans le groupe de Blicquy à Ormeignies, Irchonwelz, Aubechies 1977–1980. *Helenium* 22: 104–34.

Feinman, G., and J. Neitzel 1984. Too many types: an overview of sedentary prestate societies in the Americas. In *Advances in Archaeological Method and Theory*, Schiffer, M.B. (ed.), Vol. 7, pp. 39–102. Orlando: Academic Press.

Ferguson, R.B. (ed.) 1984. *Warfare, Culture, and Environment*. Orlando: Academic Press.

Firbas, F. 1949. *Spät- und Nacheiszeitliche Waldgeschichte Mitteleuropas Nördlich der Alpen*. Jena: Fischer.

Firth, R. 1959. *Social Change in Tikopia*. New York: Macmillan.

Fischer, A. 1982. Trade in Danubian shaft-hole axes and the introduction of neolithic economy in Denmark. *Journal of Danish Archaeology* 1: 7–12.

Fitter, A. 1978. *An Atlas of the Wild Flowers of Britain and Northern Europe*. London: Collins.

Flannery, K. (ed.) 1976. *The Early Mesoamerican Village*. New York: Academic Press.

Forbes, H. 1982. *Strategies and Soils: Technology, Production and Environment in the Peninsula of Methana, Greece.* Ann Arbor: University Microfilms International.

Ford, R. 1979. Gathering and gardening: trends and consequences of Hopewell subsistence strategies. In *Hopewell Archaeology: the Chillicothe Conference*, Brose, D., and Greber, N. (eds.), pp. 234–8. Kent (Ohio): Kent State University Press.

Fortes, M. 1962. Introduction. In *The Developmental Cycle in Domestic Groups*, Goody, J. (ed.), pp. 1–14. Cambridge: Cambridge University Press.

Frechen, J. 1965. Petrographische Untersuchung von Steingerät bzw. dessen Rohmaterial. In *Müddersheim, eine Ansiedlung der jüngeren Bandkeramik im Rheinland*, by K. Schietzel, pp. 39–42. Cologne: Böhlau.

Frenzel, B. 1966. Climatic change in the Atlantic/sub-Boreal transition on the Northern Hemisphere: botanical evidence. In *World Climate from 8000–O BC*, Sawyer, J.S. (ed.), pp. 99–123. London: Royal Meteorological Society.

Fried, M., M. Harris, and R. Murphy 1967. *War: the Anthropology of Armed Conflict and Aggression.* Garden City (NY): Natural History Press.

Fröhlich, S. 1985. Die jungsteinzeitliche Siedlung "Im Hassel" bei Heede, Landkreis Emsland. In *Ausgrabungen in Niedersachsen, Archäologische Denkmalpflege 1979–1984*, Wilhelmi, K. (ed.), pp. 111–14. Stuttgart: Konrad Theiss.

Gabałówna, L. 1970. Jama A ze spalonym zbożem z osady kultury pucharów lejkowatych na stanowisku 1 w Radziejowie Kujawskim (Informacja Wstępna). *Prace i Materiały Muzeum Archeologicznego i Etnograficznego* (archaeological series) 17: 157–63.

Garbett, G. 1981. The elm decline: the depletion of a resource. *New Phytologist* 88: 573–85

Gehl, O. 1974. Die Jagd- und Haustiere der steinzeitlichen Siedler von Basedow. *Bodendenkmalpflege in Mecklenburg* 1973: 67–87.

1976. Die steinzeitliche Siedlung Stinthorst bei Waren/Müritz im Spiegel des Säugetierfundgutes. *Bodendenkmalpflege in Mecklenburg* 1975: 39–53.

1980. Nutzung von Haus- und Wildtieren nach dem Knochenfundgut der neolithischen Siedlung bei Glasow und der Randow, Kreis Pasewalk. *Bodendenkmalpflege in Mecklenburg* 1979: 39–48.

Gendel, P.A. 1984. *Mesolithic Social Territories in Northwestern Europe.* Oxford: British Archaeological Reports (International Series 218).

Geupel, V. 1981. Zum Verhältnis Spätmesolithikum–Frühneolithikum im mittleren Elbe-Saale-Gebiet. In *Mesolithikum in Europa*, Gramsch, B. (ed.), pp. 105–12. Potsdam: Museum für Ur- und Frühgeschichte, Veröffentlichungen 14/15.

Godłowska, M. 1985. Bemerkungen zur Nutzung der Salzquellen im Neolithikum von Malopolska. *Jahresschrift für mitteldeutsche Vorgeschichte* 68: 121–9.

Goodenough, W.H. 1956. Residence rules. *Southwestern Journal of Anthropology* 12: 22–37.

1961. Review of 'Social structure in southeast Asia'. *American Anthropologist* 63: 1341–7.

Goody, J. 1962. The fission of domestic groups among the LoDagaba. In *The Developmental Cycle in Domestic Groups*, Goody, J. (ed.), pp. 53–91. Cambridge: Cambridge University Press.

Goody, J. (ed.) 1962. *The Developmental Cycle in Domestic Groups.* Cambridge: Cambridge University Press.

Gould, R.A. 1975. Ecology and adaptive response among the Tolowa Indians of Northwestern California. *Journal of California Anthropology* 2: 148–70.

Gradmann, R. 1933. Die Steppenheide-Theorie. *Geographische Zeitschrift* 39: 265–78.

Grayson, D.K. 1979. On the quantification of vertebrate archaeofaunas. In *Advances in Archaeological Method and Theory*, Vol. 2, Schiffer, M. (ed.), pp. 200–37. New York: Academic Press.

Green, S.W. 1979. The agricultural colonization of temperate forest habitats: an ecological model. In *The Frontier: Comparative Studies*, Savage, W., and Thompson, S. (eds.), Vol. 2, pp. 69–103. Norman: University of Oklahoma Press.

1980a. Toward a general model of agricultural systems. In *Advances in Archaeological Method and Theory*, Schiffer, M.B. (ed.), Vol. 3, pp. 311–55. New York: Academic Press.

1980b. Broadening least-cost models for expanding agricultural systems. In *Modeling Change in Prehistoric Subsistence Economies*, Earle, T.K., and Christenson, A.L. (eds.), pp. 209–41. New York: Academic Press.

Green, S.W., and K.E. Sassaman 1983. The political economy of resource management:a general model and application to foraging societies in the Carolina Piedmont. In *Ecological Models in Economic Prehistory*, Bronitsky, G. (ed.), pp. 261–90. Tempe: Arizona State University Anthropological Research Paper 29.

Gregg, S.A. 1986. *Forager/Farmer Interaction: Processes in the Neolithic Colonization of Central Europe*. Ann Arbor: University Microfilms International.

Greig, J. 1982. Past and present lime woods of Europe. In *Archaeological Aspects of Woodland Ecology*, Bell, M., and Limbrey, S. (eds.), pp. 23–55. Oxford: British Archaeological Reports (International Series 146).

Griffin, P.B. 1984. Forager resource and land use in the humid tropics: the Agta of Northeastern Luzon, the Philippines. In *Past and Present in Hunter Gatherer Studies*, Schrire, C. (ed.), pp. 95–121. Orlando: Academic Press.

Grigson, C. 1969. The uses and limitations of differences in absolute size in the distinction between the bones of aurochs (*Bos primigenius*) and domestic cattle (*Bos taurus*). In *The Domestication and Exploitation of Plants and Animals*, Ucko, P., and Dimbleby, G. (eds.), pp. 277–94. London: Duckworth.

Grooth, M. T. de 1977. Silex der Bandkeramik. In *Die Neolithische Besiedlung bei Hienheim, Ldkr. Kelheim. I. Die Ausgrabungen am Weinberg 1965 bis 1970*, by P.J.R. Modderman, pp. 56–70. Leiden: Institute for Prehistory (Analecta Praehistorica Leidensia 10).

Grygiel, R. 1980. Jama ze spaloną pszenicą kultury pucharów lejkowatych z Opatowic, woj. włocławskie. *Prace i Materialy Muzeum Archeologicznego i Etnograficznego* (archaeological series) 26: 41–55.

1986. The Household Cluster as a Fundamental Social Unit of the Brześć Kujawski Group of the Lengyel Culture. *Prace i Materialy Muzeum Archeologicznego i Etnograficznego* (archaeological series) 31: 43–334.

Grygiel, R., and P. Bogucki 1986. Early Neolithic sites at Brześć Kujawski, Poland: preliminary report on the 1980–1984 excavations. *Journal of Field Archaeology* 13(2): 121–37.

Gulliver, P.H. 1971. *Neighbours and Networks: the Idiom of Kinship in Social Action among the Ndendeuli of Tanzania*. Berkeley-Los Angeles-London: University of California Press.

Günther, K. 1976. *Die jungsteinzeitlichen Siedlung Deiringsen/Ruploh in der Soester Börde*. Münster: Westfalisches Landesmuseum für Vor- und Frühgeschichte (Bodenaltertumer Westfalens 16).

Hageman, B.P. 1969. Development of the western part of the Netherlands during the Holocene. *Geologie en Mijnbouw* 48: 373–88.

Hallam, S. 1975. *Fire and Hearth: a Study of Aboriginal Usage and European Usurpation in Southwestern Australia*. Canberra: Australian Institute of Aboriginal Studies (Australian Aboriginal Studies 58).

Hamond, F.W. 1978. Regional survey strategies: a simulation approach. In *Sampling in Contemporary British Archaeology*, Cherry, J., Gamble, C., and Shennan, S. (eds.), pp. 67–85. Oxford: British Archaeological Reports (British Series 50).

1980. The interpretation of archaeological distribution maps: biases inherent in archaeological fieldwork. *Archaeo-Physika* 7: 193–216.

1981. The colonisation of Europe: the analysis of settlement process. In *Pattern of the Past: Studies in Honour of David Clarke*. Hodder, I., Isaac, G., and Hammond, N. (eds.), pp. 211–78. Cambridge: Cambridge University Press.

Handwerker, W.P. 1983. The first demographic transition: an analysis of subsistence choices and reproductive consequences. *American Anthropologist* 85(1): 5–27.

Hardesty, D.L. 1977. *Ecological Anthropology*. New York: John Wiley and Sons.

Harner, M. 1975. Scarcity, the factors of production, and social evolution. In *Population, Ecology, and Social Evolution*, Polgar, S. (ed.), pp. 123–38. The Hague–Paris: Mouton.

Harris, M. 1974. *Cows, Pigs, Wars, and Witches: The Riddles of Culture*. New York: Vintage Books.

1984. A cultural materialist theory of band and village warfare: the Yanomamö test. In *Warfare, Culture, and Environment*, Ferguson, R.B. (ed.), pp. 111–40. Orlando: Academic Press.

Hartmann-Frick, H. 1969. Die Tierwelt im neolithischen Siedlungsraum. In *Ur- und frühgeschichtliche Archäologie der Schweiz*, vol. 2, pp. 17–32. Basel.

Heinrich, D., and J. Lepiksaar 1979. Die Fischreste von Bistoft LA 11. In *Socio-ekonomiska Strukturer i Tidigt Neolitikum och deras Förutsättningar*, by L. Johansson, pp. 112–17. Göteborg: Institute for Archaeology, University of Göteborg.

Hensel, W., and S. Milisauskas 1985. *Excavations of Neolithic and Early Bronze Age Sites in South-Eastern Poland*. Wroclaw: Ossolineum.

Heybroek, H.M. 1963. Diseases and lopping for fodder as possible causes of a prehistoric decline of *Ulmus*. *Acta Botanica Neerlandica* 12: 1–11.

Higham, C. 1967. Stock rearing as a cultural factor in prehistoric Europe. *Proceedings of the Prehistoric Society* 33: 84–106.

Higham, C., and M.A. Message 1969. An assessment of a prehistoric technique of bovine husbandry. In *Science in Archaeology*, Brothwell, D., and Higgs, E. (eds.), pp. 315–30. New York: Praeger.

Hingst, H. 1971. Eine jungsteinzeitliche Siedlung aus Büdelsdorf, Kr. Rendsburg. *Germania* 49: 219–20.

Hodder, I., and C. Orton 1976. *Spatial Analysis in Archaeology*. Cambridge: Cambridge University Press.

Hopf, M. 1981. Die Pflanzenreste aus Schernau, Ldkr. Kitzingen. In *Eine Siedlung der mittelneolithischen Gruppe Bischheim in Schernau, Ldkr. Kitzingen*, by J. Lüning, pp. 152–60. Kallmunz/Opf.: Michael Lassleben (Materialhefte zur Bayerischen Vorgeschichte 44).

Howell, J.M. 1982. Neolithic settlement and economy in northern France. *Oxford Journal of Archaeology* 1(1): 115–18.

1983. *Settlement and Economy in Neolithic Northern France*. Oxford: British Archaeological Reports (International Series 157).

Hubbard, R.N.L.B. 1975. Assessing the botanical component of human palaeoeconomies. *Bulletin of the Institute of Archaeology* (London) 12: 197–205.

1980. Development of agriculture in Europe and the Near East: evidence from quantitative studies. *Economic Botany* 34(1): 53–67.

Hübner, K.-D. 1980. Untersuchungen an Knochen von Raubtieren und von Biber vom vorgeschichtlichen Siedlungsplatz Hüde am Dümmer/Niedersachsen. University of Kiel: unpublished Staatsexamenarbeit.

Hughes, I. 1977. *New Guinea Stone Age Trade. The Geography and Ecology of Traffic in the Interior*. Canberra: Australian National University, Research School of Pacific Studies.

Hüster, H. 1983. Die Fischknochen der neolithischen Moorsiedlung Hüde I am Dümmer, Kreis Grafschaft Diepholz. *Neue Ausgrabungen und Forschungen in Niedersachsen* 16: 401–80.

Ilett, M., C. Constantin, A. Coudart, and J.P. Demoule 1982. The late Bandkeramik of the Aisne Valley: environment and spatial organisation. *Analecta Praehistorica Leidensia* 15: 45–61.

Isbell, W.H. 1978. Environmental perturbations and the origins of the Andean state. In *Social Archaeology: Beyond Subsistence and Dating*, Redman, C., et al. (eds.), pp. 303–13. New York: Academic Press.

Iversen, J. 1941. Landnam i Danmarks stenalder: land occupation in Denmark's Stone Age. *Danmarks Geologiske Undersøgelse*, Series II, No. 66, pp. 1–68.

   1973. The development of Denmark's nature since the last glacial. *Danmarks Geologiske Undersøgelse*, Series V, No. 7c, pp. 7–125.

Jankowska, D. 1980. *Kultura Pucharów Lejkowatych na Pomorzu Środkowym. Grupa łupawska.* Poznań: Adam Mickiewicz University (Archaeological Series 17).

Jarman, H.N. 1976. Early crop agriculture in Europe. In *Origine de l'Élevage et de la Domestication*, Higgs, E. (ed.), pp. 116–42. Nice: Union International des Sciences Préhistoriques et Protohistoriques (Colloque XX, IX Congrès).

Jarman, M.R., G.N. Bailey, and H.N. Jarman 1982. Early European Agriculture. Its Foundation and Development. Cambridge: Cambridge University Press.

Jażdżewski, K. 1938. Cmentarzyska kultury ceramiki wstęgowej i związane z nimi ślady osadnictwa w Brześciu Kujawskim. *Wiadomości Archeologiczne* 15: 1–105.

   1981. Über sogennante Sieb- und Rauchergefässe aus Mitteleuropa. In *Beiträge zur Ur- und Frühgeschichte*, Kaufmann, H., and Simon, K. (eds.), pp. 325–54. Berlin (Arbeits und Forschungsberichte zur Sächsischen Bodendenkmalpflege, Beiheft 16).

Jochim, M.A. 1976. *Hunter-Gatherer Subsistence and Settlement: a Predictive Model.* New York: Academic Press.

   1979a. Caches and catches: ethnographic alternatives for prehistory. In *Ethnoarchaeology. Implications of Ethnography for Archaeology*, Kramer, C. (ed.), pp. 219–46. New York: Columbia University Press.

   1979b. Breaking down the system: recent ecological approaches in archaeology. In *Advances in Archaeological Method and Theory*, Schiffer, M.B. (ed.), volume 2, pp. 77–117. Orlando: Academic Press.

   1981. *Strategies for Survival. Cultural Behavior in an Ecological Context.* New York-London: Academic Press.

Jodłowski, A. 1976. *Technika Produkcji Soli na Terenie Europy w Pradziejach i we Wczesnym Średniowieczu.* Wieliczka (Poland): Muzeum Żup Krakówskich (Studia i Materiały do Dziejów Żup Solnych w Polsce 5).

   1977. Die Salzgewinnung auf polnischen Boden in vorgeschichtlicher Zeit und im frühen Mittelalter. *Jahresschrift für mitteldeutsche Vorgeschichte* 61: 85–103.

Johansson, F. 1979. Die Knochenfunde von Säugetieren und Vögeln von Bistoft LA 11. In *Socio-Ecknomiska Strukturer i Tidigt Neolitikum och deras Förutsättningar*, by L. Johansson, pp. 98–111. Göteborg: Institute for Archaeology, University of Göteborg.

Johansson, L. 1979. *Socio-Ekonomiska Strukturer i Tidigt Neolithikum och deras Förutsättningar.* Göteborg: University of Göteborg, Institute of Archaeology.

   1981. Bistoft LA 11. Siedlungs- und Wirtschaftsformen im frühen Neolithikum Norddeutschlands und Südskandinaviens. *Offa* 38: 91–115.

Jones, R. 1973. The Neolithic Palaeolithic and the hunting gardeners: man and land in the Antipodes. In *Quaternary Studies. Selected Papers from the IX INQUA Congress*, Suggate, R., and Cresswell, M. (eds.), pp. 21–34. Wellington: Royal Society of New Zealand. Bulletin 13.

Jorde, L.B. 1977. Precipitation cycles and cultural buffering in the prehistoric Southwest. *For Theory Building in Archaeology*, Binford, L.R. (ed.), pp. 385–96. New York: Academic Press.

Jørgensen, G. 1977. Et kornfund frå Sarup. Bidrag til belysning af Tragtbaegerkulturens agerbrug. *KUML* 1976: 47–84

1982. Korn frå Sarup. Med nogle bemaerkningen om agerbruget i yngre stenalder i Danmark. *KUML* 1981: 221–31.

Jürgens, A. 1978/9. Rössener Siebe aus Aldenhoven. *Kölner Jahrbuch für Vor- und Frühgeschichte* 16: 17–20.

1979. Die Rössener Siedlung von Aldenhoven, Kreis Düren. In *Beiträge zur Urgeschichte des Rheinlandes* III, pp. 385–505. Cologne: Rheinland-Verlag (Rheinische Ausgrabungen 19).

Kampffmeyer, U. 1983. Die neolithische Siedlungsplatz Hüde I am Dümmer. In *Frühe Bauernkulturen in Niedersachsen*, Wegner, G. (ed.), pp. 119–34. Oldenburg: Staatliches Museum für Naturkunde und Vorgeschichte.

Kaufmann, D. 1978. Ergebnisse der Ausgrabungen bei Eilsleben, Kr. Wanzleben, in den Jahren 1974 bis 1976. *Zeitschrift für Archäologie* 12: 1–8.

1983. Die ältestlinienbandkeramischen Funde von Eilsleben, Kr. Wanzleben, und der Beginn des Neolithikums im Mittelelbe-Saale-Gebiet. *Nachrichten aus Niedersachsens Urgeschichte* 52: 177–202.

Keene, A. S. 1981. *Prehistoric Foraging in a Temperate Forest: a Linear Programming Model.* New York: Academic Press.

Kerkhoff-Hader, B. 1980. *Lebens- und Arbeitsformen der Töpfer in der Südwesteifel. Ein Beitrag zur Steinzeugforschung in Rheinland.* Bonn: Rohrscheid (Rheinisches Archiv 110).

Kind, C.-J., and E. Schmidt 1983. Die Ausgrabungen bei Ulm-Eggingen. *Denkmalpflege in Baden-Württemburg* 13: 168–73.

Klichowska, M. 1976. Aus palaeoethnobotanischen Studien über Pflanzenfunde aus dem Neolithikim und der Bronzezeit auf polnischen Boden. *Archaeologia Polona* 17: 27–67.

Knörzer, K.-H. 1971. Urgeschichtliche Unkräuter in Rheinland. Ein Beitrag zur Entstehung der Segetalgesellschaften. *Vegetatio* 23: 89–111.

1973. Pflanzliche Grossreste. In *Der Bandkeramische Siedlungsplatz Langweiler 2*, by Farruggia, J., Kuper, R., Lüning, J., and Stehli, P., pp. 139–52. Cologne: Rheinland Verlag.

1974. Bandkeramische Pflanzenfunde von Bedburg-Garsdorf, Kreis Bergheim/Erft. *Beiträge zur Urgeschichte des Rheinlandes* I, pp. 173–92. Cologne: Rheinland Verlag (Rheinische Ausgrabungen 15).

Kozłowski, S.K. 1973. Introduction to the history of Europe in the early Holocene. *The Mesolithic in Europe*, Kozłowski, S.K. (ed.), pp. 331–66. Warsaw: Warsaw University Press.

1975. *Cultural Differentiation of Europe between the 10th and 5th Millennia B.C.* Warsaw: University of Warsaw Press.

Kristiansen, K. 1982. The formation of tribal systems in later European prehistory: Northern Europe 4000–500 BC. In *Theory and Explanation in Archaeology*, Renfrew, C., Rowlands, M.J., and Segraves, B. (eds.), pp. 241–79. New York: Academic Press.

Kruk, J. 1973. *Studia Osadnicze nad Neolitem Wyżyn Lessowych.* Wrocław: Ossolineum.

1980. *Gospodarka w Polsce Poludniowo-Wschodniej w V–III Tysiącleciu p.n.e.* Wrocław: Ossolineum.

Kruk, J., and S. Milisauskas 1979. Befestigungen der späten Polgár-Kultur bei Bronocice (Polen). *Archäologisches Korrespondenzblatt* 9: 9–13.

1981. Wyżynne osiedle neolityczne w Bronocicach, woj. kieleckie. *Archeologia Polski* 26: 65–113.

Kruk, J., and S. Milisauskas 1985. *Bronocice. Osiedle Obronne Ludności Kultury Lubelsko-Wołyńskiej (2800–2700 lat p.n.e.).* Wrocław: Ossolineum.

Kubasiewicz, M. 1956. O metodyce badań wykopaliskowych szczątków kostnych zwierzęcych. *Materiały Zachodnio-Pomorskie* 2: 235–44.

Kulczycka-Leciejewiczowa, A. 1979. Pierwsze społeczeństwa rolnicze na ziemiach polskich. Kultury kręgu naddunajskiego. *Prahistoria Ziem Polskich II*. *Neolit*, Hensel, W. and Wiślański, T. (eds.), pp. 19–164. Wrocław: Ossolineum.

Kunstadter, P. 1984. Cultural ideals, socioeconomic change, and household composition: Karen, Luan, Hmong, and Thai in northwestern Thailand. In *Households, Comparative and Historical Studies of the Domestic Group*, Netting, R., Wilk, R., and Arnould, E. (eds.), pp. 299–329. Berkeley-Los Angeles-London: University of California Press.

Kuper, R., and J. Lüning 1975. Untersuchungen zur neolithischen Besiedlung der Aldenhovener Platte. *Ausgrabungen in Deutschland* 1: 85–97.

Kuper, R., and W. Piepers 1966. Eine Siedlung der Rössener Kultur in Inden (Kreis Jülich) und Lamersdorf (Kreis Düren). Vorbericht. *Bonner Jahrbücher* 166: 370–6.

Kuper, R., H. Löhr, J. Lüning, P. Stehli, and A. Zimmerman 1977. *Der bandkeramische Siedlungsplatz Langweiler 9, Gem. Aldenhoven, Kr. Düren*. Bonn: Rheinland-Verlag (Rheinische Ausgrabungen 18).

La Fontaine, J.S. 1978. Introduction. In *Sex and Age as Principles of Social Differentiation*, La Fontaine, J.S. (ed.), pp. 1–20. London–New York–San Francisco: Academic Press (A.S.A. Monograph 17).

Lamb, H.H. 1984. *Climatic History and the Future*. Princeton: Princeton University Press.

Lech, J., and A. Leligdowicz 1980. Die Methoden der Versorgung mit Feuerstein und die lokalen Beziehungen zwischen Siedlungen und Bergwerken im Weichsel gebiet während des 5. bis 2. Jt. v. u. Z. In *Urgeschichtliche Besiedlung in ihrer Beziehung zur naturlicher Umwelt*, Schlette, F. (ed.), pp. 151–84. Halle/Saale: Martin-Luther-Universität (Wissenschaftliche Beiträge 1980/6 L15).

Lefferts, H.L. 1977. Frontier demography: an introduction. In *The Frontier: Comparative Studies*, Miller, D., and Steffen, J. (eds.), Vol. 1, pp. 33–56. Norman: University of Oklahoma Press.

Leibenstein, H. 1976. *Beyond Economic Man*. Cambridge (Mass.): Harvard University Press.

Lenneis, E. 1982. Die Siedlungsverteilung der Linearbandkeramik in &ocu.sterreich. *Archaeologia Austriaca* 66: 1–19.

Levin, R.I., and C.A. Kirkpatrick 1975. *Quantitative Approaches to Management* (third edition). New York: McGraw-Hill.

Lewis, H.T. 1973. *Patterns of Indian Burning in California: Ecology and Ethnohistory*. Ramona (California): Ballena Press (Anthropological Papers 1).

Lichardus, J. 1976. *Rössen–Gatersleben–Baalberge. Ein Beitrag zur Chronologie des mitteldeutschen Neolithikums und zur Entstehung der Trichterbecher-Kulturen*. Bonn: Habelt (Saarbrücker Beiträge zur Altertumskunde 17).

Lička, M. 1981. Neolithic settlement site at Mšeno by Mělník, Bohemia. In *Nouvelles Archéologiques dans la République Socialiste Tchèque*, Hrala, J. (ed.), pp. 24–5. Prague-Brno: Institute of Archaeology, Czechoslovak Academy of Sciences.

Lightfoot, K.G., and G.M. Feinman 1982. Social differentiation and leadership development in pithouse villages in the Mogollon region of the American Southwest. *American Antiquity* 47: 64–86.

Linares, O. 1976. 'Garden hunting' in the American tropics. *Human Ecology* 4: 331–49.

Linke, W. 1976. *Frühestes Bauerntum und Geographische Umwelt*. Paderborn: Schöningh (Bochumer Geographische Arbeiten 28).

Louwe Kooijmans, L.P. 1976. Local developments in a borderland, a survey of the Neolithic at the Lower Rhine. *Oudheidkundige Mededelingen* 57: 227–97.

    1980a. Archaeology and coastal change in the Netherlands. *Archaeology and Coastal Change*, Thompson, F.H. (ed.), pp. 106–33. London: The Society of Antiquaries of London (Occasional Paper, new series, I).

1980b. Het onderzoek van neolithische nederzettingsterreinen in Nederland anno 1979. *Westerheem* 29: 93–136.

1987. Neolithic settlement and subsistence in the wetlands of the Rhine/Meuse delta. In *European Wetlands in Prehistory*, Coles, J., and Lawson, A. (eds.) pp. 227–51. Oxford: Oxford University Press.

Love, T.F. 1977. Ecological niche theory in sociocultural anthropology: a conceptual framework and an application. *American Ethnologist* 4: 27–41.

Lüning, J. 1968. Die Michelsberger Kultur. Ihre Funde in zeitlicher und räumlicher Gliederung. *Berichte der Römisch-Germanischen Kommission* 48: 1–350.

1980. Getreideanbau ohne Düngung? *Archäologisches Korrespondenzblatt* 10: 117–22.

1981. *Eine Siedlung der mittelneolithischen Gruppe Bischheim in Schernau, Ldkr. Kitzingen.* Kallmunz/Opf.: Michael Lassleben. (Materialhefte zur Bayerischen Vorgeschichte 44).

1982a. Siedlung und Siedlungslandschaft in bandkeramischer und Rössener Zeit. *Offa* 39: 9–33.

1982b. Research into the Bandkeramik settlement of the Aldenhovener Platte in the Rhineland. *Analecta Praehistorica Leidensia* 15: 1–29.

Lüning, J., and P.J.R. Modderman 1982. Hausgrundrisse der ältesten Bandkeramik aus Schwanfeld, Landkreis Schweinfurt, Unterfranken. In *Das archäologische Jahr in Bayern 1981*, Christlein, R. (ed.), pp. 66–7. Stuttgart: Konrad Theiss.

Lüning, J., and H. Zürn 1977. *Die Schussenrieder Siedlung "Im Schlösslesfeld", Markung Ludwigsburg.* Stuttgart: Landesdenkmalamt Baden-Württemburg (Forschungen und Berichte zur Vor- und Frühgeschichte in Baden-Württemburg, Volume 8).

Lüttschwager, H. 1967. Kurzbericht über Tierfunde aus meso- und neolithischen Moorsiedlungen in Schleswig-Holstein. *Schriften des Naturwissenschaftlichen Vereins für Schleswig-Holstein* 37: 53–64.

Madsen, T. 1978. Toftum – ein neues neolithisches Erdwerk bei Horsens, Ostjutland (Danemark). *Archäologisches Korrespondenzblatt* 8: 1–7.

1982. Settlement systems of early agricultural societies in East Jutland, Denmark: a regional study of change. *Journal of Anthropological Archaeology* 1: 197–236.

Madsen, T., and J.E. Petersen 1984. Tidligneolitiske anlaeg ved Mosegården. Regionale og kronologiske forskelle i tidligneolithikum. *KUML* 1982–3: 61–120.

Magny, M. 1982. Atlantic and Sub-boreal – dampness and dryness? In *Climatic Change in Later Prehistory*, Harding, A. (ed.), pp. 33–43. Edinburgh: Edinburgh University Press.

Mania, D. 1973. Eiszeitliche Landschaftsentwicklung im Kartenbild, dargestellt am Beispiel des mittleren Elbe-Saale-Gebiet. *Jahresschrift für Mitteldeutsche Vorgeschichte* 57: 17–47.

Mania, D., and J. Preuss 1975. Zu Methoden und Problemen ökologischer Untersuchungen in der Ur- und Frühgeschichte. In *Symbolae Praehistoricae*, Preuss, J. (ed.), pp. 9–59. Berlin: Akademie Verlag.

Maruszczak, H. 1983. Procesy rzezbotwórcze na obszarze Polski w okresie ostatniego zlodowacenia i w holocenie. In *Czlowiek i Środowisko w Pradziejach*, Kozlowski, J.K., Kozlowski, S.K. (eds.), pp. 35–42. Warsaw: Państwowe Wydawnictwo Naukowe.

Mazurowski, R. 1983. Bursztyn. In *Czlowiek i Środowisko w Pradziejach*, Kozlowski, J.K., and Kozlowski, S.K. (eds.), pp. 177–88. Warsaw: Państwowe Wydawnictwo Naukowe.

Meadow, R.H. 1976. Methodological concerns in zoo-archaeology. In *Problèmes Ethnographiques des Vestiges Osseux (Thèmes Spécialisés)*, pp. 108–23. Nice: IXe Congrès, Union International de Sciences Préhistoriques et Protohistoriques.

Meiklejohn, C., C. Schentag, A. Venema, and P. Key 1984. Socioeconomic change and patterns of pathology and variation in the Mesolithic and Neolithic of Western Europe:

some suggestions. In *Palaeopathology at the Origins of Agriculture*, Cohen, M. and Armelagos, G. (eds.), pp. 75–100. Orlando: Academic Press.

Meillassoux, C. 1972. From reproduction to production. *Economy and Society* 1: 93–105.

Mellars, P.A. 1975. Ungulate populations, economic patterns, and the Mesolithic landscape. In *The Effect of Man on the Landscape: the Highland Zone*, Evans, J., Limbrey, S., and Cleere, H. (eds.), pp. 49–56. London: Council for British Archaeology, Research Report 11.

1976. Fire ecology, animal populations, and man: a study of some ecological relationships. *Proceedings of the Prehistoric Society* 42: 15–46

Mellars, P.A., and S.C. Reinhardt 1978. Patterns of Mesolithic land-use in southern England: a geological perspective. In *The Early Postglacial Settlement of Northern Europe*, Mellars, P. (ed.), pp. 243–93. London: Duckworth.

Meniel, P. 1984. Les faunes du Rubané Récent de Menneville "Derriere le Village" et de Berry-au-Bac "La Croix Maigret" (Aisne). *Revue Archéologique de Picardie* 1984 (1/2): 87–93.

Midgley, M. 1985. *The Origin and Function of the Earthen Long Barrows of Northern Europe*. Oxford: British Archaeological Reports (International Series 259).

Milisauskas, S. 1977. Adaptations of the early Neolithic farmers in central Europe. In *For the Director: Research Essays in Honor of James B. Griffin*, Cleland, C.E. (ed.), pp. 295–316. Ann Arbor: Museum of Anthropology, University of Michigan (Anthropological Papers 61).

1978. *European Prehistory*. New York: Academic Press.

1982. A study of prehistoric social organization in Europe. *Reviews in Anthropology*, 9(2): 109–16.

1983. Bandkeramische Obsidianartifakte aus Olszanica. *Archäologisches Korrespondenzblatt* 13: 171–5.

Milisauskas, S., and J. Kruk 1982. Die Wagendarstellung auf einem Trichterbecher aus Bronocice in Polen. *Archäologisches Korrespondenzblatt* 12: 141–4.

1984. Settlement organization and the appearance of low level hierarchical societies during the Neolithic in the Bronocice microregion. *Germania* 62: 1–30.

Minnis, P. 1985. *Social Adaptation to Food Stress. A Prehistoric Southwestern Example*. Chicago and London: University of Chicago Press.

Modderman, P.J.R. 1958/9. Die geographische Lage der bandkeramischen Siedlungen in der Niederlanden. *Palaeohistoria* 6: 1–6.

1970. *Linearbandkeramik aus Elsloo und Stein*. Leiden: Institute of Prehistory (Analecta Praehistorica Leidensia 3).

1971. Bandkeramiker und Wandernbauerntum. *Archäologisches Korrespondenzblatt* 1: 7–9.

1972. Die Hausbauten und Siedlungen der Linienbandkeramik in ihren westlichen Bereich. In *Die Anfänge des Neolithikums vom Orient bis Nordeuropa*, Schwabedissen, H. (ed.), pp. 77–84. Cologne: Böhlau.

1974. Die Limburger Keramik von Kesseleyk. *Archäologisches Korrespondenzblatt* 4: 5–11.

1976. Abschwemmung und neolithische Siedlungsplätze in Niederbayern. *Archäologisches Korrespondenzblatt* 6: 105–8.

1977. *Die Neolithische Besiedlung bei Hienheim, Ldkr. Kelheim, I. Die Ausgrabungen am Weinberg 1965 bis 1970*. Leiden: Institute of Prehistory (Analecta Praehistorica Leidensia 10).

1982. Bandkeramische Siedlungen in den südlichen Niederlanden und im donaubayerischen Gebiet: zur Umwelt, Verbreitung, und Struktur. *Offa* 39: 35–8.

1985. Die Bandkeramik im Graetheidegebiet, Niederländisch Limburg. *Bericht der Römisch-Germanischen Kommission* 66: 25–121.

Moore, J. 1981. The effects of information networks in hunter-gatherer societies. In
   Hunter-Gatherer Foraging Strategies, Winterhalder, B., and Smith, E.A. (eds.), pp.
   194–217. Chicago: University of Chicago Press.
   1985. Forager/farmer interactions: information, social organization, and the frontier. In
   The Archaeology of Frontiers and Boundaries, Green, S., and Perlman, S. (eds.), pp.
   93–112. Orlando: Academic Press.
Morren, G. E. B. 1984. Warfare on the highland fringe. The case of the Mountain Ok. In
   Warfare, Culture, and Environment, Ferguson, B. (ed.), pp. 169–207. Orlando:
   Academic Press.
Mueller, B. 1983. Untersuchungen an Fischknochen aus den neolithischen Moorsiedlungen
   Heidmoor (Berlin-Krs. Segeberg) und Oldesloe-Wolkenwehe (Krs. Stormarn). Kiel:
   unpublished Examensarbeit zum 1. Staatsexamen für Lehramt an Gymnasien.
Müller, H.-H. 1964. *Die Haustiere der Mitteldeutschen Bandkeramiker*. Berlin: Deutsche
   Akademie der Wissenschaften.
Nagel, E. 1980. Ein Siedlungsplatz der Trichterbecherkultur in Glasow, Kreis Pasewalk.
   Bodendenkmalpflege in Mecklenburg 1979: 7–38.
Naroll, R. 1962. Floor area and settlement population. *American Antiquity* 27: 587–9.
Netting, R. 1974. Agrarian ecology. *Annual Review of Anthropology* 3: 21–56.
Netting, R., R. Wilk, and E. Arnould (eds.) 1984. *Households. Comparative and Historical
   Studies of the Domestic Group*. Berkeley-Los Angeles-London: University of California
   Press.
Newell, R.R. 1970. The flint industry of the Dutch Linearbandkeramik. In
   Linearbandkeramik aus Elsloo und Stein, by P.J.R. Modderman, pp. 144–83. Leiden:
   Institute of Prehistory (Analecta Praehistorica Leidensia 3).
   1973. The post-glacial adaptations of the indigenous population of the north-west
   European plain. In *The Mesolithic in Europe*, Kozłowski, S.K. (ed.), pp. 399–440.
   Warsaw: University of Warsaw Press.
   1981. Mesolithic dwelling structures: fact and fantasy. In *Mesolithikum in Europa*,
   Gramsch, B. (ed.), pp. 235–84. Potsdam: Museum für Ur- und Frühgeschichte,
   Veröffentlichungen 14/15.
   1984. On the Mesolithic contribution to the social evolution of western European society.
   In *European Social Evolution*, Bintliff, J. (ed.), pp. 69–82. Bradford: University of
   Bradford.
Nielsen, P.O. 1985. De første bønder. Nye fund fra den tidligste Traegtbaegerkultur ved
   Sigersted. *Aarbøger for nordisk Oldkyndighed og Historie* 1984: 96–126.
Nilius, I. 1973. Die Siedlung der Trichterbecherkultur bei Gristow, Kr. Griefswald.
   Zeitschrift für Archäologie 7: 239–70.
   1975. Bemerkungen zu einigen auffalligen Keramikfunden in der Trichterbechersiedlung
   von Gristow, Kreis Greifswald. In *Symbolae Praehistoricae*, Preuss, J. (ed.), pp.
   123–32. Berlin: Akademie-Verlag (Wissenschaftliche Beiträge der
   Martin-Luther-Universität 1975/1 L11).
Nilius, I., and D. Warnke 1984. Ein eingetiefter Gebäudegrundriss der mittelneolithischen
   Trichterbecherkultur von Ralswiek, Kreis Rügen. *Bodendenkmalpflege in Mecklenburg*
   1983: 83–101.
Nilsson, T. 1964. Standardpollendiagramme und C^{14}Datierungen aus dem Agerøds mosse
   in mittleren Schonen. *Lunds Universitet Arsskrift* (N.F. 2) 59 (7): 1–52.
Niquet, F. 1963. Die Pröbegrabungen auf der frühbandkeramischen Siedlung bei Eitzum,
   Kreis Wolfenbüttel. *Neue Ausgrabungen und Forschungen in Niedersachsen* 1: 44–74.
Nobis, G. 1975. Zur Fauna des Ellerbekzeitlichen Wohnplatzes Rosenhof in Ostholstein I.
   (Grabung 1968–1973). *Schriften des Naturwissenschaftlichen Vereins für
   Schleswig-Holstein* 45: 5–30.
   1977. Die Fauna. In *Die Schussenrieder Siedlung "Im Schlösslesfeld", Markung
   Ludwigsburg*, by Lüning, J., and Zürn, H., pp. 82–90. Stuttgart: Landesdenkmalamt

Baden-Württemburg (Forschungen und Berichte zur Vor- und Frühgeschichte in Baden-Württemburg, Volume 8).

Odum, E.P. 1971. *Fundamentals of Ecology*. Philadelphia: W.B. Saunders.

Ottaway, B. 1973. Earliest copper ornaments in northern Europe. *Proceedings of the Prehistoric Society* 39: 294–331.

Patzelt, G., and S. Bortenschlager 1973. Die postglazialen Gletscher und Klimaschwankungen in der Venedigergruppe (Hohe Tauern, Ostalpen). *Zeitschrift für Geomorphologie* (N.F.) 16: 25–72.

Pavlů, I. 1981. The Neolithic site at Vochov by Plzeň. In *Nouvelles Archéologiques dans la République Socialiste Tchèque*, Hrala, J. (ed.), pp. 21–3. Prague-Brno: Institute of Archaeology, Czechoslovak Academy of Sciences.

Payne, S. 1973. Kill-off patterns in sheep and goat: the mandibles from Asvan Kale. *Anatolian Studies* 23: 281–303.

Peterson, J.T. 1978a. *The Ecology of Social Boundaries*. Urbana: University of Illinois Press (Illinois Studies in Anthropology 11).

1978b. Hunter-gatherer/farmer exchange. *American Anthropologist* 80(2): 335–51.

Piening, U. 1979. Neolithische Nutz- und Wildpflanze aus Endersbach, Rems-Murr-Kreis, und Ilsfeld, Kreis Heilbronn. *Fundberichte aus Baden-Württemburg* 4: 1–17.

Pipkin, J. 1981. Cognitive behavioral geography and repetitive travel. In *Behavioral Problems in Geography Revisited*, Cox, K., and Golledge, R. (eds.), pp. 145–81. New York and London: Methuen.

Pirożnikow, E. 1983. Seed bank in the soil of stabilized ecosystem of a deciduous forest (Tilio-Carpinetum) in the Białowieża National Park. *Ekologia Polski* 31(1): 145–172.

Pleinerová, I. 1981. Neolithic settlement site at Březno. In *Nouvelles Archéologiques dans la République Socialiste Tchèque*, Hrala, J. (ed.), pp. 32–3. Prague-Brno: Institute of Archaeology, Czechoslovak Academy of Sciences.

Poplin, F. 1975. La faune danubienne d'Armeau (Yonne, France). In *Archaeozoological Studies*, Clason, A.T. (ed.), pp. 179–92. Amsterdam-New York: North Holland/Elsevier.

Preuss, J. 1980. *Die altmarkische Gruppe der Tiefstichkeramik*. Berlin: Deutscher Verlag der Wissenschaften (Veröffentlichungen des Landesmuseums für Vorgeschichte in Halle 33).

Price, T.D. 1978. Mesolithic settlement systems in the Netherlands. In *The Early Postglacial Settlement of Northern Europe*, Mellars, P. (ed.), pp. 81–113. London: Duckworth.

1981a. Regional approaches to human adaptation in the Mesolithic of the North European Plain. In *Mesolithikum in Europa*, Gramsch, B. (ed.), pp. 217–34. Potsdam: Museum für Ur- und Frühgeschichte, Veröffentlichungen 14/15.

1981b. Swifterbant, Oost Flevoland, Netherlands: excavations at the river dune sites, S21–S24, 1976. *Palaeohistoria* 23: 75–104.

Price, T.D., and E. Brinch Petersen 1987. A Mesolithic camp in Denmark. *Scientific American* 256 (3): 112–21.

Quitta, H. 1960. Zur Frage der ältesten Bandkeramik in Mitteleuropa. *Prähistorische Zeitschrift* 38: 1–38, 153–89.

1970. Zur Lage und Verbreitung der bandkeramischen Siedlungen im Leipziger Land. *Zeitschrift für Archäologie* 4: 155–76.

Ralska-Jasiewiczowa, M. 1983. Isopollen maps for Poland: 0–11000 years BP. *New Phytologist* 94: 133–75.

Randsborg, K. 1975. Social dimensions of early Neolithic Denmark. *Proceedings of the Prehistoric Society* 41: 105–17.

1980. Resource distribution and the function of copper tools in Early Neolithic Denmark. In *The Origins of Metallurgy in Atlantic Europe*, Ryan, M. (ed.), pp. 303–18. Dublin: Irish Stationery Office.

Rappaport, R. 1968. *Pigs for the Ancestors*. New Haven: Yale University Press.

Rawitscher, F. 1945. The hazel period in the postglacial development of forests. *Nature* 156: 302–3.

Reidhead, V.A. 1980. The economics of subsistence change. In *Modeling change in Prehistoric Subsistence Economies*, Earle, T.K., and Christenson, A.L. (eds.), pp. 141–86. New York: Academic Press.

Reinerth, H. 1939. Ein Dorf der Grosssteingräberleute. Die Ausgrabungen des Reichsamtes für Vorgeschichte am Dümmer. *Germanenerbe* 4: 226–42.

Renfrew, C. 1973. *Before Civilization*. New York: Alfred A. Knopf.

    1976. Megaliths, territories, and populations. In *Acculturation and Continuity in Atlantic Europe*, de Laet, S.J. (ed.), pp. 298–320. Brugge: De Tempel (Dissertationes Archaeologicae Gandenses XVI).

Renfrew, J.M. 1973. *Palaeoethnobotany*. New York: Columbia University Press.

Richtofen, B. von 1930. Zur bandkeramischen Besiedlung im Bereich der unteren Weichsel und Oder. *Blätter für deutsche Vorgeschichte* 7: 18–52.

Riley, D., and A. Young 1968. *World Vegetation*. Cambridge: Cambridge University Press.

Roever, J.P de 1979. The pottery from Swifterbant – Dutch Ertebølle? *Helenium* 19: 13–36.

Romanow, J., K. Wąchowski, and B. Miszkiewicz 1973. *Tomice, Pow. Dzierzoniów. Wielokulturowe Stanowisko Archeologiczne*. Wrocław: Ossolineum.

Rothmaler, W., and I. Natho 1957. Bandkeramische Kulturpflanzreste aus Thüringen und Sachsen. *Beiträge zur Frühgeschichte der Landwirtschaft* 3: 73–98.

Rovner, I. 1983. Plant opal phytolith analysis: major advances in archaeobotanical research. In *Advances in Archaeological Method and Theory*, Vol. 6, Schiffer, M.B. (ed.), pp. 225–66. New York: Academic Press.

Rowley-Conwy, P. 1981. Slash and burn in the temperate European Neolithic. In *Farming Practice in British Prehistory*, Mercer, R. (ed.), pp. 85–96. Edinburgh: Edinburgh University Press.

    1982. Forest grazing and clearance in temperate Europe with special reference to Denmark. In *Archaeological Aspects of Woodland Ecology*, Limbrey, S., and Bell, M. (eds.), pp. 199–215. Oxford: British Archaeological Reports (International Series 146).

    1984. The laziness of the short-distance hunter: the origins of agriculture in western Denmark. *Journal of Anthropological Archaeology* 3: 300–24.

Sahlins, M.D. 1961. The segmentary lineage, an organization of predatory expansion. *American Anthropologist* 63: 322–45.

    1963. Poor man, rich man, big man, chief: political types in Melanesia and Polynesia. *Comparative Studies in Society and History* 5: 285–303.

Sangmeister, E. 1951. Zum Charakter der bandkeramischen Siedlung. *Bericht der Römisch-Germanischen Kommission* 33: 89–109.

Saur, R. 1980. Die knochenreste der Paar- und Unpaarhufe der neolithischen Moorsiedlung Hüde I am Dümmer. University of Kiel: unpublished Staatsexamenarbeit.

Schirnig, H. 1979. Das 'Huntedorf' bei Lembruch am Dümmer. In *Grosssteingräber in Niedersachsen*, Schirnig, H. (ed.), pp. 235–38. Hildesheim: August Lax.

Schlicht, E. 1979. Handels- und Kulturbeziehungen auf Grund von Importfunden aus niedersachsischen Grosssteingräbern. In *Grosssteingräber in Niedersachsen*, Schirnig, H. (ed.), pp. 169–78. Hildesheim: August Lax.

Schuldt, E. 1974. Die steinzeitliche Inselsiedlung im Malchiner See bei Basedow, Kreis Malchin. *Bodendenkmalpflege in Mecklenburg* 1973: 7–65.

Schultze-Motel, J. 1980. Neolithische Kulturpflanzenreste von Eilsleben, Kr. Wanzleben. *Zeitschrift für Archäologie* 14: 213–16.

Schütrumpf, R. 1972. Stratigraphie und pollenanalytische Ergebnisse der Ausgrabung des Ellerbek-zeitliche Wohnplatzes Rosenhof (Ostholstein). *Archäologisches Korrespondenzblatt* 2: 9–16.

Schütrumpf, R., and B. Schmidt 1977. Die Zusammenarbeit zwischen Vegetationsgeschichte und Dendrochronologie, aufgezeigt an zwei ausgewahlten Beispielen. In *Dendrochronologie und Postgläziale Klimaschwankungen in Europe*, Frenzel, B. (ed.), pp. 28–42. Wiesbaden: Franz Steiner Verlag.

Schwabedissen, H. 1957/8. Die Ausgrabungen im Satruper Moor. *Offa* 16: 5–28.

    1966. Ein horizontierter 'Breitkeil' aus Satrup und die mannigfachen Kulturverbindungen des beginnenden Neolithikums im Norden and Nordwesten. *Palaeohistoria* 12: 409–68.

    1981. Ertebølle/Ellerbek – Mesolithikum oder Neolithikum? In *Mesolithikum in Europa*, Gramsch, B. (ed.), pp. 129–42. Potsdam: Museum für Ur- und Frühgeschichte (Veröffentlichungen 14/15).

Schwarz-Mackensen, G. 1975. Die bandkeramische Siedlung in Schladen, Kr. Wolfenbüttel (früher Kr. Goslar). *Nachrichten aus Niedersachsens Urgeschichte* 44: 23–34.

    1982. Die Linienbandkeramik in Norddeutschland – Umwelt, Wirtschaft, und Kultur der frühen Ackerbauern. *Bericht der naturhistorischen Gesellschaft zu Hannover* 125: 161–81.

    1983. Zu den Grabungen der frühbandkeramischen Siedlung bei Eitzum, Kreis Wolfenbüttel, in den Jahren 1956 bis 1958. *Nachrichten aus Niedersachsens Urgeschichte* 52: 209–27.

Schwarz-Mackensen, G., and W. Schneider 1983. Wo liegen die Hauptliefergebiete für das Rohmaterial donaulandischer Steinbeile und -äxte in Mitteleuropa? *Archäologisches Korrspondenzblatt* 13: 305–14.

Seehafer, K. 1980. *Der Dümmer See in Farbe*. Stuttgart: Kosmos.

Selye, H. 1956. *The Stress of Life*. New York: McGraw-Hill.

Service, E.R. 1962. *Primitive Social Organization*. New York: Random House.

Shackleton, N., and C. Renfrew 1970. Neolithic trade routes realigned by oxygen isotope analysis. *Nature* 228: 1062–4.

Shennan, S.J. 1978. Archaeological 'cultures': an empirical investigation. In *The Spatial Organisation of Culture*, Hodder, I. (ed.), pp. 113–39. London: Duckworth.

    1982. The emergence of hierarchical structure. In *Ranking, Resource and Exchange*, Renfrew, C., and Shennan, S.J. (eds.), pp. 9–11. Cambridge: Cambridge University Press.

Sherratt, A.G. 1976. Resources, technology, and trade. In *Problems in Economic and Social Archaeology*, Sieveking, G., Longworth, I., Wilson, K. (eds.), pp. 557–81. London: Duckworth.

    1980. Water, soil, and seasonality in early cereal cultivation. *World Archaeology* 11: 313–30.

    1981. Plough and pastoralism: aspects of the secondary products revolution. In *Pattern of the Past: Studies in Honour of David Clarke*, Hodder, I., Isaac, G., and Hammond, N. (eds.). pp. 261–305. Cambridge: Cambridge University Press.

    1983. The secondary exploitation of animals in the Old World. *World Archaeology* 15: 90–104.

Simkins, P.D., and F.L Wernstedt 1971. *Philippines Migration: Settlement of the Digos-Padada Valley, Davao Province*. New Haven: Yale University Southeast Asia Studies 16.

Simmons, I.G. 1969. Evidence for vegetation changes associated with Mesolithic man in Britain. In *The Domestication and Exploitation of Plants and Animals*, Ucko, P., and Dimbleby, G. (eds.), pp. 113–19. London: Duckworth.

Simmons, I.G., and G.W. Dimbleby 1974. The possible role of ivy (*Hedera helix L.*) in the mesolithic economy of western Europe. *Journal of Archaeological Science* 1: 291–6.

Skaarup, J. 1973. *Hesselø–Sølager. Jagdstationen der südskandinavischen Trichterbecherkultur*. Copenhagen: Archaeologiske Studier I.

Smith, A.G. 1970. The influence of Mesolithic and Neolithic man on British vegetation: a discussion. In *Studies in the Vegetational History of the British Isles*, Walker, D., and West, R. (eds.), pp. 81–96. Cambridge: Cambridge University Press.

Soudský, B. 1962. The Neolithic site of Bylany. *Antiquity* 36: 190–200.

1966. *Bylany. Osada Nejstaršich Zemĕdelců z Mladší Doby Kamenné*. Prague: Czechoslovakian Academy of Sciences.

Soudský, B., and I. Pavlů 1972. The Linear Pottery Culture settlement patterns in central Europe. In *Man, Settlement, and Urbanism*, Ucko, P., Tringham, R., and Dimbleby, G. (eds.), pp. 317–28. London: Duckworth.

Stampfli, H.R. 1965. Tierreste der Grabung Müddersheim, Kr. Düren. In *Müddersheim, eine Ansiedlung der jüngeren Bandkeramik im Rheinland*, by Schietzel, K., pp. 115–23. Cologne: Böhlau.

Starkel, L. 1983. Paleogeografia i klimat późnego plejstocenu i holocenu. In *Czlowiek i Środowisko w Pradziejach*, Kozlowski, J.K. and Kozlowski, S.K. (eds.), pp. 14–31. Warsaw: Państwowe Wydawnictwo Naukowe.

Starling, N.J. 1983. Neolithic settlement patterns in central Germany. *Oxford Journal of Archaeology* 2(1): 1–11.

1984. Neolithische Siedlungsentwicklung im Saalegebiet. *Archäologisches Korrespondenzblatt* 14: 251–9.

1985. Social change in the later Neolithic of Central Europe. *Antiquity* 59: 30–8.

1987. The Neolithic Höhensiedlungen of Central Germany. *Enclosures and Defences in the Neolithic of Western Europe*, Burgess, C., Topping, P., and Mordant, C. (eds.), in press. Oxford: British Archaeological Reports (International Series).

Strathern, A. (ed.) 1982. *Inequality in New Guinea Highlands Societies*. Cambridge: Cambridge University Press.

Tauber, H. 1965. Differential pollen distribution and the interpretation of pollen diagrams. *Danmarks Geologiske Undersøgelse* Series II, No. 89, pp. 7–69.

1981. ^{13}C evidence for dietary habits of prehistoric man in Denmark. *Nature* 292 (5821): 332–3.

Taute, W. 1966. Das Felsdach Lautereck, eine mesolithisch-neolithisch-bronzezeitliche Stratigraphie an der Oberen Donau. *Palaeohistoria* 12: 483–504.

1980. *Das Mesolithikum in Süddeutschland. Teil 2: Naturwissenschaftliche Beiträge*. Tübingen: Institut für Urgeschichte (Tübingen Monographien zur Urgeschichte).

Tetzlaff, W. 1978. Wyniki badań wykopaliskowych osady kultury pucharów lejkowatych w Mrowinie, woj. Poznań, przeprowadzonych w latach 1973–75. *Sprawozdania Archeologiczne* 30: 57–70.

1981. Osada kultury pucharów lejkowatych w Mrowinie, woj. poznańskie. In *Kultura Pucharów Lejkowatych w Polsce*, Wiślański, T. (ed.), pp. 171–90. Poznań: Polish Academy of Sciences.

Thomas, R. B., B. Winterhalder, and S.D. McRae 1979. An anthropological approach to human ecology and adaptive dynamics. *Yearbook of Physical Anthropology* 22: 1–46.

Tringham, R.E. 1968. A preliminary study of the Early Neolithic and latest Mesolithic blade industries in southeast and central Europe. In *Studies in Ancient Europe*, Coles, J., and Simpson, D. (eds.), pp. 45–70. Leicester: Leicester University Press.

1971. *Hunters, Fishers, and Farmers of Eastern Europe, 6000–3000 B.C.* London: Hutchinson.

1983. The development of the household as the primary unit of production in Neolithic and Eneolithic South-east Europe. Paper presented at the 48th Annual Meeting of the Society for American Archaeology, Pittsburgh, April 1983.

Troels-Smith, J. 1960. Ivy, mistletoe, and elm: climatic indicators – fodder plants. *Danmarks Geologiske Undersøgelse* Series IV, Vol. 4, No. 4, pp. 1–32.

Vang Petersen, P. 1984. Chronological and regional variation in the late Mesolithic of eastern Denmark. *Danish Journal of Archaeology* 3: 7–18.

Vayda, A. 1976. *War in Ecological Perspective.* New York: Plenum.

Velde, P. van de 1979a. The social anthropology of a Neolithic graveyard in the
   Netherlands. *Current Anthropology* 20: 37–58.

   1979b. *On Bandkeramik Social Organization.* Leiden: Institute of Prehistory (Analecta
   Praehistorica Leidensia 12).

Verdon, M. 1982. Where have all the lineages gone? Cattle and descent among the Nuer.
   American Anthropologist 84: 566–79.

Voss, J. 1982. A study of western TRB social organization. *Berichten van de Rijksdienst voor
   het Oudheidkundig Bodemonderzoek* 32: 9–102.

Voss, K.L. 1965. Stratigrafische Notizen zu einem Langhaus der Trichterbecherkultur bei
   Wittenwater, Kr. Uelzen. *Germania* 43: 343–51.

Waddell, E. 1975. How the Enga cope with frost: responses to climatic perturbations in the
   central Highlands of New Guinea. *Human Ecology* 3: 249–73.

Wallace, R.L. 1983. *Those Who Have Vanished. An Introduction to Prehistory.* Homewood
   (Illinois): Dorsey Press.

Watson, J.B. 1983. *Tairora Culture. Contingency and Pragmatism.* Seattle and London:
   University of Washington Press.

Watson, J.P.N. 1979. The estimation of relative frequencies of mammalian species:
   Khirokitia 1972. *Journal of Archaeological Science* 6: 127–37.

Wawrzykowska, B. 1981. Osada kultury pucharów lejkowatych w Brąchnówku, woj.
   Toruń. In *Kultura Pucharów Lejkowatych w Polsce*, Wiślański, T. (ed.), pp. 109–18.
   Poznań: Polish Academy of Sciences.

Whittle, A. 1977. Earlier Neolithic enclosures in north-west Europe. *Proceedings of the
   Prehistoric Society* 43: 329–48.

   1985. *Neolithic Europe. A Survey.* Cambridge: Cambridge University Press.

Wiel, M.A. van der 1982. A palynological study of a section from the foot of the
   Hazendonk. *Review of Palaeobotany and Palynology* 38: 35–90.

Wilk, R.R., and W.L. Rathje (eds.) 1982. *Archaeology of the Household: Building a Prehistory
   of Domestic Life.* Beverly Hills: Sage Publications (American Behavioral Scientist, Vol.
   25, No. 6).

Wilke, P.J., and R.E. Taylor 1971. Comments on isochronous interpretation on
   radiocarbon dates. *Plains Anthropologist* 16: 115–16.

Willerding, U. 1980. Zum Ackerbau der Bandkeramiker. In *Beiträge zur Archäologie
   Nordwestdeutschlands und Mitteleuropas*, Krüger, T., and Stephan, H.G. (eds.), pp.
   421–56. Hildesheim: August Lax (Materialhefte zur Ur- und Frühgeschichte
   Niedersachsens 16).

   1983. Zum ältesten Ackerbau in Niedersachsen. In *Frühe Bauernkulturen in Niedersachsen*,
   Wegner, G. (ed.), pp. 179–219. Oldenburg: Staatliches Museum für Naturkunde und
   Vorgeschichte.

Willms, C. 1982. *Zwei Fundplätze der Michelsberger Kultur aus dem westlichen Münsterland
   gleichzeitig ein Beitrag zum neolithischen Silexhandel in Mitteleuropa.* Hildesheim:
   August Lax (Münstersche Beiträge zur Ur- und Frühgeschichte 12).

   1985. Neolithischer Spondylusschmuck. Hundert Jahre Forschung. *Germania* 63:
   331–43.

Wiślański, T. 1969. *Podstawy Gospodarcze Plemion Neolitycznych w Polsce
   Pólnocno-Zachodniej.* Wrocław: Ossolineum.

   1974. Kultura ceramiki wstęgowej rytej na Ziemi Pyrzyckiej. In *Studia Archaeologica
   Pomeranica*, F. Lachowicz (ed.), pp. 53–77. Koszalin: Muzeum of Archaeology and
   History.

   1979. Kształtowanie się miejscowych kultur rolniczo-hodowlanych. Plemiona kultury
   pucharów lejkowatych. In *Prahistoria Ziem Polskich II. Neolit*, Hensel, W. and
   Wiślański, T. (eds.), pp. 165–260. Wrocław: Ossolineum.

1980. Siedlungsverhältnisse in der Pyritzer Ebene zur Zeit des Neolithikums. In *Urgeschichtliche Besiedlung in ihre Beziehung zur naturlichen Umwelt*, Schlette, F. (ed.), pp. 95–123. Halle/Saale: Martin-Luther-Universität (Wissenschaftliche Beiträge 1980/6 L15).

Wobst, H.M. 1977. Stylistic behavior and information exchange. In *For the Director: Research Essays in Honor of James B. Griffin*, Cleland, C.E. (ed.), pp. 317–42. Ann Arbor: Museum of Anthropology, University of Michigan (Anthropological Papers 61).

Wojciechowski, W. 1973. *Osada Ludności Kultury Pucharów Lejkowatych w Janówku, Pow. Dzierzoniów*. Wroclaw: University of Wroclaw Press (Acta Universitatis Wratislaviensis 183, Studia Archeologiczne 6).

Woude, J.D. van der 1984. *Holocene Palaeoenvironmental Evolution of a Perimarine Fluviatile Area*. Leiden: Institute of Prehistory (Analecta Praehistorica Leidensia 17).

Zabłocki, J., and J. Żurowski 1934. Znaleznienie zapasów *Lithospermum* w dwu stanowiskach kultury małopolskiej. *Materiały Prehistoryczne (Kraków)* 1: 1–27.

Zeist, W. van, and R.M. Palfrenier-Vegter 1981. Seeds and fruits from the Swifterbant S3 site. *Palaeohistoria* 23: 105–68.

Zimmerman, W.H. 1980. Ein trichterbecherzeitlicher Hausgrundriss von Flögeln – Im Ortjen, Kr. Cuxhaven. In *Beiträge zur Archäologie Nordwestdeutschlands und Mitteleuropas*, Krüger, T., and Stephan, H.-G. (eds.), pp. 474–89. Hildesheim: August Lax (Materialhefte zur Ur- und Frühgeschichte Niedersachsens 16).

Zipf, G. 1949. *Human Behavior and the Principle of Least Effort*. Cambridge (Mass.): Addison-Wesley.

Zöller, H. 1977. Alter und Ausmass postgläzialer Klimaschwankungen in der Schweizer Alpen. In *Dendrochronologie und Postgläziale Klimaschwangungen in Europa*, Frenzel, B. (ed.), pp. 271–81. Wiesbaden: Franz Steiner Verlag.

Zvelebil, M., and P. Rowley-Conwy 1984. Transition to farming in northern Europe: a hunter-gatherer perspective. *Norwegian Archaeological Review* 17: 104–28.

INDEX

244

For EU product safety concerns, contact us at Calle de José Abascal, 56–1°,
28003 Madrid, Spain or eugpsr@cambridge.org.

www.ingramcontent.com/pod-product-compliance
Ingram Content Group UK Ltd.
Pitfield, Milton Keynes, MK11 3LW, UK
UKHW030900150625
459647UK00021B/2707